Lectures in Macroeconomics

Lectures in Macroeconomics

A Capitalist Economy Without Unemployment

Kazimierz Łaski

Edited by
Jerzy Osiatyński
and
Jan Toporowski

Translated from Polish by
James West

OXFORD
UNIVERSITY PRESS

OXFORD
UNIVERSITY PRESS

Great Clarendon Street, Oxford, OX2 6DP,
United Kingdom

Oxford University Press is a department of the University of Oxford.
It furthers the University's objective of excellence in research, scholarship,
and education by publishing worldwide. Oxford is a registered trade mark of
Oxford University Press in the UK and in certain other countries

Published in the United States of America by Oxford University Press
198 Madison Avenue, New York, NY 10016, United States of America

British Library Cataloguing in Publication Data
Data available

Library of Congress Control Number: 2018965984

ISBN 978–0–19–884211–8

Printed and bound by
CPI Group (UK) Ltd, Croydon, CR0 4YY

Contents

Contents

List of Figures

List of Figures

List of Tables

Editor's Introduction

0.1 Łaski's Family, Education, Surviving the Holocaust, and First Post-war Engagements

The lectures that follow are the fruit of the final years of an extraordinary life devoted to political economy and understanding ideas that were tested not only in scholarship but also in tragic adversity. In particular the lectures reflect their author's close collaboration with Michał Kalecki in the last decade and a half of Kalecki's life.[1]

Kazimierz Łaski was born in a Polish southern city of Częstochowa into a lower-middle class family as Hendel Cygler. His father, Szmul, was a shop-keeper, and his mother, Rywa, ran a small shirt-sewing shop. The family could afford a maid, and sent Hendel and his older brother, Majer Godel, to the local *lyceum* school. The school, combined with the care of his Catholic maid who read for him Polish folk stories and tales, sang local songs and constantly talked to him, removed any trace of Jewish accent from his spoken Polish. Although well read in Polish literature and history, he was more interested in mathematics and science than arts.

Early in the World War II, his parents were deported and gassed in Treblinka and his brother was killed by the Germans. Łaski's then girlfriend, subsequently wife (from 1947) and lifelong true companion, Irena Wolfowicz, found refuge from the Nazis at a convent in Warsaw. In March/April 1943, with assistance of the Polish Underground State, Łaski was given a false Roman Catholic birth certificate and residence registration documents issued in the name of a man his age. That, together with the aforementioned fluency in the Polish language and his blue eyes, as he later recalled, allowed him to survive the Holocaust under the Nazi occupation in Poland. He was the sole survivor of his family and relatives that had numbered about thirty people. In the course of the Warsaw Uprising (August 1–October 3, 1944) he fought in a combat unit of the People's Army and was wounded in the last days of the

[1] The author is grateful for helpful comments to Amit Bhaduri, Martin Riese, Jan Toporowski, and Herbert Walter.

Uprising.[2] After the war, Łaski kept his assumed name, although he never denied his family one.

The first university to open in Poland after the war was in Lublin and Łaski went there intending to study medicine. However, in Lublin he met people from his combat troop in the Warsaw Uprising, and a close friend from before the war. They all argued that a civil war had started in the country and the obligation of the left was to fight for the new Poland, not to study. Łaski was persuaded (for reasons he later could not well explain even to himself and those closest to him) and in February 1945 he took a job in the Economic Department of the Ministry of Public Security. He worked there until 1950 as the head of a section that reviewed projects of new legislation that prior to being enacted were circulated through all ministries.

0.2 From Marx to Lifelong Engagement with Kalecki

Although Łaski never finished his secondary education, once the war ended university enrolment was opened also for those who had finished only the first grade of secondary schools. Thus in the Autumn 1945 he started studying economics at the Polish Workers' Party Academy for Political Science in Warsaw. At about the same time he read Kautsky's *Economic Doctrines of Karl Marx* which impressed him "not only because it explained past economic and social development but, moreover, also its future."[3] Thus "enlightened" by

---

[2] The People's Army (AL) was the second-largest underground combat formation fighting against Nazi occupants (1943–5). It was formed by the communist Polish Workers Party. The dominant Polish armed resistance movement was the Home Army (AK, 1942–5) which was loyal to the Polish Government-in-Exile, and constituted the armed wing of the "Polish Underground State." In his interview given to Kowalik, his friend and close collaborator, when asked why he did not join the AK and fought instead in the AL formation, Łaski replied:

It was known that on the whole the Home Army did not readily enrol Jews and I had no such option. Moreover, I was aware of what Poland was during the interwar period, and especially in the years before the war, and did not idealize it. Political forces that sought to restore the pre-war system in Poland were not appealing to me. By nature I tended left. Vaguely but clearly left. My contacts were with the People's Army and not with the Home Army and I did not seek contact with the latter. I knew the People's Army had not pressed to start the Warsaw Uprising. But when it broke out I had no doubt whatsoever that I must fight in it. There was no time then for exploring political differences. Our participation in the Warsaw Uprising was accepted by the Home Army High Command and that was enough for us. (Łaski and Kowalik 2011: 21–2)

Kowalik started interviewing Łaski in 2010 but never really finished. After Kowalik's death in 2012 Łaski asked Osiatyński to revise and copy-edit the interview which he thought unpublishable in its 2011 form. However, revising it required Łaski to fill in many factual gaps and provide additional information. Because of Łaski's many other pressing engagements, and then his death in 2015, this interview has not been revised.

[3] Łaski and Kowalik (2011: 27–8).

Kautsky, he turned to volumes II and III of Marx's *Das Kapital* which he read in German. In 1947 he started attending a seminar at the Central Committee of the Polish Workers Party that discussed Marx's theory. The seminar was run by Wlodzimierz Brus.[4]

In 1948 Łaski got his first university degree (the Academy had no licence to confer Masters degrees on its students). The following year he started teaching as Brus's assistant at the Main School of Planning and Statistics (SGPiS). In 1950 the Academy was turned into the Institute for Training Scientific Cadres (IKKN, renamed in 1954 into Institute for Social Sciences), and Łaski and Brus also taught there, as did Oscar Lange, the godfather of the concept of Market Socialism, who from 1951 had taught the history of economic thought in IKKN.

The subject of Łaski's first lectures was Marx's schemes of reproduction which he used to discuss intersectoral balances and economic development. Marx's schemata were also the key analytical framework of Łaski's master's dissertation, and then of his doctoral thesis on capital accumulation and economic dynamics in the course of the fast industrialization of Poland in the 1950s. He was awarded his PhD at the Main School of Planning and Statistics in 1954. Soon after he was appointed to the position of assistant professor and then to a full professorship. At the Main School in 1959–68 he headed the Chair of Political Economy, and in 1961–3 he served as the School's deputy rector for the curriculum and research.

Łaski himself segmented his research output into three periods: (i) prior to Kalecki, (ii) with Kalecki, and (iii) after Kalecki.[5] In November 1955 Kalecki

---

[4] Wlodzimierz Brus (Beniamin Zylberberg, 1921–2007) was then an editor of *Nowe Drogi*, the main theoretical monthly of the Polish Communist Party, which called itself the Polish Workers' Party. He was Łaski's first great mentor and with years became his true friend. An economist and high-ranking Communist Party functionary, after Stalin's death in 1953 Brus became a revisionist and ardent supporter of economic decentralization that would combine central planning with market mechanisms. Following political and anti-Semitic purges in Poland in 1968, in 1972 he emigrated to Britain where he taught at the universities of Glasgow and Oxford. Brus's 1951 PhD thesis was on "The Law of Value in the Socialist Economy." The Marxist law of value and the scope of its operation in a command economy became the central subject of his studies, including his most influential work, published in 1961, *The Market in the Socialist Economy* (for an English translation see Brus 1972). He saw "the system of functioning of the socialist economy . . . [as] the mechanism of allocation of resources and co-ordination of economic activity" (Brus 1993: 379) and argued that both democracy and market mechanisms were indispensable in a socialist system (a view that converged with the main thesis of the Kalecki's 1956 paper on "Workers' Councils and Central Planning," see Kalecki 1992). This specific perspective of economic and political reasoning also explains why much of the Polish post-1956 economic decentralization debate was conceived in terms of the "role of law of value in a centrally planned economy"—a terminology that was hardly understandable to Western contemporary economics (see Osiatyński, in: Kalecki 1992: 276; for more on Brus, see his 1993 autobiographical paper, and Toporowski 2007).

[5] Kalecki returned to Poland in February 1955 having spent nine years in the Secretariat of the United Nations in New York where he was deputy director of its Economic Department. He became personal advisor to the Deputy Prime Minister Hilary Minc whose career as the political and economic overlord of the Polish economy was coming to an end. Kalecki's other assignment was to examine economic developments in Western countries. For more on Kalecki's work for the United Nations, see Kalecki 1993A: Part 3, and the corresponding editor's notes therein.

gave two lectures at the Institute for Social Sciences (the former Academy of Political Sciences where Łaski had studied) on the "Impact of Militarization on the Business Cycle after the Second World War."[6] Łaski and others in the lecture hall knew well who the lecturer was. They also knew, however, that he was not a Communist Party member and this filled the hall of aspiring Communist scholars with an aura of some mistrust in the speaker. This is how half a century later Łaski remembered this first encounter with Kalecki:

> It is difficult to describe the first impression Kalecki's lecture made upon me. I saw in front of me a man of rather small stature who spoke in a loud voice, but was intellectually a kind of sorcerer who played with the familiar schemes of reproduction but used them for asking the most important and pertinent economic questions in order to arrive at conclusions that were completely opposed to the canons of the 'Marxian faith' ... I was amazed. Kalecki's logic was flawless, but "that which must not, cannot be." I looked for the trick and believed for a while to have found it. Kalecki slightly redefined the notion of two departments by assuming that they were vertically integrated, each of them producing only final goods, while in Marx's schemes of reproduction the first sector produces not only final goods but also intermediary goods for both sectors. However, I realized very quickly that my criticism was childish. The small change introduced by Kalecki clarified immensely the meaning of Marx's schemes of reproduction and put in the centre of analysis the relation between investment goods (produced by Department 1) and consumption goods (produced by Department 2), i.e. the relation which became the cornerstone of Kalecki's theory of effective demand in the early 1930s.[7]

In June 1956, at the Second Congress of Polish Economists, Kalecki read his paper on the "Dynamics of Investment and National Income in a Socialist Economy."[8] This time Łaski was truly impressed. First, because Kalecki's conclusions clearly contradicted the sacred dogma on the necessity of the faster development of the department producing investment goods than the department producing consumption goods. Second, because of the analytic apparatus used by Kalecki, closely akin to Marx's schemata of reproduction. This was territory well known to Łaski who immediately saw the essence of Kalecki's argument, appreciated the importance of its conclusions, and in the course of Congress strongly supported Kalecki. Many years later Łaski admitted that this second encounter with Kalecki constituted a watershed in his development as a macroeconomist.[9]

In the academic year 1961/2, as the SGPiS's deputy rector, Łaski persuaded Kalecki to accept a professorship at SGPiS and start regular teaching there.

---

[6] See Kalecki (1991).   [7] Łaski (2006 as reproduced in Łaski 2015: 7).
[8] See Kalecki (1956 (1992: Part 4 and the corresponding editor's notes, pp. 360–2)); see also Łaski (2006). Kalecki first read that paper at the meeting of the Polish Economist Association, on September 20, 1955 (see Kalecki 1992: 363–5).
[9] See Łaski and Kowalik (2011: 39); see also Kalecki (1968 (1991)).

That was a telling experience, recalled Łaski, since having already accepted the offer, Kalecki changed his mind because, he argued, he would need a few years to prepare a single lecture-course. Kalecki's reluctance arose because he only taught what was his own contribution to macroeconomics. Following the publication, in 1963, of his *Introduction to the Theory of Growth in a Socialist Economy* Kalecki taught in one term only his theory of business cycle and economic dynamics, and in the other term only his theory of growth in a socialist economy.

Łaski also persuaded Kalecki to be the intellectual leader of a small research center on underdeveloped economies. The center was set up jointly by SGPiS and Warsaw University. Łaski was one of the center's founders. Kalecki was chairman of its research board (of which Łaski was a member) and took an active interest in the activities of the center. As recalled by Ignacy Sachs, Kalecki's close collaborator and director of the center:

> The standards imposed by Kalecki were stringent and his criticism was very sharp. But he was so generous with his time and so objective in his judgments that most of us considered his proverbially uncompromising attitude as a unique opportunity to learn from him. Some of Kalecki's own papers were prompted by the research projects carried out at the center."[10]

Following Kalecki's regular teaching at SGPiS and at the center, Łaski became a member of the inner circle of Kalecki's collaborators, and especially of a team that focused on the theory of growth of a socialist economy. In 1962 Łaski and Brus authored one of the key presentations at the Congress of International Economic Association in Vienna, which addressed "Problems in Economic Development." Later Łaski published several papers on factors of growth in a socialist economy, on the relation between foreign trade and the rate of economic growth, on the impact of the choice of methods of production on full employment, and on the proportions of growth of investment and consumption in the context of growth acceleration under unemployment and under full employment.

Those studies in growth theory culminated in Łaski's 1965 *Outline of the Theory of Socialist Reproduction*. It developed and extended Kalecki's formal analysis of factors of growth in a socialist economy and examined the relationships between current investment and consumption. The *Outline* was considered in Poland a classic work on the theory of growth in socialism and was used as a textbook at Polish universities. Together with Kalecki's 1963 *Introduction*, both books provided the formal basis for criticism of the ill-balanced proportions of gross national output in Poland in the 1960s that led to shortages of consumer goods.

[10] Sachs (1977: 48).

Following the publication of those books a workshop was organized to study problems of growth and long-term planning of a socialist economy. The workshop was co-chaired by Kalecki and Łaski and attended by Kalecki's collaborators from the Planning Commission, the Economic Council, which advised the Government, the teaching staff from Łaski's chair of political economy at SGPiS, and by lecturers from other universities. Under Kalecki's intellectual leadership the workshop discussed in detail Kalecki's *Introduction* (which they also taught in their courses). The workshop's output was published in numerous journals, and gave rise to some revisions in the second edition of the *Introduction* (Kalecki 1967), as well as in the aforementioned publications by Łaski:[11]

> The significance of [Łaski's] studies went far beyond academia. They set theoretical limits to voluntary economic decision-making and demanded that central planners accept the constraints imposed by cost-benefit analysis . . . Kalecki, Łaski, and their close collaborators asked the political decision-makers who insisted on ever-larger investments to consider the resulting short-term changes in consumption. Although from today's perspective, the practical impact of the suggested constraints on politically motivated investment decisions was negligible, this insubordination of elite economics professors infuriated the communist political leadership. At the same time, however, this distinguished Poland from other centrally planned countries, paving new ways in economic theorizing. Moreover, a quarter of a century later, in Poland those post-1956 bulwarks of economic "revisionism" facilitated the country's transition from a centrally planned to a market economy. The study *From Marx to the Market* (Brus and Łaski 1989) gives an excellent account of the rather dramatic end to the totalitarian socialist search for economic rationality and social justice under totalitarian socialism.
>
> (Osiatyński 2015: 3–4)

In 1960 as a Ford scholar Łaski visited the Institute de sciences économiques appliqués in Paris, in 1964 he was visiting professor at the Institute for Higher Studies and Scientific Research in Vienna, and in the academic year 1966/7 he taught at École Practique des hautes études at the Sorbonne. Hardly aware of the anti-Semitic campaign that began in Poland in 1967 following the Arab–Israeli Six-Day War, he returned with his family to Poland in the late summer of 1967 to find himself in an alien and hostile environment at SGPiS, an environment totally different to what it had been a year earlier when he left to teach at the Sorbonne. At the end of the year he surrendered his Communist Party card explaining this was no longer the party he entered in 1946. The following year Kalecki's network of intellectual associates was purged from membership in the ruling party and positions in the universities on the pretext that they were sowing "intellectual confusion" among young people

---

[11] For more on the Seminar's output see editor's notes to Kalecki (1993: 249–52).

and party cadres, even though Kalecki and his associates took a definitely pro-socialist stance. But the real reason was their intellectual autonomy and determination to disagree with the authoritarian aspects of the system. In protest Kalecki resigned from his professorship at SGPiS and went into early retirement.

0.3 Teaching and Developing Kalecki's Theories after 1968

In November 1968 Łaski emigrated to Austria. He left Poland with a letter of recommendation from Kalecki. In Vienna Łaski knew Joseph Steindl personally as they had met in the early 1960s. Steindl had been Kalecki's friend and admirer since World War II when they were both working at the Oxford Institute of Statistics, and he visited Kalecki in Poland in the mid-1960s. Steindl worked in the Austrian Institute of Economic Research, which was expanding its newly established Department for International Comparative Studies. Franz Nemschak, the director of the Institute, was searching for new qualified staff for this Department. Thus, on the recommendation of Steindl and Kalecki, two weeks after arriving in Vienna Łaski was offered a senior research fellowship at the Austrian Institute. In 1973 the Department became the Vienna Institute for Comparative Economic Studies (WIIW), where he worked until his retirement and where in 1991–6 he served as its research director.

However, Łaski thought of himself first of all as an academic teacher and he sought a professorial position. In 1971 he assumed the chair of economics at Johannes Kepler University in Linz where he taught until retirement in 1991. The other chair of economics in Linz University was held by an outstanding economist, Kurt W. Rothschild. Like Steindl, Rothschild had escaped to Britain from Austria in 1938, spent the war years at the University of Glasgow and collaborated with the Oxford Institute of Statistics where Kalecki was working.[12] Rothschild and Łaski were both of a leftish persuasion, with solid backgrounds in mainstream macro- and microeconomics. In Łaski's opinion the two together made "a rather interesting constellation. My personal experience with reforming the centrally planned economy made me very cautious regarding radical reforms that aimed at revolutionary betterment of the world, and I was, and still am, against such revolutionary attempts. I think gradual improvements bring better results than grand schemes of salvation of the world. Rothschild was politically more radical. However, regarding economic views, I was more radical than him" (Łaski and

---

[12] I am grateful to Jan Toporowski for drawing my attention to that link between Rothschild, Kalecki, and Steindl.

Kowalik 2011: 54–5). Over the years Łaski and Rothschild became good friends.

In Linz, next to mainstream macroeconomics, Łaski taught the theories of Keynes, Kalecki's theory of business cycles and economic dynamics, and Marxian economics. Together with Rothschild they ran a regular seminar for postgraduate students. Several of his former students became university professors, economic policymakers, and government officials. Reflecting on that work Łaski wrote:

> Together with Kurt Rothschild we offered at the Linz University, to about twenty generations of students, not only a critical review of mainstream economics but also a radical theoretical alternative in the form of Kalecki's theory. I have made it my duty to pass on Kalecki's teaching to others, and looking back I have the feeling that my effort was not fruitless. (Łaski 2006, as in 2015: 9)

When in Linz, Łaski continued his involvement with the Vienna Institute for which he served as a research consultant. Alongside analytical papers, the Institute published regular surveys of economic developments in East European countries. Under Łaski's intellectual leadership in the 1970s and 1980s the Institute argued for market-oriented reforms and an alternative policy framework in those countries. Increasingly disillusioned by successive failures of attempted reforms there, Brus and Łaski wrote their study *From Marx to the Market* that examined the axioms at the root of the failure of the Marx-inspired socialist economic system, as well as of the market-oriented attempts to reform it.[13] The authors' concern with basic socialist values, such as full employment, equal opportunities, social care, etc., made them put forward a model of what they called a decentralized "market socialism proper." The publication of the book coincided, however, with the fall of communism in Poland, shortly to be followed in other countries in the region and their transition to free-market capitalism.

Following the collapse of communism, Łaski and the Vienna Institute focused on the transition of Central and East European countries to market capitalism. Łaski was a hard critic of the Washington-Consensus-oriented shock therapies, especially in his home country. He proposed a far milder strategy of restoring a short-period equilibrium in Poland at the start of transition, when on the invitation of the Poland's minister for planning he prepared a report on the expected results of the "shock-therapy package." In that report he wrote among other things:

> I came to the conclusion that GDP would fall over 1990 by 15 percent to 20 percent instead of the tacitly assumed (although not published) 5 percent...In

---

[13] Their book should be read together with Brus's 1993 autobiographical paper, "The Bane of Reforming the Socialist Economic System."

fact, in 1990 GDP fell by 11.6 percent and in 1991 by another 7 percent. As far as I know, there was no other economist to foresee this development ... My expertise was of course completely ignored and shelved.[14]

He and his team in WIIW foresaw a prolonged recession that would follow shock therapies applied in the region, and they tried to prevent it. Only with EU accession of those countries that began in 2004, and the accompanying large EU financial assistance, has the economic situation in the region significantly improved.

By emphasizing the role of effective demand in macroeconomics and economic policymaking, Łaski gave the output of the Vienna Institute a rather unique trademark. This, as well as the accuracy of forecasts based on those theoretical foundations, made the Institute a respected research center in the field of study of economic and social developments in East European countries before, during, and after their transition to capitalist system.

In Linz and Vienna Łaski advocated adapting Kalecki's theoretical framework to new economic realities and used that framework to examine economic developments in the United States and Western Europe. Among his papers on that subject Łaski selected two in which he believed he had achieved some progress. He wrote:

Keynes's teaching was absorbed by mainstream economics and emasculated (contrary to Kalecki's, which was simply ignored). The spectacular result of this operation was *inter alia* the aggregate demand versus aggregate supply analysis, with macroeconomic equilibrium being achieved similarly to that in a market for an individual good, by the right price adjustment. Together with Amit Bhaduri and Martin Riese (Bhaduri et al. 1999) we proved that the whole construction suffers from a basic inconsistency. It did not change academic teaching in any way; there exists almost no macroeconomic textbook that does not repeat the evident mistake demonstrated by us. At the seminar devoted to the centenary of Kalecki's birthday (1999) I presented the paper, "Three Ways to ... Unemployment" (Łaski 2000) in which I argued that in the majority of countries practical economic policymaking does not only disregard Kalecki's proposals for full employment but that it simply contradicts his advice. In that paper I disclosed that the propensity to save started to play an important role that had not been known previously. In some countries (such as in the United States) the decline in the savings rate gave a push to consumption growth in the late 1990s which in turn led to an increase in investment and accelerated growth of GDP. In some other countries (e.g., Germany) the increase in the savings rate limited the consumption growth and was conducive, under low propensity to invest, to a slowing down of the GDP growth and increasing unemployment.   (Łaski 2006, as in 2015: 9–10)

---

[14] Łaski (2006 (2015): 10). The summary of his report was published in 1990 and earned Łaski high respect for the accuracy of its analysis and recommendations (see Łaski (1990), see also Riese (2017)).

The 2008 economic crisis aroused some interest in Kalecki's theories. Łaski spared no effort to advance and popularize them in an environment in which, despite the prolonged crisis and the subsequent business recession, and despite the inability of mainstream economics to explain the causes of the crisis or provide policy recommendations as to how to overcome it, global macroeconomics continued to be dominated by the neoliberal doctrine. He believed Kalecki's theoretical framework offered chances for full employment in a capitalist economy that would meet the standards of economic efficiency, social justice, and equal opportunities. With these priorities in mind, he was consistently in favour of broad government intervention to counter high and lasting unemployment, should the need arise, even at the expense of controlled expansion of government deficits. He also advocated moderation of household income disparities.

Throughout his life Łaski was very active, giving guest lectures and attending conferences and seminars. Notwithstanding the bitter experience of 1968, with no other country did he feel as closely connected as he did with Poland. Invited by research institutions and associations, including the Polish Economist Association and the Institute for Advanced Studies of the leftist think tank in Warsaw, Krytyka Polityczna, together with the author of this Introduction, in 2013–15 he conducted a course on post-Kaleckian and post-Keynesian economics, in which prominent foreign economists were guest lecturers. Shortly before he passed away he completed his *Lectures in Macroeconomics* which represent the fruit of the last years of his life—an updated version of Kalecki's theory of business fluctuations and economic dynamics of a capitalist economy. His last professional appearance was in June 2015, at the age of 93, in Buenos Aires. At the Money and Banking Conference to commemorate the eightieth anniversary of the Central Bank of Argentina he argued for re-establishing fiscal policy in its role as an instrument for regulating the course of the business cycle and securing the maintenance of full employment.

0.4 Making the Project Take Off

A distinguishing feature of Łaski's *Lectures in Macroeconomics* is that they offer a systematic presentation of the theory of effective demand that is founded on the theory of Michał Kalecki, whose approach is in many ways richer and more comprehensive than that of John Maynard Keynes. Being a leading follower of Kalecki and his close friend and collaborator, Łaski presents Kalecki's theory—as noted by one of the Oxford University Press (OUP) external reviewers "with an amazing clarity, taking the reader from the most basic issues to rather more difficult ones with a style and a pedagogical capacity I have not seen before in other expositions of Kalecki's theory." Other OUP reviewers shared that judgment.

In his Preface to *Lectures* Łaski notes that they are merely his contribution to an international textbook in English "that a group of my colleagues and I are still developing." Apart from Łaski, the group consisted of Amit Bhaduri of the Jawaharlal Nehru University in New Delhi, Martin Riese of the Johannes Kepler University of Linz, and Herbert Walther of the Wirtschaftsuniversität in Vienna. Łaski, Riese, and Walther (the latter two being former assistants and close collaborators of Łaski) started to meet regularly from 2009, once every other week. Bhaduri joined the meetings irregularly, once or twice a year when he visited Europe, but participated in the discussions through email correspondence. Most attention was given to the 2008 financial crisis, especially its course in Greece, Spain, and Portugal, and the inability of mainstream economics to provide a satisfactory explanation for why the crisis had arisen and what were the ways out of it.

Riese and Walther recollect that in their meetings they regularly debated on Paul Krugman's *New York Times* column and the *Social Europe Journal* publications. They also discussed Thomas I. Palley's website "Economics for Democratic and Open Societies", and especially his concept of Gattopardo economics (Palley 2013), Richard C. Koo's idea of balance-sheet recession (presented in several of his papers and in his book, *The Holy Grail of Macroeconomics*, 2008), and various pieces by Jörg Bibow published by the Levy Institute of Economics. Of other readings Riese and Walther mention James Galbraith's (who always connected with Łaski when visiting Vienna), and Thomas Piketty's *Capital in the Twenty-First Century* (of which they were rather critical). Finally the group also tried to get familiar with modern finance via INET's course by Perry G. Mehrling (*Economics of Money & Banking: Part One*), "but did not endure."[15]

According to Riese and Walther the idea of writing together a non-mainstream textbook in macroeconomics that would represent the present-day development of Kaleckian economics and give an alternative insight to the crisis appeared only when the Polish edition of Łaski's book was already well advanced. Walther arranged funding for the book's English translation, which was to be discussed by its future co-authors. However, the translation was not ready before Łaski passed away. Except for a general presumption that the core of the joint project would be the Polish edition of *Lectures*, there was no discussion regarding subjects to be developed by other co-authors, nor on what should be revised in chapters already written by Łaski. Thus,

---

[15] Their email communication with Osiatyński of March 26, 2018.

notwithstanding their discussion of issues elaborated in *Lectures*, the project of writing a combined textbook never took off and with Łaski's death the opportunity of writing such a book together was gone.

Nevertheless, Łaski's textbook offers the reader a comprehensive, unique, and detailed exposition of the Kaleckian approach to macroeconomics. It also examines factors that prevent developed capitalist economies from achieving and maintaining full employment. Its clarity and pedagogical rigor of argument assist in understanding Kalecki's theory at its basic and intermediate level. Finally, it offers its readers an alternative to the mainstream economics of the present day. All these merits have been recognized by the publisher in offering this book far beyond the Polish reading audience. Of course, with the author's death, it was not possible to introduce substantial revisions or extensions, even where Łaski himself might have thought them necessary. Economics is not alone among the human sciences in that no work can be definitive. The editor of the present volume has limited his interventions to correcting some printing slips and an error in the Polish edition of *Lectures*. Jan Toporowski carefully checked the typescript and helped to put it into lucid English.

Naturally, the question arises of the relevance of Kalecki's theory and its policy recommendations in present-day finance-dominated capitalism. This is no doubt a critical question that attracts much attention among many post-Keynesians, post-Kaleckians, and other non-mainstream macroeconomists and policymakers. Their studies address many issues of which only two will be mentioned here. The first focuses on formal separation of the "real" and the "finance and banking" sub-sectors of the economy in a Kaleckian-type model, and examining their interrelations. The leading economist in that area is Amit Bhaduri (see, e.g., Bhaduri and Raghavendra 2017). The other focuses on examining the impact of financialization on the business cycle and long-run growth (see e.g., Hein 2014) and on potential measures aimed at counteracting global financialization (see e.g., Sawyer 2016 and Sawyer and Passarella 2015). Needless to say, there are many overlaps in those studies and the division suggested above is rather arbitrary.

As shown by Łaski in this book, in Kalecki's theory the key determinant of business-cycle and economic dynamics is private investment in fixed capital. Kalecki's investment decision function is determined in turn by enterprise-retained profit, the expected profitability of new investment projects, the degree of utilization of factors of production, and by technical progress. It is the "real economy" sector that rules economic dynamics and the Schumpeterian entrepreneur is the central figure on the scene. As long as the supply of credit is sufficiently accommodative to keep the long-term interest rate stable, financial and capital markets are of secondary importance only. To use Keynes's well-known prophetic warning, financial speculators are merely "bubbles on a steady stream of enterprise."[16] With the globalization of financial and capital markets the situation has radically changed and Minskian financial instability[17] has gained prominence. What is then the private investment decision function under financial capitalism? How may the Kaleckian "real economy" determinants of the private investment decision function be combined with the "investment" decision function of financial speculators implied in Minsky's "financial instability hypothesis"?

We do not have satisfactory answers to those questions yet. However, to appreciate the importance of issues which are under that debate requires a good understanding of the axiology of Kalecki's theory, of its underlying assumptions and conclusions. This is precisely what Łaski's *Lectures* offer. Even a mere summary of the above-mentioned financial studies goes well beyond the scope of this Introduction.

The full title of Łaski's book is *Lectures in Macroeconomics: A Capitalist Economy without Unemployment*, and its main concern is to demonstrate that following Kaleckian macroeconomics and its policy recommendations the achievement and maintenance of full employment in a capitalist economy is possible. Moreover, Łaski has always thought full employment was of critical importance for not merely economic reasons but primarily for political ones. In this respect he closely followed Kalecki who ends his renowned 1943 "Political Aspects of Full Employment" with the following sentence: "The fight of the progressive forces for full employment was at the same time a way of *preventing* the recurrence of fascism."[18] In Łaski's opinion, once the "golden age" of capitalist development ended in the mid-1970s the threat of a recurrence of fascism was on the rise. He was alerted by nationalist and fascist political movements gaining political ground across Europe and elsewhere, and he thought increasing unemployment, rising income disparities, and decay in common access to public services were important stimulants of those movements. His *Lectures*, in which he argues for full employment, are in a way Łaski's response as a scholar to that threat.

References

Bhaduri, Amit, Kazmierz Łaski, and Martin Riesew, 1999, "Effective Demand versus Profit Maximization in Aggregate Demand/Supply Analysis: A Dynamic Perspective," *Banca Nazionale del Lavoro Quarterly Review*, 52(210): 281–93.

[16] In his *General Theory* Keynes wrote: "speculators may do no harm as bubbles on a steady stream of enterprise. But the situation is serious when enterprise becomes the bubble on a whirlpool of speculation. When the capital development of a country becomes a by-product of the activities of a casino, the job is likely to be ill-done" (1936 (2003): 140).
[17] See Minsky (1986 and 1992). [18] Kalecki (1943 (1990): 352); Kalecki's emphasis.

Bhaduri, Amit and Srinivas Raghavendra, 2017, "Wage- and Profit-led Regimes under Modern Finance: an Exploration, Review of Keynesian Economics," 5(3): 426–38.

Brus, Wlodzimierz, 1972, *The Market in the Socialist Economy*, Routledge and Kegan, London.

Brus, Wlodzimierz, 1993, "The Bane of Reforming the Socialist Economic System," *Banca Nazionale del Lavoro Quarterly Review*, 46(187): 363–405.

Brus, Wlodzimierz and Kazimiery Łaski, 1989, *From Marx to the Market: Socialism in Search for an Economic System*, Oxford University Press, Oxford.

Hein, Eckhard, 2014, *Distribution and Growth after Keynes: A Post-Keynesian Guide*, Edward Elgar, Cheltenham.

Kalecki, Michał, 1943 (1990), "Political Aspects of Full Employment," in *Collected Works, Vol. I*, Clarendon Press, Oxford.

Kalecki, Michał, 1956 (1992), "Dynamics of Investment and National Income in a Socialist Economy," in *Collected Works, Vol. III*, Clarendon Press, Oxford.

Kalecki, Michał, 1963, revised Polish edition: 1967 (1993), "Introduction to the Theory of Growth in a Socialist Economy," in *Collected Works, Vol. IV*, Clarendon Press, Oxford.

Kalecki, Michał, 1968, (1991), "The Marxian Equations of Reproduction and Modern Economics," in *Collected Works, Vol. II*, Clarendon Press, Oxford.

Kalecki, Michał, 1990, *Collected Works, Vol. I: Capitalism: Business Cycles and Full Employment*, Clarendon Press, Oxford.

Kalecki, Michał, 1991, *Collected Works, Vol. II: Capitalism: Economic Dynamics*, Clarendon Press, Oxford.

Kalecki, Michał, 1992, *Collected Works, Vol. III: Socialism: Functioning and Long-run Planning*, Clarendon Press, Oxford.

Kalecki, Michał, 1993, *Collected Works, Vol. IV: Socialism: Economic Growth and Efficiency of Investment*, Clarendon Press, Oxford.

Kalecki, Michał, 1993A, *Collected Works, Vol. V: Developing Economies*, Clarendon Press, Oxford.

Keynes, John Maynard, 1936 (1967), *The General Theory of Employment, Interest and Money*, Macmillan, London.

Koo, Richard C., 2008, *The Holy Grail of Macroeconomics: The Lessons from Japan's Great Recession*, John Wiley, Singapore.

Łaski, Kazmierz, 1965, *Outline of the Theory of Socialist Reproduction*, Ksiazka i Wiedza, Warsaw, (in Polish).

Łaski, Kazimierz, 1990, "The Stabilization Plan for Poland," *Wirtschaftspolitische Blätter*, (5): 444–58.

Łaski, Kazimierz, 2000, "Three Ways to . . . High Unemployment," WIIW Working Paper No. 12, January.

Łaski, Kazimierz, 2006 (2015), "Kalecki's Place in my Career as an Economist," Newsletter No. 36/2006 of the European Association for Evolutionary Political Economy: http://eaepe.org/content/documents/NewsletterArchive/EAEPE_NewsletterNo36_Jul2006.pdf, reprinted in WIIW Monthly Report, No. 11, Special Issue in Memoriam Kazimierz Łaski.

Łaski, Kazimierz and Tadeusz Kowalik, 2011, Unpublished autobiographical interview (in Polish).

Minsky, Hyman P., 1986, *Stabilizing an Unstable Economy*, Yale University Press, New Haven, CT.

Minsky, Hyman P., 1992, "The Financial Instability Hypothesis," Working Paper No. 74, Levy Economics Institute of Bard College.

Osiatyński, Jerzy, 2015, "Remembering Kazimierz Łaski," WIIW Monthly Report, No. 11, Special Issue in Memoriam Kazimierz Łaski.

Palley, Thomas I., 2013, "Gattopardo Economics: The Crisis and the Mainstream Response of Change that Keeps Things the Same," IMK Working Paper No. 112.

Riese, Martin, 2017, "Kazimierz Łaski (1921–2015): 'An Old Kaleckian,'" Keynes Gesellschaft Tagung, Wien.

Sachs, Ignacy, 1977, "Kalecki on Development Planning," *Oxford Bulletin of Economics and Statistics*, 39(1): 47–56.

Sawyer, Malcolm, 2016, "Confronting Financialisation," in Arestis Philip and Malcolm Sawyer (eds), *Financial Liberalisation: Past, Present and Future*, Palgrave Macmillan, Houndmills and New York.

Sawyer, Malcolm and Marco Veronese Passarella, 2015 (2017), "The Monetary Circuit in the Age of Financialization: A Stock-Flow Consistent Model with a Twofold Banking Sector," *Metroeconomica*, reprinted in 2017, 68(2): 321–53.

Toporowski, Jan, 2007, "Wlodzimierz Brus," *Royal Economic Society Newsletter*, No. 139, London.

Preface

In 2009, the Institute of Economic Sciences at the Polish Academy of Sciences, with the cooperation of the Innovation Foundation and the Warsaw School of Social and Economic Studies, published my book entitled *Myths and Reality in Economic Policy and in Teaching Economics*. While this volume is in a sense the second edition of that publication, it is essentially a new book, with only a small part of the text left unmodified: new chapters have been added, and even the basic theoretical model is slightly different from the one proposed in *Myths and Reality*. The most significant change consists of directly addressing the issue of money and prices, which was previously left out, and an extended treatment of the distribution of national income.

Lectures in Macroeconomics: A Capitalist Economy without Unemployment is founded on the principle of aggregate demand as formulated by Michał Kalecki. It is a sad fact that Kalecki's theory, the only fully original Polish contribution to economic theory, is still missing from academic curricula, even in Poland. The objective of this book is to provide at least a partial remedy to that deficiency, offering an alternative to the current trends in teaching economics.

The present-day mainstream economics is represented by dynamic stochastic general equilibrium models (DSGE) which continue the tradition of Walrasian general equilibrium models but take into account the time factor. Amit Bhaduri points out the following key differences between the underlying assumptions of mainstream economics on the one hand and of the theory of effective demand on the other hand.[1] In the DSGE framework macroeconomic issues are examined as resulting from microeconomic decisions of a maximizing "representative agent" (and especially of a household). The main subject of study is long-term equilibrium while the question of effective demand is considered merely a short-term issue. Most mainstream economists assume that perfect flexibility of prices and wages reflects also the relative scarcity of labor and capital and thereby facilitates any necessary substitution between factors of production that, in turn, brings the economy into equilibrium at full employment. Some mainstream economists, often

---

[1] See Bhaduri (2014: 4).

called New Keynesians, allow in this neoclassical scheme for short-term failures of the price mechanism due to incomplete information which is the single exception allowed in the mainstream model.

The fundamental assumptions of the theory of effective demand are entirely different. The analogy between the part (individual household) and the whole (the national economy) is false since, for the economy as a whole, spending by one economic subject provides the income of another. Therefore autonomous spending, and especially investment spending, gives rise to a circular flow of expenditure and income and thereby generates savings which counterbalance that spending. In the theory of effective demand increased saving is a result of increased investment, and not a result of decisions of individual economic agents who choose between present and future consumption (or saving).

When an economy operates below full capacity utilization, additional income is generated by additional autonomous spending which leads to increased output because then increased demand leads to quantity adjustments that are stronger and appear sooner than price adjustments. In that way the neoclassical assumption that in the short run prices rather than quantities adjust to new short period equilibrium is inverted.

In the theory of effective demand prices adjust to money wages and the volume of output to demand. It follows that the mechanism of price setting is independent of the mechanism that determines the volume of output and employment. "More important, the real wage rate becomes an endogenous outcome of the interaction between the price level and the money wage rate, which makes the real wage rate an unsuitable policy instrument. Since the wage bargain is in money terms, only the money wage rate can be changed, with indeterminate effects on the extent of change in the price level and the real wage rate."[2]

Summing up, in a capitalist economy the key decisions are made by firms and not by households. The most important decisions relate to investment. It is these decisions, and not flexibility of prices and wages, that determine the volume of output and employment. It is so because investment determines the key part of profits which in turn—being roughly a constant part of national income (or only a slowly changing part)—determines the latter. The relation between profits and national income is a function of a gross profit mark-up on unit prime cost.

The neglect of these interdependencies meant that mainstream economics not only failed to predict the global financial crisis, but appeared helpless when confronted with it. Indeed, policymakers acting upon the recommendations of mainstream economists aggravated the downturn, transforming it into

---

[2] Bhaduri (2014).

long-term stagnation in the major capitalist economies around the world. It is these issues that are consistently referred to in my lectures.

Differences between mainstream economics and the aggregate demand principle are illustrated using the example of the ongoing crisis with its large scale unemployment, which usually soars in such situations. National income is low because private investment is low, and private investment is low because national income is low. Thus, the question arises how to break this vicious circle between private investment and national income.

The point of departure for the theory of effective demand is the Kaleckian profit equation, according to which profit, a critical measure in the capitalist economy, depends mostly on three factors: it is positively correlated with private investment and budget deficit, and negatively correlated with household savings. This equation is the guiding theme of this book, which gradually explicates and refines this relation.

The emergence of crises in capitalist economies is not an unfortunate accident, but the result of an otherwise very effective market mechanism. Thus, the maintenance of full employment requires an appropriate adjustment policy. When private investment is insufficient for the full utilization of the available workforce and capital, then, in light of Kalecki's equation, government expenditure should be increased and financed by running a budget deficit. Then, the state would be spending more than it receives in the form of its various revenues, expanding not only demand, but also profits and national income. An increased profitability of production and a higher level of production capacity utilization stimulates private investment, initiating economic recovery. Subsequently, after the economy rebounds and overall business improves, the budget deficit should be reduced or, if required, even a surplus raised. Kalecki's theoretical approach resembles that of a physician who has diagnosed the patient's illness and knows exactly how to help him.

In contrast, mainstream economists believe that the market mechanism is essentially perfect and any disturbances, including business crises, result exclusively from external factors such as inadequate behavior of economic agents or excessive governmental interference. In particular, they argue that unemployment primarily arises from high wages, while the weakness of private investment is attributable to ill-advised fiscal and monetary policies.

For a mainstream economist, the labor market is no different from other markets. If supply of labor is higher than demand, this means that the prices (think wages) are set too high. Thus, it would seem that if only workers were willing to accept lower wages, and the trade unions and legislative regulations did not stand in the way, everybody would be able to get a job. However, this line of reasoning can easily be refuted. For instance, when an excess of supply over demand makes the prices of horses go down, then also the supply of horses will decline. Even more importantly, a decreasing price of horses will not affect total demand. In contrast, the population of workers is not going to shrink with declining wages, while lower wage rates are likely to contract total consumption demand, which is mainly driven by worker earnings. It should be remembered that workers not only produce cars, but also purchase them, so if they earn less, then they also spend less on cars.

Let us consider in greater detail what would happen if workers accepted lower nominal wages. If prices decreased to the same extent as nominal wages, then real wages would remain unaffected and, at a given productivity level, the distribution of income between wages and profits and the share of profits in national income would be unaltered. As a result, if profits (predominantly dependent on private investment, which is usually planned in advance) remained unchanged, national income would also stall. The question arises as to what would happen if prices remained constant despite a decrease in nominal wages. At a given productivity level, real wages would decline and the share of profits in national income would expand. However, if in this situation profits remained at the same level, which is likely because of their above-mentioned dependence on private investment, then national income would decline rather than increase. And this eventuality is indeed inevitable when consumption falls as a result of a drop in real wages at given levels of profits and private investment. In both scenarios, a reduction in nominal wages would be an ineffective remedy: in the first case, unemployment would not be alleviated and in the second case it would further deteriorate. It can also be demonstrated that, in the example under consideration, at a given level of prices, an increase rather than a decrease in nominal (and real) wages combined with a lower share of profits in national income would reduce unemployment. At given investment levels, this would lead to expanded consumption, resulting in higher national income and higher employment. However, it should be stressed that only the first variant (in which unemployment does not increase) is realistic, as the share of profits in national income tends to be stable in the short term. In other words, under normal circumstances price levels are predominantly determined by nominal wages.

The ineffectiveness of reducing nominal wages in an attempt to combat unemployment becomes clear if one avoids the common fallacy of confusing the *share* of profits in national income with the *volume* of profits. Unemployment increases when, at constant private investment, the share of profits in national income rises, and it decreases when, at a constant share of profits in national income, private investment grows. In other words, what we need is not an increase of the share of profits in national income but an increase of profits in absolute terms, and that primarily depends on the volume of private investment.

As already mentioned, mainstream economists tend to blame weak private investment on the budget deficit and public debt. In the past, they claimed that the budget deficit would "squeeze out" private investment as the overall flow of savings was on some grounds assumed to be more or less constant and, therefore, it was argued that supporting private investment with government deficit spending would be ineffective. Nowadays, mainstream criticism of the budget deficit as a growth-stimulating instrument largely hinges on the Ricardo equivalence theorem, which posits that households continuously revise their expenditures and adjust their long-term plans by increasing savings whenever public debt increases, realizing that in the future that debt will require repayment. Under the circumstances, pursuant to the Kaleckian profit equation, an increase in budget deficit and a corresponding increase in household savings would cancel each other out, while profits and national income would remain unchanged. However, as it is shown in the presented lectures, those odd and unrealistic assumptions as to the behavior of households and other economic agents have led the advocates of such theories astray.

After the 2008 financial and economic crisis, the policymaking elites were forced to decide overnight on the choice of instruments best suited to alleviating its consequences. The sleight of hand of mainstream economists was rendered completely useless when the speculative bubble, which had been deemed utterly impossible, burst. This situation revived interest in the previously neglected Keynesian theories that assumed insufficient aggregate demand and accentuated the risk of deflation rather than inflation. Expansionary fiscal and monetary policies were suddenly embraced by the majority of countries and governments. The state, which had been accused of being the root cause of all economic ills, was called upon to counter the most devastating effects of the disaster precipitated by unbridled market mechanisms at the service of the unchecked pursuit of profit. However, state intervention was largely limited to bailing out banks or selected critical sectors of the real economy, and it was never extended to households, which suffered—and are still suffering—the brunt of the crisis. Moreover, as soon as the threat of implosion was more or less averted, market orthodoxy quickly returned to favor.

The costs of state intervention were high and led to enormous budget deficits and soaring public debt. However, it was soon pronounced that public debt was the cause rather than the effect of the crisis. Thus, governments discontinued the badly needed expansionary fiscal policies and embarked on an austerity crusade effectively stifling the budding economic recovery. At the same time, the mantra of structural reform was revived in the form of a flexible labor market, with the implication that nominal wages would lag behind real productivity and the share of workers' earnings in national income would decline. This pattern of change was in particular observed in the European Economic and Monetary Union. Dogmatism in thinking and a lack of pragmatism in the actions undertaken by the political elites turned out to be much stronger in Brussels, Frankfurt, and Berlin than in Washington.

In light of the above, is the "capitalist economy without unemployment," mentioned in the subtitle of this book, at all possible? As a matter of fact, during the first two decades following World War II such an economy did exist, so in reference to that period the question is rather rhetorical.[3] However, the issue of attaining full (or at least high) and sustainable employment by EU member states is much more complex. The conclusions that follow from the lectures presented here concern both internal and external prerequisites for achieving that goal.

One of the crucial internal preconditions is the presence of a sufficiently large domestic market, growing in step with the production potential of the economy. First, assuming a constant distribution of the benefits of technological progress between labor and capital, such a market would enable an increase in nominal wages in step with productivity expansion plus the inflation target. (This condition could not be met if unemployment were to be tackled through reducing flexible nominal wages, as real wages would then lag behind productivity growth, in practice generating more unemployment.) Second, this would mean that coherent fiscal and monetary policies can ensure macroeconomic adjustment of aggregate demand and aggregate supply. Indeed, such policies should strive to attain the highest possible level of employment in conjunction with price stability by adhering to an inflation target.

As far as fiscal policy is concerned, it should be founded on the principle of macroeconomic efficiency rather than a doctrine of "sound public finance." This goal may be achieved with a balanced budget, but it should be remembered that at a given level of spending (especially spending on welfare needs) higher employment may be attained by prioritizing direct taxes over indirect ones and by imposing progressive taxation on high incomes, and especially profits. At the same time, fiscal policy should treat a budget deficit (or a budget surplus) not as an objective in itself, but as an economic tool for adjusting aggregate demand to the existing production potential (at high levels of employment and stable prices).

In turn, the most important external prerequisite is an international financial architecture in which individual countries would be obliged to maintain roughly balanced current accounts over longer periods of time, even at the cost of employing capital controls if necessary. Thus, responsibility for trade imbalances would be borne not only by debtor countries, but also by creditor

---

[3] However, one must not neglect in this context the important role of military expenditure of the Cold War period. This was foreseen in a way by Kalecki who predicted that military spending would be the most favored field of government intervention.

economies. As a result, exchange rates could fulfill their principal role as tools ensuring an equilibrium in international trade and exchange rate speculation would be curtailed. Under these circumstances, countries having their own fiduciary currencies (that is, fiat money created by government decision) would gain the monetary independence necessary to implement active, sovereign fiscal policies in today's globalized economy. Without meeting these prerequisites, even large countries can hardly afford to pursue such policies due to the fact that fiscal stimulation may trigger tensions in the current accounts of their foreign trade balance, prompting a flight of capital, and sparking currency speculation.

The internal and external prerequisites discussed above were to a greater or lesser extent fulfilled in the 1950s and 1960s, but in the subsequent decades they were largely abandoned. The turning point was the fall of the Bretton Woods system and the advent of stagflation, when the benefits of technological progress to be distributed were offset by the losses arising from deteriorated terms of trade. The triumph of market fundamentalism coincided with the political and economic downfall of real socialism and central planning, and eventually set off a global financial crisis in 2008.

As the above prerequisites are not fulfilled within the European Union, the possibilities of implementing high employment policies by individual member states are very limited (but not entirely absent). Thus, the focus should be on revising restrictive EU policies, departing from so-called growth and stability pacts, and doing away with arbitrary caps on budget deficits and public debt. In addition, fiscal and budgetary policies ought to be better coordinated and the economic autonomy that the European Union enjoys thanks to its neutral or positive trade balance with the rest of the world should be exploited. In conclusion, a capitalist economy without unemployment is possible, but not without a change in the mindset of the political elites in European capitals, and especially in Brussels and Berlin.

As regards the other overarching goal of these lectures, it has become clear that the economic crisis has not led to a lasting revision of university teaching. Mainstream economics persists unapologetically unchanged: macroeconomic models are still based on the assumption that individuals are capable of (stochastically) predicting the future and making rational decisions based on their predictions. In the absence of uncertainty in such a theoretical setup, money is not really necessary, state intervention in the economy is regarded as harmful, and poverty and human suffering are interpreted as fortuitous events akin to natural disasters.

Not all students accept this intellectual framework and some call for curricula to include a confrontation of the various schools of economic thought. This book is intended as a humble effort to cater to those readers. It is also meant to show that economic science is not limited to the mainstream strand that is invariably taught at almost all universities and heralded in the mass media as the only science-based approach. This publication is also my contribution to an international handbook in the English language that a group of my colleagues and I are still developing.

The first impulse for writing this volume was the series of lectures I gave at the Warsaw School of Social and Economic Sciences in 2003, upon the invitation of a late friend of mine, Tadeusz Kowalik, who was then the vice chancellor of the school. He was also the first one to criticize me for insufficient attention to the issue of the distribution of national income in my *Myths and Reality in Economic Policy and in Teaching Economics*. His important advice is sorely missed in the process of evaluating the present volume.

Another important impulse for this book was provided by the lectures and seminars I gave at the "Political Critique" Institute for Advanced Studies in the years 2013–14. I would like to express gratitude to Jerzy Osiatyński for the valuable consulting and editing work that he contributed throughout the lengthy process of writing this text. Without his involvement and perseverance, this volume would not have been possible and would contain many more mistakes than it probably still does.

Kazimierz Łaski

Vienna, March 2015

1

Macroeconomic concepts and analytical tools

1.1 Basic Concepts in National Accounting

National accounting is primarily concerned with calculating the volume of output flows over a period of time (usually on an annual basis). A national economy produces a variety of goods, using all kinds of raw materials and intermediate products in the process. To be able to add up the value of those goods and estimate the cost of their production one needs prices. Indeed, national accounting would not be practicable without comprehensive statistical data on production and prices. Such data became gradually available with the development of capitalist production, as manufacturing became widespread. Thus, it comes as no surprise that national accounts emerged relatively late, when the capitalist economy had reached a certain level of maturity.

Gross domestic product (GDP) and its constituent components play a central role in macroeconomics, so let us begin with expounding several basic concepts used in national accounting, the discipline that deals with computing total output in an economy. Of fundamental importance is the notion of gross value added (GVA), occasionally also termed "gross new value created." Value added is generated in every company producing goods or services; it is the difference between the value of products made over a period of time (e.g., in a year) and the cost of the production factors used in the process of making them, excluding the depreciation of fixed assets. For instance, if a bakery produces goods of a total value of 100 euros per year and uses up flour, yeast, sugar, electricity, and other material inputs worth a total of 40 euros, then the GVA of that bakery will amount to 60 euros $(100 - 40 = 60)$. In turn, net value added is obtained by subtracting the depreciation of fixed assets (the decrease in the value of buildings, machinery, and equipment) from GVA.

The notion of GVA is much more often used than net value added, since precise measurement of depreciation is difficult.[1] Indeed, the market prices of old buildings, machines, and equipment do not reflect their depreciation over time very accurately. As a result, economists are forced to rely on alternative methods for estimating it, and especially on the tax rules specifying the rates of depreciation. Those rules prevent companies from depreciating their assets too rapidly, thus overstating costs in order to minimize taxable profits. To avoid this methodological quagmire, theoretical models typically employ the concept of gross rather than net value added.

Value added is inherent in the process of production and may be determined for every company. Subsequently, by summing the value added generated by all companies in a given economic sector or geographical region, we arrive at the total value added for that sector or region. Needless to say, from the point of view of national accounts, of utmost importance is the GVA of the entire economy, which is termed gross domestic product. GDP less total depreciation on the economy's fixed assets gives the net domestic product (NDP) of the country.

There are two basic methods of computing GDP: summing all incomes arising from production or summing all final expenditures. The first method is relatively straightforward. In purely capitalist companies, the process of producing aggregate output gives rise to compensation for workers and (gross) profits for owners. Let us designate total worker compensation as W, total (gross) profits as R, both after taxation, and total government revenues, or net taxes (taxes and social insurance contributions less government transfers and subsidies) as TN. Then, GDP can be represented as:

$$GDP = W + R + TN \tag{1.1}$$

The notion underpinning the other method of calculating GDP is final expenditure. To understand it, we first need to define the concept of final goods, which are the constituent elements of GDP. These are goods that are produced in a given country over a certain period of time and are not used up as production inputs in that country during that period. For instance, flour produced in a given year and sold to bakeries is not a final good, in contrast to flour bought directly by households. In other words, final goods include consumer goods and services purchased by households (private consumption – CP) or by the government with a view to delivering them to society (government consumption – CG), investment goods in the form of buildings, machinery, and equipment purchased by companies or the government in order to expand or replace their capital goods or increase stock levels (private and government investment – IP and IG, respectively), and exported goods (X). Thus, adopting a

---

[1] See Bhaduri (1972).

final expenditure perspective, GDP may be expressed by the following equation:

$$GDP = CP + CG + IP + IG + X - M \qquad (1.2)$$

where M denotes imported goods and services. Imports must be deducted since some final goods come from abroad or are produced by means of foreign factors of production. Such goods do not contribute to the gross value added generated in a given country. The final expenditures approach may also be given in the following form:

$$GDP = CP + IP + G + E \qquad (1.2')$$

where G stands for combined government expenditures on goods and investment $(CG + IG)$ and E stands for the balance of trade (international exchange of goods and services excluding international transfers of capital profits and labor compensation).[2,3]

The combined formulas (1.1) and (1.2') give:

$$W + R + TN = GDP = CP + IP + G + E \qquad (1.3)$$

Equation (1.3) shows that total incomes generated in the process of production of final goods are identical to the combined final expenditures of households, businesses, the government, and foreign buyers. The above identity is of paramount importance in the understanding of macroeconomic issues. For the time being, suffice it to say that the sum of all incomes and the sum of all expenditures are by definition equal; the remaining part of this book is largely devoted to explaining how this identity is arrived at. It should be borne in mind that the above equation is true for a national economy as a whole, rather than for individual companies. All firms generate gross value added (which is the source of their income), but not every firm manufactures final goods. While final goods comprise the entire output of some companies (e.g., bakeries catering to households), others may not produce final goods at all (e.g., a power plant supplying electricity only to an aluminum mill). It is theoretically possible for the gross value added generated by a company to be equal to the value of the final goods it produces, but that would be highly unusual.[4]

---

[2] Thus, the balance of trade includes, e.g., the services of freight companies, tourist agencies, etc., but excludes cross-border cash transfers between households, for example from Polish workers abroad to their families in Poland (such transfers are incorporated in the current account of the balance of payments, as discussed later in this book).

[3] All of these measures are customarily expressed at market prices, and they are also given in this sense throughout this book.

[4] This situation would occur if, and only if, the value of production factors purchased and used up by a company over a given period of time equaled the value of production factors generated in that company and used outside it over the same period. In a national economy as a whole, however (excluding international transactions and changes in stock levels), it is obvious that the quantities of intermediate products generated and used up are identical.

GDP is a measure of total output in a geographical sense. For instance, Poland's 2014 GDP provides information about the volume of value added generated in this country that year. However, to calculate the total income of Polish residents in 2014, we need to take into consideration the fact that some of them also received remuneration, such as labor compensation or capital profits (plus interest and rents) for their work performed or capital invested abroad. At the same time, a certain amount of gross value added generated in Poland that year was transferred in the form of labor compensation and capital profits to the residents of other countries. The difference between these two income flows is termed "net factor income from abroad" (NFIFA), and so the total income of Polish citizens is obtained by adding NFIFA to Poland's GDP. Traditionally, this macroeconomic concept is known as gross national product (GNP) and is given by the equation below:

$$GNP = GDP + NFIFA + net\ foreign\ aid \qquad (1.4)$$

As can be seen above, formula (1.4) includes aid received from abroad less aid granted to the rest of the world. Recently, the term gross national income (GNI) has often been used in place of GNP, but the content of both concepts is generally the same: they represent the sum of GDP and net primary incomes from other countries.

It should be emphasized that comparisons of GDP or its parts over time (e.g., GDP growth in Poland in the years 1990–2014), or space (e.g., GDP per capita in Poland vs. Germany or vs. the European Union average in 2014) are a non-trivial problem. Indeed, such comparisons are necessarily imprecise, and their results may be incoherent.

Let us consider two hypothetical GDP baskets containing two differently priced goods each; one basket for 1990 (A) and another for 2014 (B). If the product structures of the baskets are identical (e.g., the quantity of both products in basket B is three times that in basket A), then prices are practically irrelevant because the baskets may be compared directly (the real value of basket B will be three times greater than that of A). In turn, if the price structures of the goods in baskets A and B are the same (e.g., the price of good 1 is twice that of good 2 in both baskets), then a comparison of the baskets will yield coherent results even if the product structures of the baskets differ (e.g., basket B contains more units of product 1 and fewer units of product 2 relative to basket A). Indeed, under the circumstances, comparisons of the real value of baskets A and B, whether at prices of basket A or B, will lead to the same results.

However, in reality GDP baskets will have both different product and price structures because the quantities of some products increase faster than others, and the prices of products do not remain constant or change proportionally over time. Given the above, GDP comparisons will vary depending on whether they are conducted at prices of basket A or B and the results will be an approximation. The more the baskets are distant in time, the less consistent the comparison results will be, since disparities in the structure of goods and prices tend to widen over the years.[5]

Similar problems emerge if baskets A and B represent GDP per capita for two different countries (denoted as X and Y) in a given year. Comparisons of the baskets at prices of country X and country Y will lead to disparate results, with measurement differences increasing with the development gap between the two countries. The same holds true for comparisons between the GDP levels of countries X and Y conducted at prices specially constructed for the purposes of such analysis, e.g., at purchasing power parity (PPP), which reflects the purchasing power of the domestic currency relative to the US dollar or the euro.

Moreover, the results of GDP comparisons over time and space using different measures are not necessarily consistent with each other. Therefore, it may happen that the 1990–2004 GDP growth of country X as measured at constant prices in the currency of country X is higher than that of country Y as measured at constant prices in the currency of country Y, while a 1990–2004 comparison at PPP may show that the position of country X relative to country Y not only has not improved, but has deteriorated.

1.2 Non-financial and Financial Concepts

An inventory of national wealth in a closed economy will include only real elements: buildings and equipment belonging to companies as well as houses and movables belonging to households, excluding cash (coins and banknotes) and other financial instruments. This is due to the distinction between non-financial and financial concepts, which is discussed below.

Let us consider a balance sheet consisting of assets and liabilities. Assets include real wealth (WR) and financial assets (FA), while liabilities include financial liabilities (FL) and net wealth (WN). Net wealth equals real wealth if $FA = FL$. Generally, WN amounts to WR plus net financial assets, which are computed according to the formula $FN = FA - FL$. The balance sheet in question is given in Figure 1.1.

Financial assets are composed of cash and other financial resources (securities, commercial paper, bonds, etc.). In turn, financial liabilities consist of all kinds of debt. Financial assets are equal to financial liabilities only in rare instances, and only then is the net wealth of an economic agent identical to his or her real wealth. Consider a household that owns a house with an

---

[5] Differences in such estimates are presented in Figures A.1 and A.2 in Appendix 1 (pp. 9–10).

Assets	Liabilities
Real wealth (*WR*)	Financial liabilities (*FL*)
Financial assets (*FA*) (cash and other financial resources)	Net wealth (*WN*)

Figure 1.1. Balance sheet specifying the non-financial and financial assets and liabilities of an economic agent

outstanding mortgage and financial assets smaller than its debt. In that case, the net financial assets of that household ($FN = FA - FL$) will be negative ($FA < FL$) with its net wealth lower than its real wealth ($WN < WR$) as $WN = WR + FN$. On the other hand, there also exist mortgaged households having financial assets higher than their debt ($FA > FL$). Then, their net financial assets will be positive and their net wealth greater than their real wealth ($WN > WR$).

This is true for every economic agent. However, in a country's economy (excluding international transactions), and in the global economy as a whole, net wealth equals real wealth ($WN = WR$) because in this case $FA = FP$ (net financial assets by definition amount to zero). This is so because every financial asset corresponds to a financial debt—there is no debtor without a creditor. If A lends B 100 euros and receives from B a promissory note for that amount, then B is a debtor, A is a creditor, while their total net financial assets cancel out. That is why an inventory of national wealth incorporates only non-financial components, excluding financial ones, and especially cash (banknotes), since total cash outside the central bank is equal to the central bank's liabilities on account of issuing that cash.

1.3 Stocks, Flows, and Sector Balances

Stocks are economic quantities measured at a certain point in time (e.g., as of December 31, 2013). Let us assume a situation in which the real wealth of a household remains constant, but its nominal wealth changes throughout the year, for instance as a result of continuous repayment of its mortgage installments. To analyze this situation, we must consider the income and expenditure flows of that household. Flows are economic quantities that have a temporal dimension. Saying that a Polish household has an income of PLN 18,000 would be meaningless unless we know the interval over which this income is generated. In Poland a monthly salary of this magnitude would be considered very generous, while as an annual income it would be rather insubstantial, corresponding to monthly earnings of only PLN 1,500.

Changes in stocks are caused by income and expenditure flows. In particular, stocks increase when income exceeds expenditures and decrease when expenditures exceed income. Let us now consider changes in the balance of income and expenditures of an economic agent. Such a balance will show a surplus if expenditures are lower than income, or a deficit if income is lower than expenditures. A surplus will add to the net assets of the economic entity, while a deficit will decrease them. But also in this case, the sum total of surpluses and deficits in a country's economy (excluding international transactions) or in the global economy will equal zero due to the fact that every surplus can be linked to a deficit and every deficit to a surplus. Indeed, the expenditure of one economic agent is the income of another, just as there is no buyer without a seller and vice versa.

By way of illustration, let us divide the national economy (excluding international transactions) into the private and government sectors. The taxes collected by the government constitute its revenue, at the same time being the expenditure of the private sector. On the other hand, the government sector's expenditures are nothing else than the income of the private sector (arising out of transfers, such as salaries and welfare payments, and the sale of goods and services to the government, etc.). If the government's annual budget is balanced, then also the annual budget of the private sector will be balanced. However, if the government runs a budget deficit (spends more than its tax receipts), then the budget of the private sector will show a surplus of income over expenditure. Let us denote government deficit by D (where $D = G - TN$). If $D > 0$, then the financial assets of the private sector and its net wealth (at a given level of real wealth) will increase by $\Delta FN = D$. In turn, the government's net financial liabilities, and also its debt (at a given level of real wealth), will expand by the same amount. The same reasoning applies in the case of a government budget surplus, or $D < 0$. All other things being equal, this would imply an increase in the net financial assets and net wealth of the government sector by $|D|$, and a corresponding deficit of the private sector (a decline in its net financial assets and net wealth).

Finally, analysis incorporating the balance of foreign trade requires the addition of one more sector, that is, the rest of the world. The financial balance of the incomes and expenditures of these three sectors considered together is by definition equal to zero:

Balance of the private sector + Balance of the government sector + Balance of the rest of the world = 0

As follows from the above formula, if one of these sectors, e.g., the private sector, reports a positive balance (its income exceeds expenditures, leading to a surplus), then at least one of the remaining sectors (government or the rest of the world) must run a deficit. Therefore, there are some inescapable relationships between the surpluses (i.e., savings) and deficits of individual sectors, reflected in the resulting changes in the net wealth and debt levels of those sectors. Regrettably, those relationships are often ignored or overlooked in the public debate, giving rise to grave errors in economic policymaking.

Appendix 1. Comparison of Two Baskets of Goods over Time and Space

Let us consider two goods: good 1 with price $_Ap_1$ and good 2 with price $_Ap_2$. There are an infinite number of combinations of quantities of good 1 (q_1) and good 2 (q_2) that at prices $_Ap$ produce the value ZA:

$$q_{1A}p_1 + q_{2A}p_2 = ZA$$

A simple rearrangement of this equation leads to:

$$q_2 = \frac{ZA}{_Ap_2} - q_1 \frac{_Ap_1}{_Ap_2} \tag{A1.1}$$

(A1.1) is the equation of the segment KL in Figure A.1.1 with a slope of tan α, determined by the price ratio of $_Ap_1/_Ap_2$. All points along the segment KL represent baskets containing different quantities of goods 1 and 2 whose combined value amounts to ZA. One of such baskets is basket A represented by point A with the coordinates $q_1 = 0F$ and $q_2 = 0E$.

Let us now consider price $_Bp_1$ of good 1 and price $_Bp_2$ of good 2. Obviously, there is also an infinite number of combinations of quantities of goods 1 and 2 which at prices $_Bp$ amount to the value ZB:

$$q_{1B}p_1 + q_{2B}p_2 = ZB$$

which again can be transformed to:

$$q_2 = \frac{ZB}{_Bp_2} - q_1 \frac{_Bp_1}{_Bp_2} \tag{A1.2}$$

(A1.2) is the equation of the segment MN (in Figure A.1.1) with a slope of tan β determined by the price ratio of $_Bp_1/_Bp_2$. All points lying on the segment KL represent baskets containing different quantities of goods 1 and 2 whose combined value amounts to ZB. One of such baskets is basket B represented by point B with the coordinates $q_1 = 0H$ and $q_2 = 0G$. Let us assume that $0H > 0L$ and $0G < 0E$, which means that basket B contains more of good 1 and less of good 2.

Thus, we have two baskets containing goods 1 and 2: basket A lying on the segment KL and basket B lying on the segment MN. They can represent two baskets of goods for one country in different periods of time or for two different countries in the same period. The fundamental difficulty in comparing baskets A and B is that the price systems $_Ap$ and $_Bp$ differ.

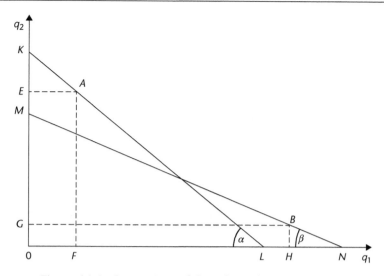

Figure A1.1. Comparison of the values of baskets A and B

Since the angle α is greater than β, then $(_Ap_1/_Ap_2) > (_Bp_1/_Bp_2)$, which means that in the price system $_Ap$ a unit of good 1 is valued higher than a unit of good 2 relative to the price system $_Bp$. Points K and L represent the same total basket value as point A because all of them are located along the segment KL. Point K represents a basket containing only good 2 valued in the $_Ap$ price system; the quantity of that good amounts to $0K$ ($0K = ZA/_Ap_2$). In turn, point L represents a basket containing only good 1, also valued in the $_Ap$ price system; the quantity of that good amounts to $0L$ ($0L = ZA/_Ap_1$).

Similarly, points M and N represent the same value as point B because they are all located along the segment MN. Point M represents a basket containing only good 2 valued according to the $_Bp$ price system; the quantity of that good amounts to $0M$ ($0M = ZB/_Bp_2$). In turn, point N represents a basket containing only good 1, also valued according to the $_Bp$ price system; the quantity of that good amounts to $0N$ ($0N = ZB/_Bp_1$).

As can be seen, $0K > 0M$, so in terms of the quantity of good 2 basket A (equivalent to basket K in the $_Ap$ price system) is greater than basket B (equivalent to basket M in the $_Bp$ price system). However, at the same time $0L < 0N$, so in terms of the quantity of good 1 basket A (equivalent to basket L in the $_Ap$ price system) is smaller than basket B (equivalent to basket N in the $_Bp$ price system).

Thus, it appears that comparisons of the value of baskets A and B by means of seemingly strictly physical measures (quantities of goods 1 or 2) lead to contradictory results. This is due to the fact that points K and L (equivalent to point A) are assessed according to the $_Ap$ price system, while points M and N (equivalent to point B) are assessed according to the $_Bp$ price system

This difficulty will also persist, albeit in a slightly different form, if the baskets are evaluated in terms of comparable prices (as it is done in practice). Let us use $_Ap$ prices as a comparable price system (both baskets will be valued at $_Ap$ prices). Taking as a point of departure Figure A1.1, this operation is represented by moving the segment KL with a

9

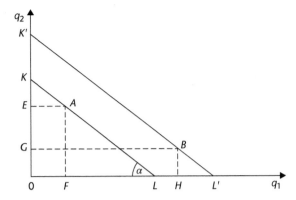

Figure A1.2. Basket B is greater than basket A in the $_Ap$ price system

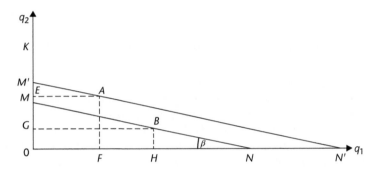

Figure A1.3. Basket B is smaller than basket A in the $_Bp$ price system

slope tan α to the right so that it touches point B (as shown in Figure A1.2). The segment $K'L'$ is parallel to the segment KL. The value of all points lying on the segment $K'L'$ (designated as $_AZB$) is higher than that of the points located on the segment KL. This means that the value of basket B is greater than that of basket A.

Now let us use $_Bp$ prices as a comparable price system (both baskets will be valued at $_Bp$ prices). Then, in Figure A1.1 the segment MN with a slope tan β will move to the right, so that it touches point A (as shown in Figure A1.3). The segment $M'N'$ is parallel to the segment MN. The value of all points along the segment $M'N'$ (designated as $_BZA$) is higher than that of the points along the segment MN. This means that the value of basket B is smaller than that of basket A.

As it can be seen, measurement results depend on the price system adopted for comparison purposes. The more disparate the price systems are, the more likely it is that the obtained results will be contradictory. If the compared periods are relatively close or the compared countries not very different, the changes in price relations will not be as dramatic as those shown in Figure A1.1. Thus, the results obtained using different price systems will still be different, but not necessarily contradictory.

2

Surplus of consumer goods and how it can be turned into a profit

2.1 Introductory Notes

The subject matter of these lectures is the capitalist economy rather than an abstract economy. Obviously, one can study the economy in the abstract, arguing that in every economic system decisions are made as to what to produce, how to produce it, and how to distribute the output among the members of society. In every society people have to work to obtain the goods necessary to meet their needs, and so they use means of production, which are in a sense more efficient extensions of the human hands. However, very general conclusions of this kind would not be of much help in elucidating how the various types of economies operate or in identifying ways of improving their operation.

Does the capitalist economy have anything in common with the centrally planned economy? Undoubtedly so. But can their common features help in understanding the problems currently besetting the former, and can they facilitate finding optimum solutions to these difficulties "here and now"? The answer to this question is negative since the two types of economic systems are not only different from one another, but also fundamentally contradictory in many aspects.

The three defining features of the capitalist economy are:

1) predominant market production
2) labor treated as a commodity
3) presence of two major social classes: capitalists and workers.

The first point implies that manufactured goods are not meant to be consumed directly by the producers, but are sold to essentially anonymous buyers in the market. While in pre-capitalist economies market production was negligible, it became ubiquitous in the capitalist economy, with household production reduced to a marginal phenomenon. The capitalist economy is also characterized by advanced division of labor, involving not only the production of consumer and investment goods, but also raw materials and intermediate products. This division of labor is not officially instituted, but rather brought about through markets, which provide a meeting place for the sellers and buyers of the various goods. Indeed, in the capitalist economy, with the predominant role of market production, the market is the fundamental coordination mechanism for the activity of producers and sellers. Each of them acts in their own interest, without regard for the others, but their actions are interconnected. In this sense, the market is a prodigious mechanism coordinating decisions that are at the same time independent and interdependent. However, as we shall see, this unique and irreplaceable mechanism is not free of certain major disadvantages and necessitates compliance with a specific set of rules, sometimes also requiring direct state intervention.

The predominance of market production, which is the second fundamental trait of the capitalist economy, implies paid labor. This means that labor carries a price in the form of remuneration for the time devoted by workers to performing the tasks assigned by their employers. Still, it is a very special commodity. In contrast to other services, labor (or, to be exact, the workforce which performs it) is not generated in the same way as other commodities. As a result, the labor market must not be treated just as any other kind of market. For instance, if demand for draft horses decreases, their prices go down and their supply declines in the process of adjustment to demand. On the other hand, if demand for labor services contracts and wages are reduced, what declines is not the population of workers, but rather aggregate demand, as wages are the chief driver of the latter.

The underlying class structure of capitalist society, which is the third fundamental feature of the capitalist economy, predominantly consists of capitalists, who own the means of production, and workers, who do not. However, in order to put their means of production to use, capitalists must purchase labor services. In turn, workers are economically forced to sell their services. Thus, the class division is determined by capital ownership, especially with respect to large manufacturing or service companies. Indeed, to acquire or establish such firms, it is necessary to make considerable financial outlays, which are typically beyond the reach of ordinary workers. Obviously, it may happen that enterprising individuals of modest financial means eventually become capitalists or owners of large companies, but they are exceptions to the rule. And the rule is that most capitalists are people who had some initial capital to begin with, usually inherited from their ancestors. Furthermore, the financial markets are mostly accessible to individuals who can offer some collateral in the form of assets owned by them.

While it is not impossible to advance from one class to the other, this is difficult. However, even in the most extreme capitalist systems there are some intermediate social groups, such as craftsmen, professionals, and family-run farms. Such groups also include workers with very high salaries, and those individuals who inherited considerable financial assets.

It should also be emphasized that while generally the incomes of capitalists are much higher than those of workers, there are some workers in top-earning positions whose incomes may be substantially higher than those of small capitalists. Thus, income disparities do not always run along the lines of class divisions. As we shall see, increasing income inequalities play a major role in the way the capitalist economy functions.

2.2 Surplus of Consumer Goods

Michał Kalecki, the pioneer of the effective demand theory, used to tell an anecdote that can be recounted as follows. There is a railroad line that is heavily underused because unemployment is high and the business climate in the region is bad. The question is what can be done? The provocative answer given by Kalecki was: build another railroad line, next to the existing one. The project will generate contracts for railroad tracks, sleepers, construction work, etc., which will stimulate business around the old line. Steelworks, manufacturers of sleepers, construction companies, etc., will need raw materials to complete these contracts. The increased employment and additional incomes will in turn stoke consumer demand. Therefore, also demand for railroad transport will increase, and the old line will be used more intensively. But what can be done once the construction of the new line is completed, the contracts expire, and people start losing jobs again? According to Kalecki, yet another railroad line should be built next to the other ones! Obviously, the above anecdote should not be taken literally. In real life it does not make much sense to construct new railroad lines along old, underused ones. Instead, the message is that a fuller utilization of the existing production potential depends directly on its expansion. The anecdote also demonstrates that the relationship between so-called common sense and the principles of economic development is not always straightforward.

Indeed, common sense may not be sufficient for scientific reasoning, not only in economics. For instance, we all know from our everyday experience that a coin tossed out of a window will drop to the ground faster than a feather tossed at the same time out of the same window. And yet, if the coin and feather are placed inside a vacuum tube, both will fall at equal speed and come to the bottom at exactly the same time. The scientific principle inferred from this experiment is that gravity acts on all objects in the same way. As can be seen, our experience is not always consistent with the scientific theories that explain it.

The main lesson that may be drawn from Kalecki's anecdote is that in a national economy income is determined by spending. This stands in stark contrast to our experience. In our everyday lives it is our spending that is dependent on income, and not the other way round. But it is not so in a national economy as a whole. Here, income is exactly equal to expenditures, within the limits of existing production capacity. I will try to illustrate this thesis using a simplified and rather abstract but instructive example.

Let us begin with a very basic model, in which the national economy consists exclusively of one bakery with an owner who pursues profit. The bakery is vertically integrated in the sense that it has its own mill, wheat fields, etc. In this case, its final product equals gross value added because it does not purchase any commodities from the outside. While this model is unrealistic, it serves well as an introduction to further analysis. Let us assume that the daily production capacity of this bakery is 1,200 loaves of bread at an employment of $L_c = 100$ workers at the various levels of production, with each worker being paid $w = 8$ loaves a day. The output per worker is $x = 12$ loaves. If the bakery works at full capacity, it produces $L_c x = 100(12) = 1,200$ loaves of bread and its workers can purchase $L_c w = 100(8) = 800$ loaves, which leads to a surplus of $L_c(x - w) = 100(12 - 8) = 400$ loaves of bread (the owner's consumption is ignored for the sake of simplicity). This surplus cannot be sold within the bakery and it constitutes a potential profit that may be realized only if there are customers with an adequate purchasing power. Therefore, as long as those 400 loaves remain unsold, there is no profit, and without a profit bread production does not make sense for the owner. The very important conclusion here is that what is needed to turn the commodity surplus into an actual profit is demand from outside the bakery. This example also shows that the bakery's supply itself cannot generate sufficient demand that would guarantee utilization of the total production potential of the bakery.

The question arises as to whether the above conclusions hold only for our extravagant assumption that the entire national economy consists of one vertically integrated bakery. Actually, it is not the case. If we assume the existence of any number of vertically integrated companies making consumer goods, then the situation that was observed for the bakery will also apply to all of them. The workers of a company cannot purchase everything that they produce and there will always be a surplus of commodities. The only difference is that now the employees of the bakery are not limited to buying bread alone, meat packers do not have to buy only meat, and the workers of furniture or computer factories may purchase goods other than furniture and computers, etc. Nevertheless, their overall purchasing power will not suffice to buy all the consumer goods produced and realize the profits embodied in the commodity surpluses of all the companies.

Our example shows that a vertically integrated sector of consumer goods will inevitably lead to a surplus of commodities that cannot be sold within the consumer sector. This surplus could be sold, turning potential profits into real ones, only outside of this sector. It also follows from the above that the supply of goods in the consumer sector left to its own devices will not generate a corresponding demand. This conclusion contradicts Say's law, according to which supply creates its own demand whereby each seller is also a buyer.

However, one could argue that our conclusion depends on the fact that real wages of 8 loaves of bread a day are simply too low. Indeed, at wages equal to 12 loaves of bread no external demand would be necessary because there would be no surplus of commodities. That is undoubtedly true, but then the owner of the bakery would not have any motivation to run the company and bear the related risk, either. Also the depreciation of machinery at all levels of production would not be allowed for. On the other hand, the lower the real wages, the higher the commodity surplus to be sold. For instance, at real wages of 6 loaves of bread, the commodity surplus would amount to $L_c(x-w) = 100$ $(12-6) = 600$ loaves of bread (rather than 400). Thus, it appears that the issue under consideration cannot be resolved by adjustment of real wages.

To solve the problem of selling the surplus of consumer goods and realizing the "locked" profits, we need to take into account the existence of firms producing non-consumer goods. Let us consider a vertically integrated factory making investment goods, such as machinery and equipment (including construction). The real wages in that factory are the same as in the bakery. The question now arises as to the size of investment workforce L_i that would provide purchasing power sufficient for absorption of the commodity surplus at full production capacity of the bakery. Thus, the desired L_i should fulfil the condition:

$$L_i w = L_c(x - w) \tag{2.1}$$

Dividing both sides by w, we arrive at:

$$L_i = L_c \frac{(x - w)}{w} \tag{2.1'}$$

In this case, $(x-w)/w = (12-8)/8 = \frac{1}{2}$, which means that employment at the factory must be equal to half the employment at the bakery. Indeed, if the factory employs $L_i = 50$ workers, they earn $L_i w = 50(8) = 400$ loaves of bread, which exactly corresponds to the commodity surplus at full capacity of the bakery. If the factory employed 60 workers, then the commodity surplus would fall short by 80 loaves as $60(8) = 480$ loaves of bread. In turn, if the factory employed only 40 workers, not all surplus would be sold as $40(8) = 320$

loaves (there would be 80 loaves of unsold bread). The first case will give rise to insufficient supply of goods and (at fixed wages) long lines of customers in stores, while the other case will lead to insufficient purchasing power and a glut of commodities. The unbiased reader will agree that capitalist economies typically correspond to the second case involving a buyer's market, goods waiting for customers, and workers looking for employment.

Let us return to the question posed above: Is this predicament not caused by "rigid wages"? What would happen if in a buyer's market and at insufficient investment real wages were reduced to, e.g., 6 loaves of bread? Then, demand for the commodity surplus at an employment of $L_i = 40$ would amount to $40(6) = 240$ loaves of bread (a decrease from $40(8) = 320$), while the commodity surplus at full capacity production would increase from $100(12 - 8) = 400$ to $100(12 - 6) = 600$ loaves of bread.

Thus, the introduction of "flexible real wages" in place of rigid ones would not improve the situation, but further aggravate it. A critical reader could argue that the obtained results are also affected by the fact that employment at the factory remained unchanged at 40 workers. If investment were sufficiently increased, the entire commodity surplus would be sold and the problem of low demand would disappear. Indeed, the value of the fraction $(x - w)/w$ at a real wage of 6 loaves of bread would be $(12 - 6)/6 = 1$, so L_i should equal L_c and amount to 100 workers employed in an investment factory. Thus, if investment workforce increased from 40 to 100 workers, then the entire surplus of consumer goods would be marketable. This indeed would be the case, but due to increased investment rather than to lower real wages. Since the final result depends on the volume of investment, a drop in real wages from 8 to 6 loaves of bread would actually make things more difficult, because at the original real wages it would have been enough to increase employment in the investment factory from 40 to 50 (rather than 100) workers.

Even more importantly, the question is whether a decrease in real wages would influence employment in the factory of investment goods, and, if so, in what way. This issue is linked to the determinants of investment decisions, and at this point a conclusive answer may not yet be given. However, it should be emphasized that this largely depends on companies' expectations concerning the future, which are going to be rather pessimistic: indeed, decreasing wages automatically impairs the sales of consumer goods and leads to lower utilization of production capacity. Under the circumstances companies will be rather reluctant to invest in expanding their production potential.

Figure 2.1 gives a visual representation of the problem of commodity surplus and the conditions under which it may be sold. The radius $C = xL_c$ denotes the output of the bakery at employment L_c and productivity x. The latter is represented by the slope of radius C, i.e., by $\tan \beta$. The segment $0M$ represents maximum employment at the bakery ensuring full utilization of its

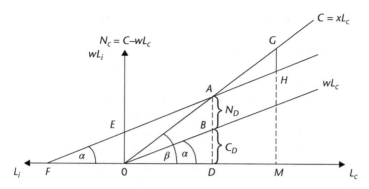

Figure 2.1. Surplus of consumer goods and conditions under which it can be sold

production capacity. It is assumed that the product wage-rate, w, is equal to tan α. Therefore the radius with the slope tan α represents the wage bill corresponding to any given volume of employment. If employment in the bakery is $0D$, its wage bill, which represents the internal consumption of the bakery, is $C_D = w(0D)$. The segment parallel to this radius and passing through point E transects the radius C at point A and the L_i axis at point F. The segment $OE = w(0F)$ represents the demand for consumer goods generated by the investment goods factory: since $(OE/OF) = \tan \alpha$, then $OE = \tan \alpha$ (OF). On the supply side, this corresponds to the segment $AB = N_D (x - w)0D$, which represents the surplus of consumer goods of the bakery at employment $0D$. Thus, condition (2.1) is fulfilled.

In turn, at maximum employment $0M$ and real wages $w = \tan \alpha$, the commodity surplus $N_M = GH$ would not be marketable. Furthermore, if other things being equal real wages declined, then the slope of the radius wL_c would be smaller and the corresponding point A would move towards the point of origin along the radius C. The unsalable surplus of consumer goods (GH) would then expand rather than shrink. In contrast, given $L_i = 0F$, a rise in real wages, leading to a larger angle α, could create a market for the commodity surplus GH. Keeping the segment $0F$ constant, we could increase the slope of the radius wL_c and of the parallel segment EH to a position in which the latter would transect the radius C at point G. Then, at a given $L_i = 0F$, we would arrive at a level of employment L_i that would be adjusted to full employment in the bakery, $L_c = 0M$.

Formula (2.1), which specifies the condition of consistency in the consumption goods market, deserves closer analysis. In our approach, the volume of investment expressed on the left side of (2.1) determines the marketable volume of commodity surplus. This is the most important element of the effective demand theory: investment spending is the decisive factor determining the volume of aggregate output, and thus also aggregate income. However, the surplus of consumer goods, N_c, which corresponds to the difference between total output of the bakery and its costs of production, may also be interpreted as a profit, or internal savings. This interpretation is characteristic of all varieties of mainstream economics. According to that interpretation, these are real rather than potential profits, or savings, since any amount of commodities may be sold provided that prices are flexible. In turn, these profits (savings) determine the volume of investment: the greater they are, the greater the investment. Thus we return to Say's world, in which the problem of insufficient aggregate demand simply does not exist.

In a moneyless economy, goods are exchanged for other goods. If a shoemaker in need of a pair of trousers and a tailor in need of a pair of shoes come to the market, then they can directly exchange trousers for shoes. In this model, the problem of demand does not exist as the seller is also a buyer, and the buyer is also a seller. In economics many misunderstandings arise due to the fact that the above model of moneyless exchange is also thought to be valid in a monetary economy. It is believed that money simply facilitates exchange enabling trade even if the demand and supply of both exchange partners do not match.

While this is true, money leads to splitting the unitary act of direct exchange of goods into two independent acts: sale of goods and acquisition of goods, which has some major ramifications. The seller of shoes (or trousers) receives money, but he or she does not have to spend it immediately (e.g., the money may be kept until the next day, month, or year). The seller may also refrain from spending that money altogether, saving it for posterity, etc. Therefore, at a given period of time sales may not be followed by purchases, which was impossible in a moneyless economy. There are also acts of purchase without immediately preceding sales, when a buyer spends money obtained from a sale in the past or funds offered by the banking system which creates money. Therefore, both sales without immediately following purchases and purchases without directly preceding sales may co-exist as individual events in a given period of time.

However, for the economy as a whole these values may differ only in the sense of intended sale and purchase transactions. Taking into consideration all acts of sale and purchase *ex post*, they have to be equal to each other by definition. Thus, there must exist a mechanism that ensures that intended acts of sale and purchase, which are usually not correlated with each other, become balanced *ex post*.

Let us formulate the problem under consideration in more specific terms. If somebody receives a monetary income and does not spend it on consumption, then the resulting surplus is defined as savings. Let us call such a surplus intended savings. On the other hand, there also exist monetary expenditures not directly fuelled by an income (e.g., investments financed entirely by loans extended by the banking system). The overall values of intended savings and planned investments do not necessarily equal each other, but actual saving must be equal to actual investment. Thus, one of the leading themes of our analysis is an explanation of how these values, which are not necessarily equal *ex ante*, become equal *ex post*.

The differing explanations of this problem provided by the effective demand theory and mainstream economics lie at the heart of these lectures. However, we are still missing one essential element of the puzzle, which prevents us from proceeding in this discussion: prices. So far, we have been using the notion of real wages (expressed as loaves of bread), but in reality wages must be measured in nominal or money terms, just as profits and savings. Also the relationship between savings and investment may be seriously addressed only if both are expressed as nominal values. Therefore, prior to further explication of the effective demand theory, we need to introduce the notion of prices.

3

Prices and the distribution
of national income

3.1 Cost- and Demand-determined Pricing Systems

In Kalecki's theory of prices, goods are divided into two major groups: one contains industrial products, construction activity, and services, and the other consists of agricultural produce and all types of raw materials, including energy carriers. Goods classified in the first group are intermediate and final products (we shall call them "finished goods"), while goods in the second group are raw materials. This distinction is important because the prices of these two groups of goods are determined by different sets of factors.

This difference is primarily due to supply conditions. The supply of finished goods is elastic, also in the short term, because their producers usually have considerable reserve output capacity. Thus, an increased demand typically leads to a greater supply rather than higher prices. In contrast, the supply of raw materials is largely constrained by production capacity, monopolistic practices, or state regulations. This situation is presented in Figure 3.1, showing the relationship between the quantity q of a good and its price p. In panel A, supply is represented by the segment SS. When demand increases from D_1 to D_2, then prices rise from p_1 to p_2 in the short term during which supply remains at the level q_0. In Panel B, supply is represented by the horizontal segment SS. When demand increases from D_1 to D_2, prices remain at the level p_0, while quantity rises from q_1 to q_2. In the case of finished goods, supply and demand are typically balanced through quantity adjustment at a given price. In contrast, an equilibrium level for raw materials and agricultural produce is attained through price adjustment.

World prices of raw materials are very sensitive to demand because their supply in relation to changes in their price is inelastic, at least in the short term. This is particularly evident in agriculture; for instance if demand for meat goes up, it takes a rather long time for the production of livestock to

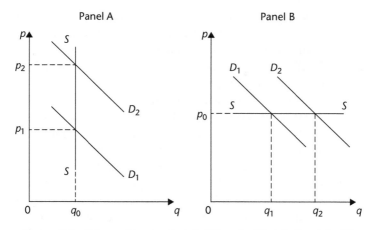

Figure 3.1. Prices of raw materials (A) and of finished goods (B)

catch up. In the case of natural resources, increased production often requires the discovery of new deposits involving long-term investments. In the case of petroleum, the factors at play include both supply constraints and oligopolistic practices, and elements of competition resulting from the activity of those oligopolies.

In contrast to raw materials, the supply of finished goods is elastic, mostly as a result of imperfect competition. A typical modern industrial sector is dominated by a small number of large companies (rather than a large number of small firms). This situation is a far cry from the model of perfect competition in which an individual manufacturer provides a small proportion of overall supply without affecting the prices. Under perfect competition, for small firms, market prices are external determinants, while costs are the limiting factors. The position of an oligopolistic company is different. It has a significant market share and is capable of producing more goods than it does, but that would affect the prices it can command. Moreover, such a company must not disregard the reactions of other oligopolists offering similar products, to which it could lose customers. In this situation, the optimum price setting strategy is based on unit variable costs plus a profit margin (mark-up). That margin must cover not only the depreciation of equipment and buildings, but also other fixed costs.

Thus, the prices of finished goods are set by manufacturers by adding a mark-up to unit variable costs, taking into account competition. At those prices, the manufacturer is ready to supply any quantity of goods that can be absorbed by the market. In practice, this implies that companies usually keep some inventories of goods and have reserve production capacity. They decrease their inventories when demand is greater than expected and increase them in the opposite case. Adjustment to market needs occurs mostly through quantity rather than pricing. A distinction between these two types of reactions to changes in demand is a characteristic feature of the effective demand theory; it is generally ignored in mainstream economics in which price-based adjustment almost always takes precedence.

Let us consider the issue of pricing finished goods more formally. Why do companies tend to take into account variable (labor or raw materials) rather than fixed costs (overheads such as costs of used machines and equipment, of long-term loans, etc.)? In the short term, they have some influence over their variable costs, while their overheads are predetermined. Therefore, they take into consideration those price-setting factors which depend on their current decisions and ignore those which do not. Variable costs are determined by the output volume (quantity of goods produced) and include the costs of labor, raw materials, and intermediate goods. As production capacity is typically underused, unit labor costs (at given wages) will be constant, at least up to the full utilization of production capacity. At given prices of materials, one can also assume that unit material costs will remain invariable. As a result, the relationship between unit variable costs and output volume may be presented as in Figure 3.2.

Initially, the curve representing unit variable costs, DB, runs parallel to the horizontal axis, which shows that they are constant throughout the first interval. Subsequently, the cost of each additional unit produced (i.e., its marginal cost) begins to rise, implying an increase in unit variable costs, as the company approaches its production capacity (an output volume equal to the segment $0A$). However, since companies rarely reach their production

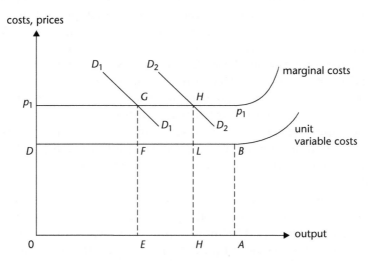

Figure 3.2. Prices of finished goods as a function of unit variable costs and output volume

capacity, the focus is on the segment between points 0 and A. To cover fixed costs and provide for profits, the company adds a mark-up to unit variable costs, amounting to the segment Dp_1. The segment p_1p_1 is the supply curve. If the demand for the company's products corresponds to the curve D_1D_1, then the company sells the quantity $0E$ at a price of p_1. The surplus thus obtained is represented by the area of the rectangle Dp_1GF. It covers the fixed costs and provides for a profit. If demand increases and the demand curve moves to D_2D_2, then the company sells the quantity $0H$ at the same price (p_1), while the surplus increases by the area of the rectangle $FGHL$. These considerations convey the idea of quantity adjustment of supply to demand at a given price level.

Kalecki assumes that in the process of price setting companies take into account two factors: the average variable costs (also called average prime costs), u, and the average prices in a given sector, $\bar{p}$. According to Kalecki, "the firm must make sure that the price does not become too high in relation to prices of other firms, for this would drastically reduce sales." On the other hand, the price should not become "too low in relation to its average prime cost, for this would drastically reduce its profit margin."[1] These conditions are met by the formula:

$$p = mu + n\bar{p} \tag{3.1}$$

where m and n are positive values and $n < 1$.[2] In a given sector, companies have different average variable costs due to varying degrees of their technological advancement. Therefore, their positions in relation to the average price $\bar{p}$ differ, which is reflected in the parameters m and n. However, one may calculate average values for a given sector, that is, average variable costs $\bar{u}$, as well as average parameters $\bar{m}$ and $\bar{n}$. Furthermore, let us consider a representative company in which m, n, and price correspond to the average values. The formula for calculating cost-determined prices for that representative company is as follows:[3]

$$\bar{p} = \bar{m}\bar{u} + \bar{n}\bar{p}$$

and consequently

$$\bar{p} = \frac{\bar{m}}{1-\bar{n}}\bar{u} \tag{3.2}$$

---

[1] Kalecki (1954 [1991]: 211).
[2] This postulate becomes clear when it is assumed that the price $p = \bar{p}$; indeed, at n higher than 1, the coefficient m could not be positive.
[3] See Lopez and Assous (2010: 72).

where the term $[\bar{m}/(1-\bar{n})] > 1$ represents the degree of monopoly. "The average price, $\bar{p}$, is proportionate to the average unit prime cost $\bar{u}$ if the degree of monopoly is given. If the degree of monopoly increases, $\bar{p}$ rises in relation to $\bar{u}$."[4] At a given degree of monopoly, the relation of total revenues of an industrial sector to its total variable costs is stable. Thus, if the degree of monopoly, $[\bar{m}/(1-\bar{n})]$, increases or decreases, then the ratio of revenues to costs (i.e., profitability) rises or declines accordingly. Of course, as has been stressed, the above considerations presuppose elastic supply ensured by reserve production capacity.

Kalecki enumerated three major factors affecting the degree of monopoly in developed capitalist economies. The most important of them is the advancing process of concentration of firms, giving rise to huge corporations manufacturing a significant proportion of output in a given sector. These corporations are also usually technological leaders and are aware of the fact that their pricing has a considerable impact on the average price, $\bar{p}$. As the latter influences the behavior of smaller companies, they will be forced to follow suit. Thus, taking advantage of their dominant position, large corporations can set their prices at a higher level than is otherwise possible. Such a situation can also lead to overt, or, more often, covert price-fixing schemes among major corporations in various industries.

Another factor affecting the degree of monopoly is the replacement of price competition with ubiquitous advertising, sales agents, and customer services, accompanied by a simultaneous decrease in the quality, and especially durability, of products. The idea is that the customer should repurchase the product after a relative short period of time.

The third factor contributing to the degree of monopoly is the bargaining power of workers, which is positively correlated with the presence and power of trade unions and negatively correlated with unemployment. Over the past years, in the developed countries the bargaining power of workers has considerably decreased. The number of trade union members in relation to total workers has declined and globalization has led to greater competition from the less developed nations where wages typically are a fraction of those in the developed countries. Thus, the weakening of workers' bargaining power has certainly led to higher monopoly of late.

In his theory of product pricing, Kalecki deliberately gives up the profit maximization principle: "In view of the uncertainties faced in the process of price fixing it will not be assumed that the firm attempts to maximize its profits in any precise sort of manner."[5] This is an important point as it may

---

[4] Kalecki (1954 [1991]: 214).
[5] Kalecki (1954 [1991]: 210). [Translator's note: Kalecki used the term "price fixing" in the sense of "price setting."]

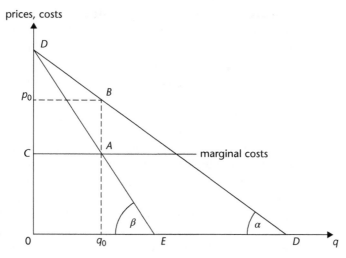

Figure 3.3. Total revenue, marginal revenue, and marginal costs for a monopolist

suggest that companies behave irrationally and accept profits that are lower than those they would be able to achieve. Indeed, both the quantity and price commanded by the monopolist, presented in Figure 3.3, are suboptimal. Let us now assume that the monopolist knows exactly the average and marginal variable costs, as well as demand (*DD*), as presented in Figure 3.3.

The segment *DD* represents price as a linear function of sales. The lower the price p ($p < OD$), the greater the quantity q may be sold, which implies a lack of a straightforward relationship with total revenues. If a small price reduction leads to a considerable rise in the quantity of products sold, then the revenue, $U = pq$, will increase, but it will decline otherwise. It is even more difficult to predict the implications of quantity and pricing changes for profits. The solution would be to find such a combination of the variables p and q for which profit would be maximized, which happens at the point where a revenue increase is equal to the corresponding increase in marginal costs.

Let the price function be expressed as:

$$p = A - bq \tag{3.3}$$

where the angle α, $\tan \alpha = b$, represents the slope of the segment *DD*. Thus, multiplying the price by the volume of output, we arrive at the revenue U:

$$U = pq = (A - bq)q = Aq - bq^2 \tag{3.4}$$

The relationship between revenue and output volume can be found by calculating the derivative of U with respect to q:

$$\frac{dU}{dq} = A - 2bq \tag{3.5}$$

25

This derivative, or marginal revenue, is represented by the segment DE in Figure 3.3; its slope is represented by angle β, $\tan \beta = 2b$. Thus, the slope of the segment DE is greater than that of the segment DD; the former intersects the horizontal axis halfway the $0D$ interval. Finally, Figure 3.3 also shows marginal costs, which are equal to average variable costs at a distance of $0C$ from the horizontal axis.

The above data are sufficient to find the maximum profit, which is the combination of the price p and the quantity q at which an increase in revenue (marginal revenue dU/dq) equals the increase in marginal costs. In this case, marginal costs are represented by the segment parallel to the horizontal axis, which means that the above condition is satisfied by point A. At the quantity q_0 the price is p_0, while the total profit is equal to the area of the rectangle p_0BAC, which is the difference between total revenue (the rectangle $0p_0Bq_0$) and total variable costs (the rectangle $0CAq_0$). Indeed, in the event of an output volume lower than q_0 the profit will decline as the company forfeits a revenue increase that would exceed the increase in costs. In turn, in the event of an output volume greater than q_0, the profit will decline as revenue will rise more slowly than costs.

Given the fact that in the cost-based approach prices are set by adding a mark-up to marginal costs, the value of that mark-up corresponds to the degree of monopoly. Let us compare the cost-based price with the price at which the profit is maximized, given in Figure 3.3. The combination of price and output volume will overlap for these two calculation methods only in one case: if the mark-up happens to be equal to the segment AB. Mark-ups on the marginal costs that are higher or lower than AB actually reduce profits. Furthermore, it can be proven that in a situation of profit maximization, at given marginal costs, higher demand would lead not only to a higher output volume (as in the cost-based pricing approach), but also to higher prices.

As it was already noted, Kalecki justified his departure from the strict principle of profit maximization by the fact that companies operate under conditions of uncertainty. This thesis was further elaborated by Amit Bhaduri, who argued that not all information or predictions are available to everyone and not all are equally rated by companies. Naturally, companies can readily access data about their own costs, and that data are also more reliable than information concerning total demand for a product or the effect of price changes on total demand. Bhaduri termed the former type of information "hard" and the latter "soft," aptly noting that companies tend to pay more attention to hard rather than soft data. This is rational because it leads to solutions that are satisfactory from the point of view of profits in a situation where optimum price adjustment based on strict profit maximization is uncertain, costly, and slow.[6]

---

[6] See Bhaduri (1986: 82–4).

Thus, companies behave rationally by adding a mark-up to unit production costs and letting the market decide how much of the product will be sold at a given price. While this rationality is procedural rather than goal-oriented, under imperfect information the former may lead to better results than the latter, which would require all types of information to be considered as having the same weight.[7]

3.2 Distribution of National Income

The cost-based pricing approach is directly related to the division of national income into wages and profits. According to (3.2), the degree of monopoly determines the relationship between prices and variable costs, mostly in the manufacturing sectors. If this formula is applied to the entire national economy, the mark-up on the average variable costs may be expressed as a proportion of the latter. The mark-up covers profits (before depreciation, including interest on loans), R, plus fixed labor costs (salaries of white-collar workers), WU. Thus, in the entire economy, for the sum of profits and fixed labor costs, we get:

$$R + WU = (\kappa - 1)(WF + MAT) \tag{3.6}$$

where $\kappa = \overline{m}(1 - \bar{n})$ represents the degree of monopoly for the economy as a whole, WF – wages of manual workers, and MAT – costs of materials. The sum $(WF + MAT)$ corresponds to variable costs. Adding WF to both sides, we arrive at GDP or national income:

$$Y = WF + R + WU = WF + (\kappa - 1)(WF + MAT) \tag{3.7}$$

The ratio of WF to Y, denoted as ω, equals:

$$\omega = \frac{WF}{Y} = \frac{WF}{WF + (\kappa - 1)(WF + MAT)} = \frac{1}{1 + (\kappa - 1)(1 - j)} \tag{3.8}$$

where $j = (MAT/WF)$ represents the ratio of costs of materials to variable labor costs. According to (3.8), the share of wages in national income primarily depends on the degree of monopoly, κ. If it is stable, then also the share of wages in national income remains the same.[8] The other factor determining ω is the ratio j. The costs of materials are affected by the costs of raw materials, variable labor costs, and the degree of monopoly at the preceding stages of production. Therefore, at a given degree of monopoly, the ratio j depends on

---

[7] See Bhaduri (1986: 82–4).
[8] This requires maintaining certain proportions between increases in nominal wages, productivity growth, and inflation. This problem is analyzed in greater detail further on.

the ratio of prices of raw materials (affected by demand) to average variable labor costs. The third factor determining the ratio ω is the structure of production. In particular, the levels of price monopolization vary across industries, so changes in the structure of production affect κ for the entire economy.

The share of total wages ($W = WF + WU$) in national income, denoted as α, can be expressed as:

$$\alpha = \frac{WF + WU}{Y} = \omega + \frac{WU}{Y} \tag{3.9}$$

Thus, that share depends not only on ω, but also on the ratio (WU/Y), which is the share of the salaries of white-collar workers in national income. Summing up, the share of total wages in national income, α, is determined by the degree of monopoly, the ratio of raw material prices to variable labor costs, the structure of production, and the division of wages, W, into the constituent components of WF and WU.

It is generally assumed that the most important of these factors are the degree of monopoly and the average wage rate. To examine this hypothesis, let us radically simplify formula (3.9) and leave out raw materials and fixed costs of labor. The former removes the problem of demand-based pricing and the latter allows us to treat all labor costs as variable costs. This simplification must also be reflected in the price formula (3.2), which we use for analyzing the distribution of national income. For that end, let us denote prices as p, the degree of monopoly as κ, the average nominal wage rate as w, GDP in constant prices as X, and the number of workers as L. Then we arrive at:

$$p = \kappa \frac{wL}{X}$$

or

$$p = \kappa \frac{w}{x} \tag{3.10}$$

where $\bar{u}$, average variable costs, are replaced by the quotient (w/x), or unit labor cost, ulc, defined as nominal wages (per worker), w, falling on productivity per worker, x.

If the rate of growth of the variables is denoted with the operator $g(i)$, $i = p$, k, w, x, then we arrive at:

$$g(p) = g(\kappa) + [g(w) - g(x)] \tag{3.11}$$

where the term in square brackets, $[g(w) - g(x)]$, is the rate of growth of unit labor costs, $g(ulc)$. It follows from the above that strict equality of price increase $g(p)$ with unit labor costs, $g(ulc)$, occurs only if the mark-up, κ, is constant, or $g(\kappa) = 0$.

It should be borne in mind that changes in the mark-up coefficient imply changes in the distribution of national income between wages and profits. Let us denote the share of wages, $W = wL$, in gross domestic product, $Y = pX$, as α:

$$\alpha = \frac{wL}{pX} = \frac{w}{px} \tag{3.12}$$

and then substitute (3.10) for p. Then, the equation can be transformed to

$$\alpha = \frac{1}{\kappa} \tag{3.13}$$

and

$$g(\alpha) = -g(\kappa) \tag{3.14}$$

This shows that the distribution of national income between wages and profits remains constant if the degree of monopoly does not change. When the degree of monopoly increases or decreases, then the share of wages in national income decreases (increases) accordingly.

Based on (3.10), we can also obtain the factors that determine the degree of monopoly, κ:

$$p = \kappa \frac{w}{x} \tag{3.10'}$$

which means that

$$g(\kappa) = [g(p) + g(x)] - g(w) \tag{3.15}$$

Thus, it can be seen that in order to maintain a stable κ, nominal wages, $g(w)$, must rise at the same rate as the sum of changes in productivity and prices $[g(p) + g(x)]$. When nominal wages grow faster than that sum, then the degree of monopoly declines. In the opposite case, the degree of monopoly rises.

If we substitute 0 for $g(\kappa)$, then from (3.15) we obtain:

$$g(w) - g(p) = g(x) \tag{3.16}$$

At a constant degree of monopoly, real wages $g(w) - g(p)$ would grow in line with productivity. Furthermore, as the distribution of national income between wages and profits would then remain unchanged, workers and capitalists would benefit from the results of technological advancement in equal measures.

The thesis that prices are mostly determined by unit labor costs is further corroborated by the following line of reasoning: GDP is calculated in current prices and if one wants to find the real GDP increase, one needs to use

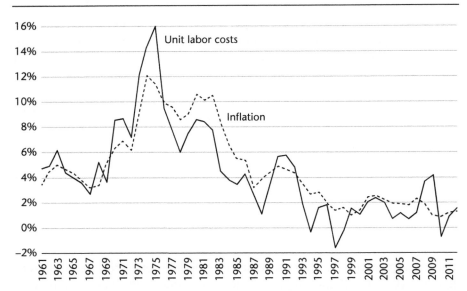

Figure 3.4. Increase in unit labor costs and prices in selected EMU countries (percentage per annum)
Source: Flassbeck and Lapavitsas, 2013, p. 8.

deflators, or price indexes.[9] In all countries GDP deflators are strongly correlated with unit labor costs (average wages divided by GDP per worker). Figure 3.4 presents mean GDP deflators and mean unit labor costs, *ulc*, defined as the sum of average gross wages for all workers divided by real GDP per worker for twelve eurozone countries (Belgium, Germany, Finland, France, Greece, Ireland, Italy, Luxembourg, Netherlands, Austria, Portugal, and Spain) over the past half-century; the figures are expressed in ECU/euros.

First of all, it should be noted that while the correlation between the two curves is definitely present, it is not perfect. This is quite understandable, since in order to focus on the most crucial factors, we deliberately ignore some other factors determining prices and the structure of national income. In the 1960s, changes in prices and unit labor costs were almost identical. Thus, in that period nominal wages changed more or less in line with productivity and prices, or, in other words, the increase in real wages approximately corresponded to the increase in productivity. In the first half of the 1970s, which saw a surge of inflation, the increase of unit labor costs even surpassed the increase of prices. Thus, in those years, real wages rose faster than productivity

[9] A deflator expresses the ratio of national income at current prices (in nominal terms) to national income at constant prices (in real terms) and so it acts as a coefficient of inflation understood as percentage change of prices of all goods contributing to GDP over the period under study. Thus, it includes both consumption and investment goods, and its magnitude depends also on the relative shares of consumption and investment in GDP.

and the degree of monopoly declined. However, since the second half of the 1970s, the rate of price increase has been almost always higher than that of unit labor costs. Thus, nominal wages have grown for the most part more slowly than the sum of inflation and productivity increases, and so the degree of monopoly has been almost uniformly on the rise.

In the 1960s, the share of total wages in national income (α) in the EU15 countries remained stable, then it grew until the mid-1970s, and has been almost invariably on the decline ever since. However, it should be stressed that the processes in question unfold slowly. The mean α for the examined group of countries amounted to 71.4 percent in the 1960s and 72.8 percent in the 1970s; thus the mean value increased by 1.4 percent over a decade, or 0.14 percent annually. Subsequently, the mean α declined to 70.1 percent in the 1980s and 67.5 percent in the 1990s (by approx. 2.7 percent in each of those decades, or 0.27 percent annually). Finally, in the 2000s, the mean α shrank by another 1.6 percent (0.16 percent annually), down to 65.9 percent.[10] As can be seen, despite the uniformly downward trend, the process has been proceeding so slowly that the assumption of a stable α in the short term causes only a slight error. This should be kept in mind. The assumption of relative stability of the share of total wages in national income plays a major role in subsequent chapters, since it is synonymous with the assumption of the short-term stability of the share of profits in GDP ($1 - \alpha$).

[10] See Statistical Annex of European Economy. Spring 2013, p. 93.

4

Profits and GDP in the basic model

4.1 Factors Determining Profits and GDP in the Basic Model

Total incomes and expenditures are by definition equal for a national economy as a whole. In the basic model, we ignore spending by the government and the rest of the world, and so we arrive at:

$$W + R = CW + CK + IP, \tag{4.1}$$

where CW and CK represent workers' and capitalists' consumption, respectively. Given that $CW + CK = CP$, formula (4.1) corresponds to formula (1.3). Subtracting the term W from both sides of (4.1), we obtain:

$$R = IP + CK - SW, \tag{4.2}$$

where workers' savings (SW) are understood as the difference between their wages and spending on consumption, $SW = (W - CW)$. Assuming initially, for the sake of simplicity, that $SW = 0$, we get:

$$R = IP + CK, \tag{4.2'}$$

which is the fundamental Kaleckian profit equation. The special role of investment in this equation becomes clear in light of the earlier discussion of the importance of external outlet markets for the surplus of consumer goods. It should be noted that the capitalists' spending on consumption and investment creates the market for the private consumption CP.

The identity represented by formula (4.2') is always true; it becomes a piece of economic theory only once it provides an explanation of the mechanism through which this identity is reached: is it profits (incomes) that determine capitalists' consumption and investment spending or, conversely, is it capitalists' spending that determines their profits? While our individual experience suggests that income precedes spending, macroeconomics takes a different stance on the issue. Kalecki asks the question as to which side of equation (4.2') is dependent on capitalists' decisions and goes on to observe that "capitalists may decide to consume and to invest more in a given period than in the preceding one, but they cannot decide to earn more."[1] According to this logic, it is private investment and capitalists' spending on consumption that determine profits rather than vice versa. Kalecki's equation constitutes the foundation of the effective demand theory expressed in the famous statement: "capitalists earn what they spend, and workers spend what they earn." In economic publications this is often called "the Kalecki principle."

When workers do not spend all they have earned, then, according to (4.2), worker savings appear, which constitutes a constraint on profits. Indeed, if workers spent all their wages, then potential profits arising out of spending, $IP + CK$, (in the sense of marketable output volume CP), would be fully realized. However, if some of those earnings are saved, that potential remains partially untapped.

At given profits, R, and their share in GDP (see pp. 28 and 32), which amounts to $(1 - \alpha)$, we can transform the previously introduced equation:

$$R = IP + CK - SW \qquad (4.2)$$

to obtain:

$$R = \frac{R}{1 - \alpha} = \frac{IP + CK - SW}{1 - \alpha} \qquad (4.3)$$

Figure 4.1 graphically presents formulas (4.2) and (4.3). Let the horizontal axis represent Y and the radius $0B$ with a slope of $(1 - \alpha)$ represent R as a linear function of Y. The distances between $0D$ and DF represent CK and IP, respectively, which means that the segment $0F$ corresponds to the sum $IP + CP$. As the segment EF is equal to SW, profit ($R = IP + CK - SW$) is expressed by $0E$. The line parallel to the horizontal axis at a distance $0E$ intersects the radius R at point B, determining $Y = 0A$. Therefore, the coordinates of point B give R and Y, which stand for profits and GDP, respectively.

Due to the fact that the radius $0G$ is inclined at an angle of 45°, also the segment AG represents $Y = 0A$. This means, in turn, that the segment BG represents wages, W, being the difference between Y and R. The difference between W and CW denotes savings out of wages, represented by the segment SW. Finally, the difference between R and CK represents profits retained by companies, RN, or their internal savings. Total private savings, $SP = RN + SW$, are by definition equal to IP and represented by the segment DF.

[1] Kalecki (1954 [1991]: 240).

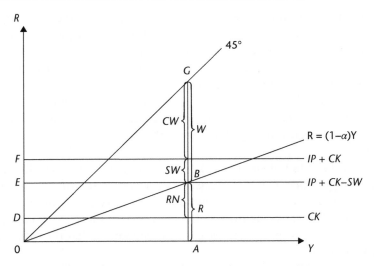

Figure 4.1. Graphical representation of Kalecki's profit equation

4.2 The Two-sector Model

The results of our analysis are now presented within a two-sector model of the economy, which shows the way in which investment spending, after accounting for worker savings, stimulates and determines consumption spending, and ultimately also the national income. The first person to use a similar model was Karl Marx. Kalecki modified it by introducing vertical integration within individual sectors, thus eliminating intermediate products, which obscured Marx's arguments, and in what follows Kalecki's model shall be used. In the model discussed herein, the economy consists of only two vertically integrated sectors. Sector 1 produces investment goods (including inventory changes), denoted as *IP*. Sector 2 produces consumer goods, denoted as *CP*. As a result of vertical integration, the final output of either sector equals its gross value added, which means that in its entirety it can be divided into the two basic types of income: wages and gross profits, denoted as *W* and *R*, respectively, with the subscripts indicating the sector. To simplify the discussion, let us assume that *CK* = 0.

Sector 1: $W_1 + R_1 = IP$
Sector 2: $W_2 + R_2 = CP$
Total: $\quad W + R = Y$

The way in which profit is determined by spending can be expressed by means of the key formula:

$$W_1 - SW \overset{\rightarrow}{=} R_2 \tag{4.4}$$

where W_1 is demand for consumer goods, which cannot be satisfied within the investment sector, and R_2 is the surplus supply of consumer goods, which cannot be sold within the consumption sector. The arrow placed above the sign of equality in formula (4.4) is of fundamental importance. It points in the direction of R_2, which means that R_2, or the profit of sector 2, is determined by $(W_1 - SW)$, i.e., by the spending on wages of sector 1, corrected for worker savings, and not vice versa. This spending stimulates employment in sector 2, which is necessary to generate a surplus equal to R_2 (sold outside sector 2). In this way, CP becomes adjusted to the level of IP, yielding the degree of production capacity utilization in the consumption sector.

Adding the term R_1 to both sides of equation (1.5), we obtain:

$$W_1 - SW + R_1 = R_1 + R_2$$
$$IP = R + SW \tag{4.5}$$

Equation (4.5) shows that private investment, IP, determines savings in the form of profits, R (on the assumption that $CK = 0$), plus worker savings, SW. The fact that investment generates the savings of companies and workers means that within a national economy, "investment finances itself." Obviously, this does not mean that each capitalist will get back as profit whatever he has spent on investment. On the contrary, he will have less money if he has financed the investment himself, or will be in debt if he has taken out a bank loan, as is usually the case. However, other capitalists will make a profit exactly amounting to his expenditure (if we ignore workers' savings, SW). We shall be returning to this interdependence in many sections further on in this book.

4.3 The Investment Multiplier: Quantity and Price Adjustment

In order to simplify our argument without detriment to the basic conclusions, capitalist consumption, CK, is generally left out from subsequent discussion, since what is of utmost importance is the investment spending of capitalists, whose objective is not mere consumption, but pursuit of wealth. Then, Kalecki's profit equation takes the following form:

$$R = IP - SW \tag{4.3'}$$

with the left side representing profits, R. Worker savings, SW, may be expressed as a proportion of worker wages, sw ($0 < sw < 1$):

$$SW = swW = sw\alpha Y$$

Thus, by substituting (4.3'), we obtain:

$$R = IP - sw\alpha Y \tag{4.5'}$$

$$Y = \frac{R}{1-\alpha} = \frac{IP - sw\alpha Y}{1-\alpha}$$

$$Y\left[\frac{(1-\alpha) + sw\alpha}{1-\alpha}\right] = \frac{IP}{1-\alpha}$$

$$Y = \frac{IP}{(1-\alpha) + sw\alpha}$$

$$Y = \frac{IP}{sp} \tag{4.6}$$

where:

$$sp = (1-\alpha) + sw\alpha \tag{4.7}$$

The coefficient sp stands for average saving propensity. Indeed, by definition $IP = SP$, and so $(IP/Y) = sp$. However, it should be kept in mind that sp is a weighted average of the propensity to save out of profits, $(1-\alpha)$, and the propensity to save out of wages, sw, so it also depends on the distribution of national income between profits and wages.

For a given sp, (4.6) can be transformed to:

$$\Delta Y = \frac{\Delta IP}{sp} \tag{4.6'}$$

which means that the increase of GDP is by a factor of $(1/sp)$ higher than that of investment ΔIP. Therefore, the ratio $(1/sp)$ is called the investment multiplier. Obviously, investment could also decrease ($\Delta IP < 0$), and then the decline of GDP would be $(1/sp)$ times greater than that of investment. Further on, we will focus on investment growth and its consequences.

The relationship between investment and GDP is graphically presented in Figure 4.2, in which Y is marked on the horizontal axis, IP is marked on the vertical axis, and $\tan \beta = sp$, $0 < \tan \beta < 1$, stands for the slope of the radius OB. It can easily be seen from the figure that if the initial position of the economy is represented by point A, at investment and GDP volumes equal to IP_0 and Y_0, respectively, then an increase in investment of ΔIP to the volume of IP_1, will move the economy to point B with GDP amounting to Y_1. It is clear that GDP growth (the segment AC) is greater than investment growth (the segment BC), as sp, or the slope of the radius OB, is less than one.

The question arises why GDP growth is a multiple of investment change, or why the ratio $(1/sp)$ is called the investment multiplier? Let us consider an

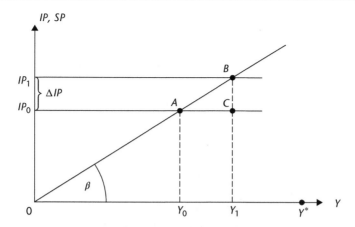

Figure 4.2. Investment multiplier

example in which the share of wages in GDP is $\alpha = 0.5$, and so also $(1 - \alpha)$ as well as $sp = (1 - \alpha) = 0.5$ (assuming as we still do that workers do not save, i.e., $sw = 0$). At $\Delta IP = 100$ euros and $sp = 0.5$, GDP will rise by 200 euros, as in this case the investment multiplier is $(1/0.5) = 2$. But what causes GDP growth to be twice as high as the investment increment?

In the first step, as a result of prior decisions, the output of investment goods increases by 100 euros, which means that gross value added (the sum of wages and profits in sector 1) also rises by 100 euros. According to our assumption that $sp = 0.5$, half of that sum turns into savings (in the form of profits), while the workers of sector 1 purchase 50 euros worth of consumer goods from sector 2. However, that does not exhaust the investment effect. Half of this income of sector 2 will be saved in the form of profits, and 25 euros will be spent by the workers of that sector to purchase more goods. Is that the end? No, as again half of this income of sector 2 will be saved in the form of profits and 12.5 euros will be spent on more consumer goods. These steps are reiterated, but since each consecutive increment amounts to only half of the preceding one, they soon cease to be of practical significance. After four steps, the additional purchases of consumer goods are equal to:

$$50 + 25 + 12.5 + 6.25 = 93.75$$

and approach 100 euros. Indeed, this represents a decreasing geometric series with the first term of 50, a quotient of 0.5, and a sum quickly approaching 100 euros. Thus, an initial investment expenditure of 100 euros triggers a cumulative process of purchasing consumer goods amounting to another 100 euros. This shows that a 100 euros increase in investment and consumption

Table 4.1. Multiplier mechanism at positive savings out of wages, $sw = 1/3$

Multiplier steps	ΔIP	ΔR	ΔSW	ΔCP
First step	100	50	16.6	33.3
Second step		16.6	5.5	11.1
Third step		5.5	1.8	3.7
Fourth step		1.8	0.6	1.2
Total	100	73.9	24.5	49.3

leads to a GDP growth of 200 euros, which was to be demonstrated. Indeed, at $sp = 0.5$ the investment multiplier is 2.

At $sw > 0$, the effects of the multiplier are similar, but their magnitude may vary. Let us assume that $sw = (1/3)$; then substituting the equation $sp = [(1 - \alpha) + sw\alpha]$, we arrive at $sp = (1/2) + (1/2)(1/3) = (2/3)$ and a multiplier of $[1/(2/3)] = 1.5$. Therefore, in the first step, an increase in private investment of $\Delta IP = 100$ euros leads to retained profits of 50 euros and worker savings of 16.6 euros. The subsequent steps of spending and the final outcomes are given in Table 4.1.

The totals are as follows: $\Delta R = 73.9$ euros plus $\Delta SW = 24.5$ euros amounts to $\Delta SP = 98.4$ euros, which is roughly equal to $\Delta IP = 100$. Furthermore, consumption grows by almost 50 euros ($\Delta CP = 49.3$ euros). The aggregate increase in incomes after the fourth step amounts to 147.7 euros and approaches $\Delta Y = 150$ euros, which is consistent with an investment multiplier of 1.5.

In both cases, the increase in private savings equals the increase in investment, which corroborates Kalecki's famous thesis according to which "in a sense, investment finances itself." Let us illustrate this process using figures from the second example. For instance, an investor takes out a bank loan amounting to 100 euros. After the loan has been spent in both sectors, the banking system receives deposits amounting to 75 euros from companies and 25 euros from workers. Thus, a total of 100 euros returns to the banking system, which corresponds to the amount of money the banks generated in the beginning.

It should be stressed here that, in contrast to common belief, the banking system is not a mechanism gathering the dispersed savings of households to make them available to investors. The banking system itself produces a purchasing power that finances investment, which in turn gives rise to private savings, including household savings. It is those savings that prevent profits from reaching the level that would ensure the maximum return on investment expenditure.[2]

The assumption that the banking system only collects savings and conveys them to investors can be easily reduced to absurdity under the assumption

---

[2] These problems are discussed in detail in Section 4.4.

that investment decisions are made exclusively on the basis of past savings. By definition, for every period of time, the following will hold true ex post:

$$IP(t) = SP(t) \tag{4.8}$$

This represents the identity of investment and private savings. Let us now imagine that in a given period investment decisions for that period, $ID(t)$, are made based on savings of the same period, $SP(t)$:

$$ID(t) = SP(t) \tag{4.9}$$

Then, equations (4.8) and (4.9) give:

$$IP(t) = ID(t) \tag{4.10}$$

However, as current investment decisions also determine the volume of future investment, we obtain:

$$ID(t) = IP(t+1) \tag{4.11}$$

By combining (4.10) and (4.11) we arrive at:

$$IP(t) = IP(t+1) \tag{4.12}$$

This implies constant investment over time, which is obviously not true since investment is one of the most variable economic phenomena. The error in the above line of reasoning is that it does not account for the fact that capitalists can invest over and above their savings by taking out loans. They can also invest less than they saved by paying off loans or increasing their deposits. Marshall's "familiar economic axiom," according to which "a man purchases labor and commodities with that portion of his income which he saves just as much as he does with that he is said to spend," is an obvious error.[3]

Does this imply that saving does not matter? Of course, this is not the case. At the beginning of our example a bank extends a loan to the investor. However, when a company applies for a loan, the bank expects collateral in the form of equity, bonds, or title deeds to real estate. The higher the equity, the easier it is for the company to access the financial market. And it should be noted that a company's equity grows primarily through retained profits. Corporate investment is always fraught with risk and the higher the equity the higher the company's readiness to make inherently risky investment decisions. As can be seen, increasing equity by retaining profits is of great importance to the company in terms of its ability and willingness to take out bank loans or, more generally, access the capital market.

In discussing the investment multiplier, we made the tacit assumption that the prices (used for measuring the examined quantities) are constant. Thus, a

---

[3] Marshall, quoted in Joan Robinson (1971: 89).

real increase in investment at a given saving rate, *sp*, leads to real GDP growth. This reaction of the economy to higher investment may be termed, after Amit Bhaduri (1986: 37ff.) "quantity adjustment" in the presence of available production capacity and labor reserves. Since the presence of these unused resources is rather typical in a capitalist economy, quantity adjustment is the rule rather than the exception. Point Y^* on the horizontal axis in Figure 4.2 represents potential GDP, which can be theoretically attained at the full utilization of production capacity. As the points representing both the starting and final GDP are positioned to the left of Y^*, there is some room for quantity adjustment.

In light of the above, some economists draw the conclusion that effective demand theory presupposes constant prices, and if the prices vary, then the theory is not applicable. It should be noted that in the 1930s, when the effective demand theory was formulated, prices were sharply declining. In fact, for the investment multiplier to be valid we do not need constant prices, but a constant distribution of GDP between wages and profits, as the saving propensity varies between these two types of income. Under pure quantity adjustment, when the distribution between wages and profits is stable, the saving rate, $sp = (1 - \alpha) + sw\alpha$, is also stable. Furthermore, a constant share of profits in GDP does not require constant prices, either, but rather a constant percentage margin (mark-up) on unit costs of labor. Whether under the circumstances prices rise or not depends on the relationship between unit costs of labor and productivity. If both of them are stable or grow at the same rate, then those costs, and also prices, are stable.

In turn, if average nominal wages grow faster than real productivity, but the difference between these two corresponds to the expected inflation rate, then the growth of unit labor costs will also correspond to the expected inflation rate (real inflation will be equal to expected inflation). As a result, average real wages will grow in line with average productivity.[4] This combination of productivity, wage, and inflation rates of growth can be most readily attained when organizations of entrepreneurs and trade unions cooperate rather than fight each other. This was one of the main characteristics of the social market economy, which was practiced for an extended period of time in Germany and Austria, but which has now become increasingly marginalized, especially in Germany. Thus, normal quantity adjustment requires, amongst others, an active incomes policy. Its absence poses the risk of

---

[4] For instance, let productivity growth be 2 percent annually, expected inflation 3 percent, and average nominal wage rise 5 percent. Then, average unit costs of labor increase by 3 percent annually and at a given percentage mark-up on those costs, also prices rise by 3 percent. Thus, the inflation expectations will be met and the average real wages will grow by 2 percent, in line with average productivity.

insufficient outlet markets or excessive inflation triggering an anti-inflationary reaction of the central bank. In both cases the quantity adjustment will be correspondingly smaller.

When the economy approaches full production capacity in the consumer goods sector, then investment growth will trigger not only quantity adjustment, even if unemployed workforce and production capacity in sector 1 are available. In this case, prices must increase in relation to unit labor costs and, at an increasing profit margin, the rise in real wages must lag behind productivity growth in order for the share of profits in GDP, $(1 - \alpha)$, to increase and, at a given sw, also for $sp = (1 - \alpha) + sw\alpha$ to adjust to the new share of investment in GDP. This is termed price adjustment. Investment growth does occur, but the multiplier effect triggered by it affects only prices, causing inflation at a given volume of consumer goods output.[5]

4.4 The Paradox of Saving

The investment multiplier presupposes a constant private saving propensity, sp, and variable private investment. However, we may also examine what happens in an economy in which the investment volume is given and sp varies. The formulas needed for this analysis are given below:

$$R = IP - SW \tag{4.3'}$$

$$R = IP - sw\alpha Y \tag{4.5'}$$

$$Y = \frac{R}{(1 - \alpha)} = \frac{IP - sw\alpha Y}{(1 - \alpha)} \tag{4.5''}$$

$$Y = \frac{IP}{sp} \tag{4.6}$$

---

[5] The issue becomes more complicated when production capacity is still available in sector 1 at full employment in the economy. It is generally assumed that in this case investment grows at the cost of constraining the output of consumer goods at a given GDP level. This also gives rise to a classic price adjustment leading to such changes in the distribution of GDP between wages and profits that adjust the saving rate sp to the higher share of investment in unchanged GDP (the problem of price adjustments was presented in the famous paper by Kaldor, "Alternative Theories of Distribution," in Kaldor (1960 [1971])).The weakness of this approach consists in the fact that in the absence of unemployment an increase in the workforce in sector 1 can take place only at the cost of a decrease in the workforce in sector 2. However, if in sector 1 capitalists offer higher wages to workers from sector 2 in order to attract them to sector 1, it is unclear why capitalists in sector 2 should not give their workers a corresponding pay rise to retain them. If such a policy is indeed used, this will lead only to inflation, and the growth of investment, which was previously assumed to take place, cannot occur. Consequently, if investment cannot grow, then the price adjustment, which is supposed to be caused by investment growth, will not take place.

where invariably:

$$sp = (1 - \alpha) + sw\alpha \qquad (4.7)$$

When sp increases, then pursuant to (4.6) GDP contracts. This formula is the traditional point of departure for analysis of the effects of sp growth: if a society wishes to increase its saving rate, then at a given IP national income will shrink. Thus, saving is not necessarily a virtue; it may also be detrimental to the economy. This is undoubtedly true. Nevertheless, the average saving rate used in the Keynesian literature does not allow for a comprehensive analysis of the mechanism underlying this effect.

It should be noted that sp depends on two factors: sw, the propensity to save out of wages, and α, the share of wages in national income. In particular, sp increases with sw as well as with $(1 - \alpha)$, that is, when the share of profits in GDP rises. As we shall see, the mechanism of national income contraction depends on whether the private saving rate, sp, increases as a result of the growth of sw, or as a result of an increase in $(1 - \alpha)$.

According to Kalecki's equation (4.3'), profits, R, decline when at a given IP savings out of wages, SW, increase. This is so because at any given level of private investment IP, private saving (the sum of retained corporate profits or internal savings, R, and worker savings, SW) is also given. At a given IP, profits, R, decrease when worker savings, SW, increase. And when profits shrink, then, according to (4.5''), $\underline{Y}$ also contracts. The case of increasing worker savings due to a higher propensity to save out of wages and the resulting decline in GDP is shown in Figure 4.3.

The initial position of the economy is represented by point A. At constant investment volume, $\overline{IP}$, profits R_0 are equal to $\overline{IP}$, assuming that $SW = 0$. If

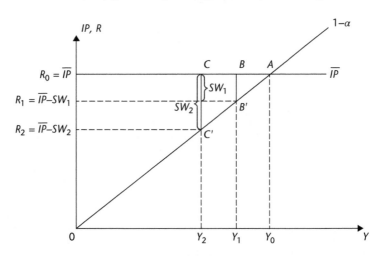

Figure 4.3. The paradox of saving at increasing SW

saving out of wages amount to the value of the segment BB' (SW_1), then profits decline to $R_1 = \overline{IP} - SW_1$, corresponding to point B'. Finally, point C' represents profits $R_2 = \overline{IP} - SW_2$, where $SW_2 = CC'$. GDP for a given profit volume is determined by the abscissa of points $A = R_0/(1 - \alpha) = Y_0$, $B' = R_1/(1 - \alpha) = Y_1$, and $C' = R_2/(1 - \alpha) = Y_2$. National income Y_1 is lower than Y_0 as at a constant share of profits in GDP, amounting to $(1 - \alpha)$, profits R_1 are lower than R_0. Similarly, $Y_2 < Y_1$ as at given $(1 - \alpha)$ we obtain $R_2 < R_1$. This type of GDP contraction is caused solely by declining private consumption, CP, at a given level of private investment, $\overline{IP}$. When investment $\overline{IP}$ is given, then also savings, SP, are given. Under the circumstances, a rise in saving propensity, sp, may be accomplished only by reducing consumption, CP. However, it is now clear that this reduction of consumption and GDP is a direct cause of the contraction in profits, R, due to an increase of SW at given private investment, $\overline{IP}$.[6]

These conclusions are not in line with natural intuition, which is reluctant to acknowledge that saving may have adverse consequences for the economy as a whole. Therefore, in economic theory this phenomenon is known as the "paradox of saving" or the "paradox of thrift." However, it may be deemed paradoxical only within the conceptual framework of the orthodox strand of economic thinking, which assumes the full use of production capacity and supply-side constraints on aggregate output. Under these assumptions, an increased propensity to save would mean that a larger part of supply-side-determined GDP is allocated to investment, and a smaller part to consumption. On the other hand, the proposition that at a given level of investment a higher saving propensity hinders profits, national income, and consumption, is entirely consistent with the theory of effective demand, according to which at given production capacity, GDP is determined by aggregate spending rather than supply constraints. Consequently, within this framework it does not make sense to consider this effect a paradox. It seems paradoxical only to the advocates of theories that assume constant full utilization of production capacity.

It should be noted that historically many economists have been forced to recognize the stimulating role of lower savings in dire economic situations, if only indirectly. Following the 2001 stock market crash in the United States, and especially following the onset of the 2008 crisis, much was said about insufficient consumer optimism and the need to improve it. But what does improved "consumer optimism" actually mean in economic terms? It means nothing else but a low propensity to save. Those who hope for greater consumer optimism in fact call for a decreased saving rate. However, if directly

---

[6] Changes in the volume of SW in Figure 4.3 imply respective changes in the sw rate. Let us join points 0 and B to form the radius $0B$ (not shown). The slope of this radius is $(1 - \alpha) + \alpha sw_1$. Thus, the segment $SW_1 = \alpha sw_1 Y_1$. Similarly, by joining points 0 and C we obtain the radius $0C$ (not shown) with a slope $(1 - \alpha) + \alpha sw_2$. As a result, the segment $SW_2 = \alpha sw_2 Y_2$.

asked whether they advocate a lower saving rate, the same persons would almost certainly deny it; being liberals they abhor the thought that a certain profligacy in the behaviour of households might turn out to be a social virtue.

Liberal economics is founded on the assumption that if everybody pursues their own interests, such as profit maximization (companies) and utility maximization (consumers), then everybody can attain the greatest possible benefits. However, household saving and social saving are two different things. If a family saves for a major purchase, for old age, or for children, then such behavior is laudable. However, if everybody follows suit, and especially if the propensity to save exceeds the companies' propensity to invest, then the outcomes are often detrimental to employment and aggregate output levels. Similarly, if one person stands up in the theater, he or she certainly has a better view of the stage. But if everyone did this, then the situation would be worse than before for everyone.

The other mechanism of saving-rate growth involves an increase in the share of profits in national income, $(1 - \alpha)$. Given our extreme assumption that capitalists do not consume, all profits are retained by companies and constitute their internal savings. More realistically, capitalists do consume part of their incomes, but the propensity to save out of profits is higher than out of wages and any increase in the share of profits in national income leads to a higher sp rate.

While a higher proportion of profits in national income detracts from consumption, the mechanism of the saving paradox is somewhat different: pursuant to (4.3′), at a lower α, profits, R, remain unchanged if the volume of savings out of wages, SW, is constant. However, constant profits imply lower total wages, and so lower consumption at a given level of savings out of wages. The problem of the distribution of national income between wages and profits is discussed in greater detail in the next section.

4.5 Nominal Wages and Employment

There is a widespread belief that unemployment is caused by high wages, which is mostly due to the fact that the labor market is often treated as any other type of market; say—as this has already been mentioned—as if it were a horse market. If the price of horses is too high and supply exceeds demand, then a decrease in price stimulates demand while constraining supply. The market relatively quickly returns to an equilibrium and demand and supply balance out at a new price.

In the past there were very many draft horses in Poland. Nowadays, there are far fewer, and their price has declined. In Austria there are even fewer draft horses, as opposed to racing horses. The former are mostly used to draw hackney carriages in Vienna and, moving very slowly and holding up traffic, they are a nuisance to motorists. The situation of workers is entirely different. Nowadays, no one in their right mind would claim that a decrease in wages will lead to a reduction in the number of workers. While arguments to that effect were indeed made in the history of economics, it was a very long time ago, and wages no longer seem to be the decisive determinant of population growth. Let us now consider why a decline in nominal wages is not an effective tool in combating unemployment.

Let us assume that nominal wages decrease at given price and productivity levels. This leads to lower unit labor costs, which at constant prices (according to our assumption) leads to a rise in profit per unit of output. And it is this effect that is advertised by all those who advocate nominal wage reductions as a means of alleviating unemployment. However, they more or less explicitly assume that aggregate demand is not a constraint on production, and so companies will be able to sell the same, or even greater, volume of goods at a given price. In turn, this is supposed to boost not only profits, but also employment. Consequently, everybody would benefit if only workers did not insist on maintaining high wages, apparently against their own interest.

If real wages are reduced in a single, not very important industry (e.g., vertically integrated factories manufacturing mustard), then the aggregate demand will indeed decrease negligibly. However, if nominal wages decline in a major sector (e.g., the vertically integrated automotive industry), then aggregate demand is bound to suffer considerably as the number of workers in that industry is very large in proportion to the aggregate workforce of the entire economy. Finally, if all industries reduce nominal wages, then the demand for consumer goods will decline in line with the change in nominal wages. As is apparent, that which can help an individual company is not necessarily beneficial for the economy as a whole. On the contrary, a decrease in unit labor costs as a result of wage cuts will not only leave unemployment unmitigated, but is likely to aggravate it.

Let us now assume that investment does not react immediately to a decrease in nominal wages. Under conditions of wage reductions and at constant prices (or at prices that decrease more slowly than wages), the demand for consumer goods from the investment sector will decrease. Therefore, the marketable surplus of consumer goods produced by the consumption sector will decrease, and production and employment in the consumption sector will fall accordingly. While the profit per unit of output will go up, and with it the savings rate,[7] at a given volume of investment, GDP and employment will decline, according to the paradox of saving.

---

[7] Let us use (4.7) to calculate the partial derivative of sp with respect to the argument α: $\partial(sp)/\partial\alpha = (sw - 1) < 0$, which means that sp is a decreasing function of α, and an increasing function of $(1-\alpha)$.

Figure 4.4 shows the situation before and after a reduction in nominal wages, with the assumption of $sw = 0$ for the sake of clarity. Thus, the slope of the radii $0A$ and $0B$ corresponds to both the share of profits in GDP, $(1 - \alpha)$, and the rate of private saving, sp. Point A represents the initial position. If the share of profits in GDP amounts to $\tan \beta_0 = (1 - \alpha_0)$ and investment is IP_0 (equal to profits R_0), then GDP amounts to Y_0. If nominal wages decrease at given productivity and price levels, the share of profits in GDP increases. Let the new share be $\tan \beta_1 = (1 - \alpha_1)$, $\alpha_1 < \alpha_0$ (and thus $(\beta_1 > \beta_0)$). At the same level of investment, IP_0, the position of the economy is now represented by point B, and GDP declines to Y_B. As a matter of fact, while the share of profits in national income has risen (profit per unit of final goods has increased), aggregate profits remain equal to IP_0. Thus, a higher share of profits in GDP is manifested primarily by a decline of GDP at a given profit volume, $R_0 = IP_0$.

This result is entirely consistent with the paradox of saving and does not require further discussion. While a reduction in nominal wages at given price levels increases profit per unit of output, unemployment rises rather than declines as a result of contracted output. Therefore, wage-cutting economic policies primarily affect workers as both their real wages and employment decrease, while capitalists gain nothing as their profits are stalled.

A condition which is necessary, but as we shall see, insufficient to avoid these adverse consequences, is an immediate increase in investment. But in actual time, this is impossible as today's investment results from yesterday's decisions. Thus, if nominal wages are declining today, they can only affect today's investment decisions. Furthermore, it is extremely unlikely for a decrease in nominal wages and output (entailing lower utilization of available

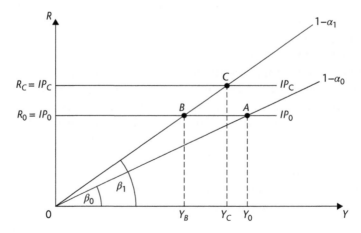

Figure 4.4. Reduction of nominal wages leads to higher unemployment rather than more jobs

production capacity) to result in positive investment decisions, with the only encouraging factor being higher profits per unit of final goods. Thus, if investment is not going to grow simultaneously with a reduction in nominal wages, it will not grow in the future either. Consequently, also in the long term the policy of nominal wage reductions is going to exacerbate rather than alleviate unemployment. Appendix 2 presents an in-depth discussion of this conclusion by comparing unemployment as understood in effective demand theory and in classical theory.

The policy of real wage reduction as a means of countering unemployment is sometimes criticized as unjust because it places the burden of remedying unemployment on workers. However, the crucial problem is that such a policy is simply ineffective.

Going back to Figure 4.4, it should be noted that even if investment increased, it may be insufficient to induce higher employment in the face of a wage reduction. If investment rose from IP_0 to IP_c, and the economy moved to point C, then at the new share of profits $(1 - \alpha_1)$, GDP would only reach Y_c, where $Y_c < Y_0$. Nevertheless, the critical question is whether under the circumstances investment is going to rise thanks to higher profits per unit of final goods, and the answer is generally no.[8]

Investments are made to maintain and expand existing production capacity, so they are essentially aimed at creating a "production effect." This is indeed the most important effect of investment, as productive capacity (second only to human capital) is the foundation of the livelihood of each society. However, so far we have not discussed this aspect of investment, focusing only on the "income effect," according to which workers employed for the completion of investment projects receive wages, which they spend purchasing the surplus of goods manufactured in the consumption sector. However, a distinction must be made between the income effect and the production effect of investment. Interestingly, when the income effect of investment is present, the production effect is not there yet. And when the production effect arrives, the income effect has already disappeared. Thus, when an investment project is being carried out, we have to deal with an income effect without a production effect. The income generated by the project implementation creates demand for the surplus of consumer goods, but does not increase that surplus. It is precisely that income which makes it possible to sell the surplus of goods which would not be marketable otherwise, given total wages of workers in the consumer sector alone. Thanks to investment-generated income, that surplus is turned into money and becomes the profit of manufacturers. In other

---

[8] The conclusions are somewhat different if one accounts for international trade. This issue will be addressed further on in this book.

words, for the economy to operate properly and effectively, we need the income effect of investment, preceding the production effect. A mutual adjustment of these two effects is theoretically possible at a constant rate of investment growth and upon meeting some additional conditions, and that requires a wise macroeconomic policy.[9]

4.6 The Capitalist Economy and the Centrally Planned Economy

The centrally planned economy, which was previously in place in Poland, was constrained on the supply side and suffered from chronic investment drive. This was caused by the ambition to quickly catch up with and surpass the most economically developed capitalist countries, which resulted in rushed industrialization and a policy of prioritizing the production of investment goods at the expense of consumer goods. However, the economic policy factors notwithstanding, the severe investment shortage and the permanent internal disequilibrium were also caused by one of the fundamental characteristics of the planned economy: the soft budget constraint of government enterprises.[10]

As a result, investment and the wages earned in the investment sector were too high with respect to the production capacity of the consumption sector as measured by the surplus of marketable consumer goods: the seller's market was prevalent. The seller was king and customers stood in long lines to purchase the goods they desired; also employers had problems with finding workers in the labor market. The low efficiency of factors of production and the absence of entrepreneurial management standards ensured full employment. However, it should be stressed that the intensity of the above processes predominantly depended on economic policy. The more rigid the plans were and the more the existing constraints were disregarded, the greater the deficiencies were, and vice versa.

In turn, the capitalist economy is constrained on the demand side, because the propensity to invest is hindered by risk and uncertainty. All entrepreneurs will think twice before they decide to engage their own or borrowed monies in new investment. While they obviously want to make a profit, they are afraid of losing their capital. Therefore, production capacity typically remains underutilized. The capitalist economy is characterized by the buyer's market: it is not customers who wait for goods, but rather goods that wait for customers. The same pertains to workers: their work is also a "commodity," and "buyers" make cautious "purchases," carefully calculating whether they really need

---

[9] See Chapter 8 concerning growth.   [10] See Kornai (1980).

what they are buying. In summary, in the capitalist economy production capacity, including labor, is underutilized, but the actually employed factors of production are used highly efficiently.

The above argument clearly points to two aspects of the mode of operation of each of those economic systems. In the capitalist economy, the suboptimal utilization of production capacity, and especially workforce, may lead to painful consequences. On the other hand, the economy is extremely flexible, able to adjust to the changing expectations and market needs almost instantaneously. Due to the tendency to underutilize production capacity inherent in the capitalist economy, state intervention is necessary to correct that tendency through appropriate economic policy. But there are no ideal solutions. It is impossible to remedy completely the undesirable tendency in this way, although rational government intervention may strengthen the positive aspects of the capitalist economy and mitigate its shortcomings.

Central planning was supposed to be a cure for a very real ailment of the capitalist economy, i.e., the absence of efficient macroeconomic coordination between savings and investment decisions. The problem with the newly fledged neoliberals today is not that they claim, quite rightly, that real socialism and the centrally planned economy proved to be inadequate remedies, but that they deny the existence of the ailment itself (underutilization of production capacity, including workforce). They probably believe that price and wage adjustments in combination with free competition ensure not only a market equilibrium, but also full utilization of the factors of production. As a result, they do not see any reason why the state should intervene to moderate the negative social consequences of unfettered market forces, such as widespread unemployment and quickly growing income inequalities reflected in the declining share of wages in GDP.[11]

This issue touches on the crucial relationship between ideology and science in economics, which we should examine more closely. It is not true that economic sciences can be completely detached from ideology. One can wish and strive for it, but it is impossible to attain, as everyone exhibits some political affinities, whether leftist or rightist. Being fully aware of the interrelationship between ideology and economic theory, Joan Robinson proposed an experiment revealing the effects of one's political and scientific views.[12]

Following the example of Joan Robinson, let us consider the shift in the beliefs of many economists after the collapse of the socialist system. For instance, let us take an economist who was an ardent advocate of the effective

---

[11] The share of wages in Polish GDP was on average 69 percent in 1992–3, 61.5 percent in 2002–3, 54.7 percent in 2007–8, and 52.3 percent in 2012–13, which means a decline of 17 percentage points over 20 years (see Statistical Annex of European Economy, 2013, Table 32).

[12] See Chapter 1, "Metaphysics, Morale, and Science" in Joan Robinson (1962).

demand theory, which justified his leftist/socialist outlook. That economist has now come to the conclusion that his previous political views were false, and has turned into a liberal. If his economic credo has completely altered, if he previously claimed that market macro-coordination was faulty in the capitalist economy and now says that the relationship between aggregate demand and supply is inconsequential, then it is clear that in his previous economic views there was hardly a shade of science and they were based on pure ideology, as are his newly found views. However, if someone has changed her political orientation, but preserved some core elements of her economic background, those elements can be deemed scientific, as they do not depend on political allegiance.

The above considerations pertain to many economists who turned overnight from more or less critical (or uncritical) believers in the centrally planned economy into staunch supporters of an unfettered market economy. In their sudden epiphany, it dawned on them that whatever the government does is evil and whatever the market does is good. In reality, errors are made not only by the government, but also by the fallible market. The crux of the matter is to strike a happy medium between spontaneous market mechanisms and deliberate government intervention. The state can neither assume the role of the market, nor can the market replace the state. What we need is a symbiosis in which the state intervenes in those areas in which the market fails.

Appendix 2. Unemployment According to the Effective Demand Theory and According to the Classical Theory

While wages are the source of effective demand, they at the same time constitute the most important element of unit production costs. The classical theory tends to neglect aggregate demand, and by the same token, the demand side of wages, overemphasizing the role of wages as an element of costs, especially pursuant to the strict principle of corporate profit maximization. A comparison of both of these aspects of labor in the effective demand theory and the classical theory allows one to clearly identify fundamental differences in the understanding of the causes of unemployment and in policy to combat them.[13]

Figures A2.1 and A2.2 present the short-term, classical production function. At given capital outlay, the volume of final production is determined by the function $Y = f(L)$, with L being the number of workers, and the only variable. $f(L)$ grows at a decreasing rate: $f' > 0$, $f'' < 0$. In other words, with employment growth, the (physical) marginal product of labor (mpl) is positive ($f' > 0$), but decreases ($f'' < 0$). The neoclassical theory

---

[13] This section draws heavily on Amit Bhaduri (1986: 70–3).

assumes that companies maximize profit in the strict sense, which implies they increase employment as long as the marginal revenue (which is equal to product price, P, in the case of free competition) is higher than the marginal cost. The marginal cost may be obtained by multiplying the inverse of *mpl* (the additional labor input necessary to produce an additional unit of output) by the nominal wage, w. The maximum profit is achieved when the marginal revenue and marginal cost converge:

$$P = w/f'(L)$$

or,

$$w/P = f'(L) \tag{A2.1}$$

where w/P, or the real wage, will be hereinafter denoted as *wr*. Pursuant to (A2.1), a company's profit reaches a maximum when the real wage, *wr*, is equal to the (physical) marginal product of labor, *mpl*.

The determination of employment based on profit maximization and by effective demand, whose central element is investment outlay, involves two different theoretical constructions yielding different results. Keynes attempted to reconcile these two different approaches by rejecting Say's law (according to which all savings automatically turn into investment), but still adhering to the principle of profit maximization. Thus, employment is first determined by effective demand (mostly by investment), and then the real wage becomes adjusted to the physical marginal product of labor generated at that employment level.[14]

In Figure A2.1, it is assumed that employment $L_0 = OC$ will lead to a GDP of $Y_0 = AC$, which satisfies both postulates proposed by Keynes. Therefore, $Y_0 = I_0/r_0$, where $I_0 = AA'$

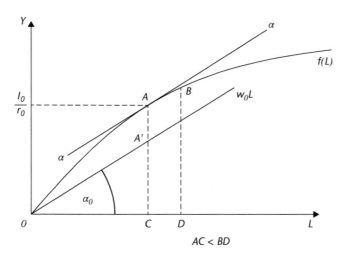

Figure A2.1. Keynesian unemployment

[14] For in-depth analysis of this Keynesian theory, see Bhaduri (1986: 70–3).

represents investment and $r_0 = AA'/AC$ the share of profits (savings) in Y_0.[15] Employment, $L_0 = 0C$, is thus determined by effective demand, with the resulting real wage being defined by the slope of the line aa, which is tangential to the curve $f(L)$ at point A and expresses the marginal product of labor, mpl, at an employment of $L_0 = 0C$. Thus, the radius $0A'$ must be parallel to the tangent line aa if the real wage wr_0 is to be equal to mpl at point A. The slope is $\tan \alpha_0$. Since $wr_0 = \tan \alpha_0$, the postulate of profit maximization required by equation (A2.1) is also met.

The segment $L_F = 0D$ is marked on the horizontal axis, with L_F designating full employment. Thus, at an employment of $L_0 = 0C$ we arrive at Keynesian unemployment, equal to $L_F - L_0 = CD$, which results from insufficient investment, I_0, at a given share of profits, r_0. To counter this unemployment, investment must exceed I_0. In turn, for proponents of the orthodox theory, the segment CD is a measure of classical unemployment, as in the classical theory with profit maximization, the volume of workforce is determined by the real wage (wr_0), which is apparently too high given the existing supply of labor.

The classical argument is presented in Figure A2.2. In this approach, to provide employment for all who are able and willing to work, the real wage should be decreased from wr_0 to wr_1, where $wr_1 = \tan \alpha_1$ with $\tan \alpha_1$ representing the slope of the line bb, tangential to the curve $f(L)$ at point B, which represents mpl (marginal product of labor) at that point. At that wage, companies will increase employment to $L_F = 0D$, and GDP will reach $Y_F = BD$. Out of that GDP, the part $B'D$ will be paid to workers in the form of real wages and is thought to be spent on consumer goods. The remaining part of GDP,

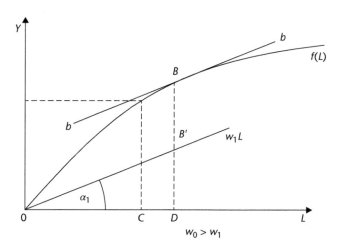

Figure A2.2. Classical unemployment

[15] Since $\tan \alpha_0$ corresponds to real wages w_0 (as $\tan \alpha_0 = A'C/0C$), and the segment $0C$ measures the volume of employment, then the product of $\tan \alpha_0 \times 0C = A'C$ gives total wages. Therefore, the difference $AC - A'C = AA'$ corresponds to aggregate profits, and since $AC = Y_0$, then AA'/AC gives the share of profits in national income.

amounting to BB', will be distributed to capitalists in the form of profits and is supposed to be saved. According to Say's law, it will be automatically reinvested.

For those who do not believe in a miraculous transformation of savings into investment and who do not see a ready outlet market for the goods represented by the segment BB', the reduction of wages to wr_1 will lead to higher rather than lower unemployment rates. At a given level of I_0 (a decrease in the real wage may affect investment with a certain delay) and at a real wage $wr_1 < wr_0$, effective demand will decline below AC as, according to Kalecki's theory (which dismisses the strict principle of profit maximization),[16] lower wages will lead to higher profits (and savings).

---

[16] The rationale behind this assumption and its implications were discussed in Section 3.1.

5

Income and GDP in the model with government

5.1 The Role of Fiscal Policy: Some Comments on the Relationship between the Government, Market, and Distribution of Income

In a free market economy, government fulfills three main economic functions. First, through fiscal policy, it influences employment, prices, and the GDP growth rate. Second, government supplements and corrects the market allocation of resources. Third, it can mitigate the degree of income disparities and assure a more socially just distribution by reallocating incomes spontaneously generated in the market economy. These lectures focus on the first function, but some comments shall also be made on the other two in so far as they are relevant to macroeconomic issues.[1]

The market as a mechanism of allocation fails both in the sphere of classic public goods, such as national defense, public safety, prevention of epidemics, etc., and in the sphere of goods generating significant externalities not reflected in the profit and loss accounts of companies, such as environmental pollution, workers acquiring qualifications on the job, an apiarist's bees pollinating farmers' crops, etc. Yet another example is the health care system. Although it may be left to the devices of the free market, it is far more effective if a sizeable proportion of health care services are provided by the government. However, the state may also fail, especially if it gives in to pressures from different interest groups. Government may become unwieldy, costly, with public officials pursuing their own ends rather than tending public interest, which is after all their *raison d'être*. The recent decades have seen a rise in the small government ideology and belief in the superiority of the market mechanism. This ideology has found particularly fertile ground in countries that in

---

[1] For an accurate and accessible discussion, see Falkinger (1995: 67–115).

the past had centrally planned economies. There the state turned out to be an extremely inefficient provider of commodities ranging from cucumbers to steel, to say nothing of the disastrous state-run retail trade system. In reality neither can the market exist without the state, nor can the state be effective without the market. Therefore, whether one likes it or not, it is necessary to arrive at a pragmatic compromise between an imperfect market and an imperfect state.

Let us now move on to the distribution function, that is, the issue of income distribution in a given society. This is of paramount importance in comparisons of wealth over time using averaged statistical indicators, such as national income per head of population or average household income. If such indicators increase in a given country, this means that the wealth of all members of society also grows, as long as income distribution remains constant or nearly so. However, if that condition is not met, then the wealth of some social groups will rise faster than that of others; indeed, a rapid accumulation of wealth by some may be accompanied by the impoverishment of others.

Let us illustrate this thesis with data showing the increase in household income disparities in the United States over the past decades (Table 5.1). While most other capitalist countries have exhibited smaller inequalities, the trend is similar around the world.

Back in 1982, the poorer half of American households received 19.7 percent of the total income generated by all households in that country, while the poorest quarter of households received only 5.7 percent of that income. In turn, the richest one-tenth of American households received 33.4 percent of total income, while the richest percentile[2] (1 percent) of households obtained 9.9 percent. This inequality deteriorated considerably by the end of the twentieth century. In 2000, the poorer half of American households received only 15.6 percent of total income, and the poorest quarter as little as 4.2 percent. As can be seen, the share of this quarter in aggregate income declined by 1.5 percentage points, which translates to a drop of 26 percent. In turn, in 2000, the richest one-tenth of American households received 42.9 percent of aggregate income, while the richest percentile obtained as much as 17.4 percent. The share of this group increased by 7.5 percentage points, or by 76 percent. Assuming equal distribution within the poor quarter of American households, one percentile of them received on average $(5.7/25) = 0.23$ percent and $(4.2/25) = 0.17$ percent of total income in the years 1982 and 2000, respectively. This means that in 1982 the average

---

[2] Percentile (or centile) is the number of observations (that can be expressed as a percentage) of the studied variable (in this case, the percentage of the total number of households) that are below a given threshold or within certain brackets of the overall percentage distribution of the independent variable (in this case, the share in national income, expressed cumulatively as a percentage).

Table 5.1. The share of selected percentiles of households in US aggregate national income in 1982 and 2000 (in percent)

Percentiles	1982	2000	Change in *pp*
0–25	5.7	4.2	–1.5
25–50	14.0	11.4	–2.6
50–90	46.9	41.4	–5.4
90–100	33.4	42.9	9.5
Breakdown of the top 10 percentiles:			
90–95	10.7	10.2	–0.5
95–99	12.9	15.3	2.4
99–100	9.9	17.4	7.5

Source: Wolff and Zachariasz (2006: Table 1).

income of households in the top percentile was $(9.9/0.23) = 43$ times higher than the average income of households in the bottom quarter, while in 2000 this disparity grew to $(17.4/0.17) = 102$ times.

The statistics for 2002 of the Internal Revenue Service of the United States report that super-rich taxpayers, accounting for 0.1 percent of the total population (148,000 persons) made on average \$3 million in 2002, up from \$1.2 million in 1980, accounting for inflation. Thus, the increase in the income of this group was approximately 2.5-fold and its share in aggregate income was 7.4 percent (more than twice the 1980 level). No other social group was able to increase its income so rapidly in that period of time.[3]

After 2000, the situation further deteriorated. In the years 2001–9, the richest decile of households seized almost 100 percent of aggregate national income increment, and as much as 120 percent in the years 2009–12. This means that the remaining nine deciles did not derive any benefits from growth in the first period, and incurred losses in the second one.[4] This stands in stark contrast to the years 1950–80, when half to three-quarters of overall income growth went to 90 percent of households.

In a liberal economy, income distribution between the various social classes and groups is conceived of as an indisputable outcome of the market mechanism, which rewards production factors according to their relative contribution to the production process measured in terms of marginal productivity. Within this framework, the problem of a fair income distribution does not exist. An income corresponding to an individual's input is by definition just, even if it implies extreme inequalities. In light of the above, calls for a more egalitarian income distribution are attributed at best to ignorance, and typically to envy. Furthermore, the liberal argument proceeds, interference with income distribution is socially detrimental because it decreases economic effectiveness by undermining the motivation of entrepreneurs, increasing

---

[3] See Johnston (2005).   [4] See Tscherneva (2014).

unemployment due to excessively high real wages compared to marginal productivity of labor, etc. However, the theoretical underpinnings of such an argument are untenable. The so-called Capital Controversies debate in the 1960s showed that those theoretical underpinnings are not internally coherent, except for an unrealistic model of an economy producing only one commodity.[5]

There are many arguments supporting the view that the more evenly income is distributed, the more just it is, irrespective of the exact understanding of the notion of justice, which may vary depending on tradition, culture, religion, and many other factors. First of all, a very uneven distribution is conducive to a high saving rate, which is not necessarily beneficial, and may be downright harmful to the economy, as was shown earlier in this book. Second, an extremely unequal income distribution poses a threat to social order. Indigent social groups, and especially young people without prospects for the future, often prove to be prone to criminal activity directed against those social groups who live in luxury. The latter take shelter in gated communities guarded by security personnel, and so cannot freely use their wealth. Third, while many claim that high income disparities are necessary to create strong motivation for entrepreneurship and promote growth, this is only one side of the coin. Given that starting a company is linked to one's willingness to take risks, the consequences of failed investments do matter. While in an economy with a very uneven income distribution an entrepreneur's failure pushes him or her very far down the social ladder, in economies with a more egalitarian income distribution the consequences of a failure are much less severe. Fourth, and most importantly, in a perfect free-market society everyone has equal opportunities to put their abilities to use. However, it is clear that rags-to-riches stories are rare exceptions to the rule. In reality, the children of affluent parents are much more likely to end up in the privileged group than those of poor parents, although there is no evidence that the children of affluent parents are more able than poorer children. This problem concerns not only individual success. Exceptional abilities are rare. So it is in the interest of the entire society to discover and develop them. It is beyond doubt that under conditions of extreme income and wealth inequalities, resulting in sizable pockets of poverty, underprivileged children, including gifted ones, will not have adequate development opportunities, with a detriment not only to them, but to society at large.

The problem of growing income disparities is addressed multiple times in the following chapters as it directly bears on the course of macroeconomic processes. For the time being, suffice it to say that numerous serious research

---

[5] For a review of this discussion see Pasinetti (2000); see also Osiatyński (1978).

results indicate that deepening inequalities in income distribution hinder economic development.[6]

5.2 Profits and GDP in a Model with Government Revenues and Spending

Taking into consideration government spending on goods and services (including collective goods and services and government investment), G, the expenditure side of the GDP equation is as follows:

$$Y = CP + IP + X - M + G \tag{5.1}$$

where CP, IP, X, and M denote, as previously, private consumption, private investment, exports, and imports, respectively.

At the same time, the income side of the GDP equation is now:

$$Y = W + R + TN, \tag{5.2}$$

where W and R stand for wages and profits after direct taxes, respectively, and TN represents net taxes in the sense of all government revenues (including net pension contributions in the pay-as-you-go system, less all cash transfers, including the costs of servicing the interest on public debt). By combining both formulas, we arrive at:

$$W + R + TN = CP + IP + X - M + G \tag{5.3}$$

For the sake of simplicity, let us maintain the assumption that all profits are saved, which gives:

$$R = IP + (X - M) + (G - TN) - (W - CP)$$
$$R = IP + E + D - SW, \tag{5.4}$$

where $D = G - TN$ denotes budget deficit, $E = (X - M)$ – net exports, and $SW = W - CP$ household savings. It follows from (5.4) that the higher private investment, export surplus, and budget deficit are, and the lower household saving is, the higher profits will be.

In the special case without the rest of the world ($E = 0$) and without government ($D = 0$), equation (5.4) will be reduced to its basic form (see p. 35):

$$R = IP - SW \tag{4.3'}$$

Under capitalism profits are primarily determined by private investment less household savings. In an open economy, profits are also affected by net

---

[6] For instance, see Nikiforos (2014), Galbraith (2012), Piketty (2014).

exports. In the model with government, profits also depend on the budget deficit: If the government spends more on goods and services than it receives from economic agents, it creates an additional market thereby increasing economic output and, by the same token, GDP. Let us now consider this issue in greater detail. First, we introduce the notion of disposable income of businesses and households:

$$YD = Y - TN = Y - tnY = (1 - tn)Y \tag{5.5}$$

where tn stands for the rate of personal income tax rate.[7]

The share of wages after taxation in disposable income, YD, shall continue to be denoted by α,[8] and the share of profits by $(1 - \alpha)$. As a result, we arrive at $W = \alpha(1 - tn)Y$ and $R = (1 - \alpha)(1 - tn)Y$, which gives:

$$Y = \frac{R}{(1 - tn)(1 - \alpha)} \tag{5.6}$$

Furthermore, (5.4) can be transformed into:

$$R = IP + X - M + G - TN - SW$$

Substituting the term mY (where $m = M/Y$ represents the import intensity of Y) for M and the term $sw\alpha(1 - tn)Y$ for savings out of wages, SW, we obtain:

$$R = IP + X + G - Y[m + tn + sw\alpha(1 - tn)] \tag{5.7}$$

where sw is the propensity to save out of wages.

Combining (5.6) and (5.7), we arrive at:[9]

$$Y = \frac{IP + X + G}{(1 - tn)sp + m + tn} \tag{5.8}$$

where $sp = (1 - \alpha) + sw\alpha$.

As can be seen from the numerator of (5.8), GDP depends on three factors: private investment, IP, exports, X, and government spending, G. The denominator of (5.8) also contains three elements: the private saving rate, sp, related to disposable income $(1 - tn)$, import intensity, m, and the tax rate, tn.

---

[7] A proportionate income tax is introduced here only for the sake of simplicity; later on, in these lectures, this simplification will be waived.

[8] This is permissible only as long as the tax rates on wages and profits are the same.

[9]
$$Y = \frac{IP + X + G - Y[m + tn + sw\alpha(1 - tn)]}{(1 - tn)(1 - \alpha)}$$

$$Y\frac{[(1 - tn)(1 - \alpha) + m + tn + sw\alpha(1 - tn)]}{(1 - tn)(1 - \alpha)} = \frac{IP + X + G}{(1 - tn)(1 - \alpha)}$$

$$Y\{(1 - tn)[(1 - \alpha) + sw\alpha] + m + tn\} = IP + X + G$$

While the numerator of (5.8) consists of external inflows to aggregate demand (i.e., all elements that add to it, except for CP), the denominator consists of aggregate demand outflows, such as savings, imports, and taxes.

In order to focus more closely on the problems of fiscal policy, for the time being we leave out the role of international trade wherever possible (it will be included only where necessary). Thus, assuming that X, M, and m all equal zero, let us illustrate the formulas introduced above with a numerical example using the following data: $IP = 20$ euros, $G = 30$ euros, $\alpha = 0.8$, $tn = 0.25$, and $sw = 0.1666$. First, we need to calculate sp, which is equal to $(1 - \alpha) + sw\alpha = 0.2 + 0.1666(0.8) = 0.333$. As a result, $(1 - tn)sp = 0.75$ $(0.333) = 0.25$, with the denominator of (5.8) being $(1 - tn)$ $sp + tn = 0.25 + 0.25 = 0.5$. Therefore, $Y = [20(IP) + 30(G)]/0.5$, hence $Y = 100$ euros. In this situation, a GDP of 100 euros is broken down into taxes $TN = 25$ euros, wages $W = 60$ euros, and profits $R = 15$ euros. The relationship between GDP distributions according to revenues and spending is shown in Figure 5.1.

Of greatest interest is the graphical illustration of Kalecki's profit equation in the model with government. The budget deficit, $D = 30(G) - 25(TN) = 5$ euros, constitutes (on top of IP) an additional element of company profits (savings), while workers' savings, $SW = 0.1666(60) = 10$ euros, reduce that profit:

$$R = IP + D - SW = 20 + 5 - 10 = 15 \ euros.$$

At the same time, since $R + SW = IP + D$, the private savings of firms (15 euros) and households (10 euros) equal the sum of private investment (20 euros) plus the budget deficit (5 euros).

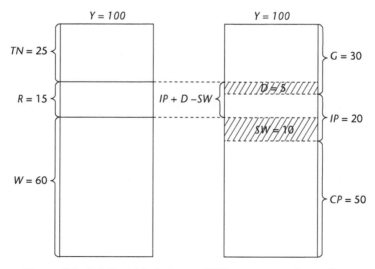

Figure 5.1. Relationship between GDP revenues and spending

5.3 The Government's Budget as an Automatic Business-cycle Stabilizer When Investment Fluctuates

Private investment fluctuations are a characteristic feature of the capitalist economy. They lead to cyclical variations in the volume of output and employment, exerting a negative influence on the overall economic situation. Therefore, one of the objectives of economic policy should be to reduce these fluctuations of output and employment at a given rate of private investment fluctuations. It appears that an income-related tax system may be helpful in attaining such a goal as long as the income tax mechanism is allowed to act without restraint.

Figure 5.2, panel A shows income tax as an increasing function of Y in the form of $TN = tnY$, with government spending on goods and services at G_0. The slope of the segment $0C$ represents the tax rate tn. At point C, government revenues and spending are balanced. For a given G_0, the lower the Y, the lower the tax revenues tnY, and so the higher the deficit, D. Panel B shows a deficit of $D = G_0 - TN$. Here, point C' corresponds to C, which means that at $Y = 0C'$ the budget is balanced, which in practice is a rare occurrence (albeit not as rare as a budget surplus). Such a budget can occasionally be seen during periods of economic prosperity with high volumes of employment and GDP.

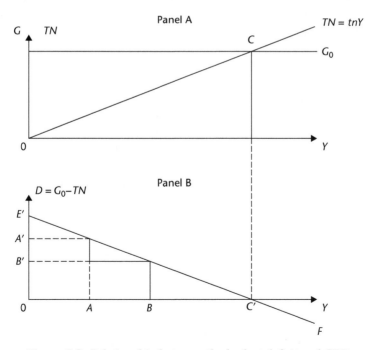

Figure 5.2. Relationship between the budget deficit and GDP

As can be seen from Figure 5.2, panel B, the budget deficit, D, is a decreasing function of Y at a given G_0. Indeed, if GDP rises from $Y=0A$ to $Y=0B$, then the budget deficit diminishes from $D=0A'$ to $D=0B'$, which explains the role of the budget as an automatic stabilizer of business cycles. When Y increases as a result of rising private investment, the deficit declines. In turn, when Y decreases as a result of shrinking private investment, the deficit increases. Therefore, both increases and decreases of Y may be to a certain extent dampened if the finance minister takes advantage of the countercyclical consequences of the budget deficit.

Let us now proceed to more detailed analysis, still assuming that X, M, and m are all zero. Then, from 5.8 we obtain:

$$Y = \frac{IP + G}{(1 - tn)sp + tn} \tag{5.9}$$

where $sp = [(1 - \alpha) + sw\alpha]$ denotes the average propensity to save out of disposable income. Given constant values of the parameters α, sw, tn, and G, equation (5.9) can be transformed to:

$$\Delta Y = \frac{\Delta IP}{(1 - tn)sp + tn} \tag{5.10}$$

Formula (5.10) represents the investment multiplier in the model with government. GDP increases by a factor of $1/[(1 - tn)sp + tn]$ times investment growth. If $tn = 0$, then:

$$\Delta Y = \frac{\Delta IP}{sp} \tag{4.6'}$$

which is the already familiar investment multiplier from our basic model. A comparison of (5.10) and (4.6') shows that in the presence of income taxation, the investment multiplier is lower than in an economy without it. Indeed, the denominator of formula (5.10) is larger than that of formula (4.6').[10]

Let us illustrate this argument with a numerical example, adopting the same parameters as before: $\alpha = 0.8$, $sw = 0.16666$, and $tn = 0.25$. Then, we obtain:

$$sp = (1 - \alpha) + sw\alpha = 0.2 + 0.1666(0.8) = 0.333$$

and:

$$[(1 - tn)sp + tn] = 0.75(0.333) + 0.25 = 0.5.$$

---

[10] Let us designate the denominator of (5.10) as z, where $z = (1 - tn)sp + tn$. Then, $z = sp$ if $tn = 0$. The derivative of z with respect to tn is $\frac{\partial z}{\partial tn} = sp + 1 > 0$, which means that z is an increasing function of tn.

Indeed, all other things being equal, the multiplier $(1/sp) = (1/0.33) = 3$, while the multiplier $\{1/[(1 - tn)sp + tn]\} = (1/0.5) = 2$. Thus, at $\Delta IP = 10$ euros, $\Delta Y = 30$ euros in the model without government, and $\Delta Y = 20$ euros in the model with government, since the increase in private investment leads to a rise in private consumption by 10 euros only.

Using (5.7) we can also calculate the change in profits, R:

$$\Delta R = \Delta IP - \Delta Y[tn + sw\alpha(1 - tn)] \tag{5.11}$$

In the example under consideration, this translates into: $\Delta R = 10 - 20$ $[0.25 + 0.166 (0.8) (0.75)] = 10 - 20 (0.25 + 0.1) = 3$ euros.

Furthermore, the change in the budget deficit amounts to:

$$\Delta D = -tn\Delta Y \tag{5.12}$$

which means that $\Delta D < 0$, or the deficit decreases with increasing GDP:

$$\Delta D = -0.25(20) = -5 \text{ euros}$$

In turn, the increase in workers' savings amounts to:

$$\Delta SW = sw\Delta W = sw\alpha(1 - tn)]\Delta Y = 0.1666(0.8)(0.75)20 = 2 \text{ euros.}$$

Thus, a rise in profits by 3 euros equals the sum:

$$\Delta IP + \Delta D - \Delta SW = 10 - 5 - 2 = 3 \text{ euros.}$$

The underlying cause of the lower investment multiplier in the model with government is the outflow of taxes at each step of the multiplier process. This outflow occurs alongside the outflow of profits (corporate savings) and worker savings, which were analyzed in detail in Chapter 4. At given government spending, G, an increase in taxation, ΔTN, implies a reduction in the budget deficit, $\Delta D < 0$, which leads to a lower growth of profits, ΔR, and of national income, ΔY, resulting from an increase in IP.

Obviously, when investment decreases, i.e., $\Delta IP < 0$, the process goes in the opposite direction: GDP decreases, but not as much as in the model without government. This is again due to the lower investment multiplier, implying a smaller decrease in GDP. Here, profits do not decline as sharply as a result of the increasing budget deficit: a contracting GDP causes a drop in tax revenues, triggering a higher budget deficit at a given level of government spending. Thus, profits arising from government spending partially compensate the contraction caused by reduced private investment. This automatic business-cycle stabilization mechanism is based on the presence of an income tax system and its effects are the stronger the more progressive that tax system is. In a period of economic prosperity, profits and high incomes grow faster than GDP, and, as a result, in a progressive income tax system, net government revenues also increase faster, decreasing the budget deficit. This entails more pronounced dampening of the growth of profits and GDP than in the case of a less progressive tax system (and especially in the case of a proportional one). These conclusions may be symmetrically applied to periods of economic downturn. In such situations, the more progressive the income tax system is, the more precipitously the government revenues decline, expanding the budget deficit, which partially alleviates profit and GDP contraction. Therefore, the degree of tax progression should be considered not only in terms of income distribution between high- and low-income groups, but also in terms of the effectiveness of business-cycle stabilization. In particular, in a flat-tax system, the automatic business-cycle stabilizer will not be very efficient, in addition to the fact that such a system will be opposed by all those who rightly advocate progressive taxation as a necessary and useful instrument of income redistribution in the market economy.

The automatic business-cycle stabilizer is based on a reduced power of investment multiplier, its constitutive factor being countercyclical changes in the budget deficit: decreases in periods of investment growth and increases in periods of investment decline. A reduced budget deficit attenuates the growth of profits and GDP during economic prosperity, while an increased deficit alleviates the contraction of profits and GDP during an economic downturn.

Finance ministers, stock market participants, and mainstream economists often evaluate the economic standing of a country based on changes in its budget deficit. They tend to perceive reductions in that deficit as a sign of economic health, and increases as a sign of malaise. Consequently, many of them call for a statutory obligation to maintain a balanced budget (or a constant budget deficit-to-GDP ratio). Irrespective of the fact that such an obligation would be impracticable, it should be noted that a fiscal policy of this kind would eliminate the automatic business-cycle stabilizer. In the event of a decline in private investment (and the resulting contraction of GDP and government revenues), the minister of finance would have to reduce government spending accordingly, further undermining economic activity. In turn, in the event of an expansion of private investment, GDP, and government revenues, the minister would be obliged to increase government spending, thus additionally stimulating the economy and aggravating business-cycle fluctuations. Indeed, such a policy could hardly be deemed consistent with the economic interest of the country.

5.4 Why Budget Deficits are Inevitable in the Capitalist Economy?

Despite being contrary to the spirit and principles of mainstream economics, the function of the budget deficit as an automatic business-cycle stabilizer is in practice accepted by international financial institutions, and especially by the EU administration (e.g., as an important element of the Maastricht criteria). At the same time, budget deficits and surpluses are expected to offset each other over the course of a business cycle so that the budget for the entire cycle should be in balance or close to it. Prior to tackling the theoretical foundations of this proposition, let us examine some empirical data on past budget deficits. Of particular interest is the 2013 UNCTAD chart reproduced in Figure 5.3 below.

Figures larger than zero correspond to surpluses, while lower than zero to deficits. Surpluses imply an increase in net financial assets, and deficits imply a rise in debt. If one ignores some small measurement errors and deviations resulting from the aggregation of large quantities, then the surpluses and deficits are mirror reflections of each other.

As foreign trade does not exist for the world as a whole, the private sector balances mirror the public-sector balances (and vice versa). The chart shows that over the past forty years the public sector has consistently exhibited deficits, while the private sector has, by necessity, recorded financial surpluses of corresponding magnitude. Since world GDP primarily represents the GDP of the largest countries, Figure 5.3 is mostly indicative of the experience of those economies. The UNCTAD analysts aptly observed that there is a difference between the periods preceding and following the year 1990. Prior to the 1990s, public-sector deficits were relatively stable: they amounted to approximately 3 percent of world GDP and were accompanied by corresponding private-sector surpluses. This situation seems normal: the private sector accumulates financial assets in the form of government securities, in this way

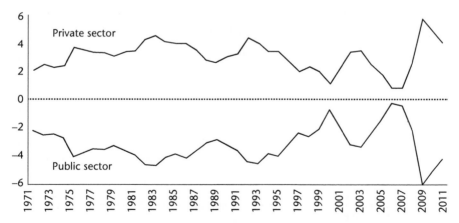

Figure 5.3. Public- and private-sector balances in the world economy, 1971–2011 (percent of world domestic product)
Source: UNCTAD Secretariat calculations, UNCTAD (2013: 16).

investing the excess of private savings over private investment.[11] However, the subsequent period reveals a much greater instability of public- and private-sector balances, with the average deficit being approximately 2 percent of the world GDP. Of special interest is the fact that marked drops in budget deficits preceded both the crisis of 2001 and the great financial crisis that began in the years 2008/9. Indeed, a decrease in the public-sector deficit by definition means a lower surplus of private savings over private investment, as well as a decline in financial assets and net private wealth of this sector.

It is also noteworthy that the European Union has exhibited a current account balance close to zero throughout its existence (at least by 2011). In the years 1961–2011, its current account balance amounted on average to only 0.3 percent of the European Union's GDP. Therefore, in this group of countries private- and public-sector balances mirrored each other as well. In the years 1974–2013, for which unified data are available, the average annual budget deficit amounted to about 4–5 percent of GDP,[12] which more or less corresponded to the surplus of private savings over private investment. Therefore, it may be concluded that over the past forty years, both in the world as a whole and within the EU-12, budget deficits have amounted to 3–5 percent of GDP on a regular basis. While budget surpluses have been occasionally recorded in individual countries in some years, they were the exception rather than the rule.

Given the above, it is indeed of utmost importance to examine the theoretical basis of the EU postulate for balanced or nearly balanced structural budgets (i.e., budgets adjusted for business-cycle fluctuations) in its member states. In this context, it seems necessary to reconsider the factors that determine the dynamics of profits and GDP in the simplest of terms. In particular, it is assumed that profits are entirely retained by private companies while workers spend all their wages on consumption. Thus, we obtain:

$$R = IP \tag{5.13}$$

and:

$$Y = \frac{R}{1 - \alpha} = \frac{IP}{1 - \alpha} \tag{5.14}$$

As was argued earlier, the cause-and-effect relationship between those variables is such that it is private investment that determines profits, and not

---

[11] Deficits of such proportions may be accompanied by sustainable economic growth and constant government debt to GDP ratios (cf. pp. 81–2).

[12] In individual decades between 1974 and 2000, the budget deficit of the EU-12 amounted to 3.8 percent, 4.1 percent, and 4.9 percent of GDP respectively, while after 2000, in two consecutive five-year periods, it was 5 percent and 2.6 percent of GDP (see Statistical Annex of European Economy, Spring 2014, p. 204).

the other way round. Furthermore, profits can be used to calculate Y, as the mark-up price-setting system implies a largely stable share of profits in GDP, equal to $1 - \alpha$.

Let us denote GDP at full employment as Y_F and the profits that enable full employment as $R_F = (1 - \alpha)Y_F$. The sum of individual investment decisions, and the resulting volume of private investment, IP, may be smaller than, equal to, or greater than R_F. If private investment were as a rule equal to R_F, then as a matter of principle the capitalist economy would exhibit full employment. This has indeed occurred in some countries for a few years, but it is a very rare phenomenon that results from factors the elaboration of which is beyond the scope of our present simple model. However, should private investment be usually greater than R_F, then as a matter of principle we would see inflation driven by aggregate demand accompanied by a seller's market and lines of buyers in front of stores. In capitalist economies, this may happen at a time of war, disaster, or social upheaval, but otherwise very rarely, while this situation was widespread in the centrally planned socialist economies (which were very different from capitalist ones). Finally, private investment may be smaller than R_F with GDP lower than Y_F. An unbiased observer will admit that the last option is typical of capitalist economies with a buyer's market, in which sellers and goods wait for customers, and workers look for employment, but do not necessarily find it. As a result, unemployment is typical of unplanned capitalist economies.

This situation is by no means accidental. While in the capitalist economy the distribution of GDP between wages and profits is relatively stable (which is reflected in the general similarity of changes in unit labor costs and GDP deflators, and thus in stable mark-ups), private investment tends to fluctuate and seldom achieves a volume sufficient for attaining R_F. This is due to the fact that investment decisions are made based on profitability calculations for each individual project, which is to be carried out under a set of forecast, but essentially unknown conditions, such as future prices, costs, and the general economic environment in the future. It is little wonder that the resulting overall volume of private investment is highly volatile. One of the inherent weaknesses of the capitalist economy is that the share of profits in GDP is largely constant in the short term irrespective of the volume of private investment.

In a rationally organized economy, the share of profits in GDP would be determined in such a way as to enable approximately full employment at each volume of private investment: then, the share of profits would have to vary and adjust to the volume of private investment. In other words, the prices and mark-ups would have to change to ensure more or less full employment at given levels of private investment. In particular, when private investment declines, consumption should increase to compensate for shortage of invest-ment. Thus, to protect employment in the face of contracting private

67

investment, wages would have to increase relative to prices, implying a drop in the mark-up.

However, in reality market forces act in the opposite direction. In the case of reduced private investment, the bargaining power of workers in the labor market is weakened. Moreover, mainstream economists believe that excessive wages lie at the core of unemployment. Under these circumstances, in periods of faltering private investment wages do not rise relative to prices; indeed, it is difficult to prevent them from falling (with respect to the existing mark-up). While according to mainstream economists the downward rigidity of wages contributes to unemployment, in fact, it is exactly the other way round—this rigidity prevents an increase in the mark-up and a further aggravation of unemployment, which is caused not by excessive wages, but insufficient private investment.

If $IP < R_F$, then $Y < Y_F$ and aggregate demand is insufficient to ensure full employment. Some of the available production capacity remains unused and, more importantly, part of the workforce remains jobless. This implies irreparable economic losses compounded by social damage because unemployment deprives people not only of jobs and incomes, but also of a traditional place in the social and family structure.

An in-depth analysis of this situation needs to take into consideration household savings, which, along with company savings (still identified with profits) play a key macroeconomic role. If $sw > 0$, then formulas (5.13) and (5.14) can be replaced by (see p. 66):

$$R = IP - SW \qquad (5.13')$$

and:

$$Y = \frac{R}{(1-\alpha)} = \frac{IP - sw\alpha Y}{(1-\alpha)}$$
$$Y = \frac{IP}{(1-\alpha) + sw\alpha} \qquad (5.14')$$

Figure 5.4 represents the economic relationships that arise between the corporate and household subsectors under the circumstances described above. At a private investment of IP_0, GDP amounts to $Y_0 = 0A$. Indeed, according to (5.13') profits (company savings) are given by $R_0 = IP_0 - SW_0 = AC - CB = AB$, which is obviously accompanied by $Y_0 = 0A$. It is noteworthy that, in contrast to the previous analysis, here profits R_0 are smaller than IP_0, as a result of which corporate investment does not fully return to the corporate sector. The difference $IP_0 - R_0$, equal to the segment BC, represents the debt of the corporate subsector to the household subsector in the form of new shares issued by firms and purchased by households or in the form of loans extended to firms by banks from the deposits of households.

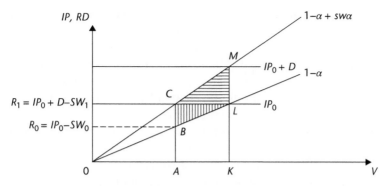

Figure 5.4. Aggregate demand gap

It should be stressed that households which put their savings at the disposal of companies do not do them a particularly generous favor: if $sw = 0$, then those savings would not arise in the first place, and companies would not be indebted to households at all. However, since $sw > 0$ then the possibility of lending those savings to the corporate subsector is of great significance as companies do own fixed assets exceeding their liabilities and as such are reliable debtors of households, and are capable of servicing their debts from future revenues.

Let us now assume that, as in the typical capitalist economy, Y_0 does not ensure adequate utilization of the production capacity of companies and a satisfactory level of employment. Let Y_1 denote a desirable GDP, but not necessarily equal to full employment GDP ($Y_0 < Y_1 \leq Y_F$). At private investment equal to IP_0 and desirable $Y_1 = OK$, profits would amount to $R_1 = KL$ and household saving to $SW_1 = LM$. These savings would be accompanied by insufficient willingness of companies to incur debt as their investment outlays and profits would still be equal to KL. This would lead to an aggregate demand gap (between desirable household savings and the willingness of companies to incur debt to households), amounting to LM. Assuming a constant IP_0, at given α and sw this gap could be filled by a budget deficit or export surplus. Leaving out the export surplus, which is not a viable alternative for all countries taken together, this gap may be bridged by the deficit $D = LM$, implying the government's readiness to incur debt of that volume. If private investment corresponded to $IP_1 = KM$, then the segment LM (equal to $IP_1 - IP_0$) would represent the willingness of companies to incur debt exactly in the amount of LM, and no budget deficit would be needed.

It should be noted that at IP_0, and given all other parameters, when the desired GDP increases from $Y_0 = OA$ to $Y_1 = OK$, the willingness of the corporate subsector to incur debt decreases (see the triangle BCL), while the aggregate demand gap (the triangle CLM) expands. The macroeconomic objective of financial policy should be to arrive at such a budget deficit that would fill the gap between household savings and companies' willingness to incur debt which arises when private investment is insufficient to obtain the desirable GDP. Thus, the budget deficit fulfills a critical macroeconomic role, as fiscal policy can modify aggregate demand. In particular, when the latter is insufficient, additional demand should be created by means of a budget deficit to bring the economy closer to full employment.

So far, we have left out foreign trade or the sector of the rest of the world. The existence of that sector does not affect our analysis when we consider all countries taken together. However, the situation is different for individual economies. Let us modify equation (5.4) to the following form:

$$[(R_F - IP) + SW_F] = D + E \tag{5.4$'$}$$

where, as before, the left side represents the balance of the private sector as the difference between the balance of the corporate subsector (usually negative) and that of the household subsector (usually positive). The balance $[(R_F - IP) + SW_F] > 0$ reflects a surplus of potential household savings over companies' willingness to incur debt, corresponding to $(R_F - IP)$, which occurs at full (or desirable) employment (see the CLM triangle in Figure 5.4). This surplus will still be termed in short the "aggregate demand gap." In the more complex model, bridging this gap requires for $D + E$ (rather than D alone) to be equal to the gap. In other words, the aggregate demand gap is to be filled not only by the budget deficit, but also by the deficit of the rest of the world.

In this context, it should be remembered that since an increase in the budget deficit causes an increase in GDP, it also entails a rise of imports by $\Delta M = mY$, with the balance of trade changing by $\Delta E = -mY$, which impairs the budget deficit mechanism. It follows from the above that an increment in the budget deficit causes the sum $D + E$ to grow at a lesser rate than D alone. Second, and more importantly, if a country is vulnerable in terms of its balance of payments, then its freedom to shape its fiscal policy is heavily constrained. Therefore, for the aggregate demand gap to be bridged one also needs coordination of the fiscal policies of the countries engaged in international trade exchange.

As far as the mercantilist policy of expanding exports to achieve export surpluses is concerned, it will also be rendered less effective by the same mechanism. Indeed, as GDP growth leads to increased government revenues $\Delta TN = tn\Delta Y$, the budget deficit mechanism deteriorates as the sum $D + E$ grows more slowly than its component E alone. However, what is of special note is that mercantilist policy affects the aggregate demand gap itself. In particular, attaining international competitiveness at the expense of limiting wage rises relative to productivity immediately hampers consumer demand. In Figure 5.4, this is illustrated by the rotation of the radii $0L$ and $0M$ upwards and to the left: their increasing slope signals a tendency for GDP to decline at given private investment. Also private investment itself is adversely affected by this policy. And when IP decreases on the left side of equation (5.4′), then the aggregate demand gap increases. As a result, mercantilist policy is either utterly ineffectual or at best modestly effective, leading to only a small uptick in aggregate demand (the sum of domestic and foreign demand).

Finally, it should be stressed that, in countries with a permanent current account deficit, the room for fiscal flexibility is very limited as the condition $D + E > 0$ must be met for the aggregate demand gap to be bridged. Consequently, if $E < 0$, then D must be greater than $|E|$. Indeed, when the budget deficit equals the absolute value of E and $E < 0$, then the sum $D + E$ amounts to 0. As can be seen, countries that are not internationally competitive need much higher budget deficits to fill (or reduce) the aggregate demand gap.

5.5 Deficit Spending or Private Investment Stimulation?

Section 5.4 explained why governments need to run budget deficits when private investment is insufficient in relation to a given rate of private saving. Thus the question arises here whether one should supplement private investment with a budget deficit, or stimulate it directly. This issue deserves careful consideration.

The most critical element of any policy aimed at full (or at least high) employment is the promotion of private investment, the key driver of the capitalist economy. This may be attained by low interest rates, monetary policies stimulating lending, and fiscal instruments, such as accelerated depreciation and similar tax incentives. However, such measures also have certain limitations. Private investment is aimed at a production effect rather than a demand effect, and its goal is to renew and expand the production stock. From this point of view we need to consider the possible limitations of stimulating private investment.

First, however, we should address the problem of employment, which has been previously left out. Let us assume that the rate of productivity growth, μ, is constant and determined by technological progress at given capital intensity, v (such technological progress is considered neutral). Let us assume that the rate of employment growth, corresponding to the rate of workforce growth, λ, is also constant. Finally, let the growth rate corresponding to the sum $\mu + \lambda$ be denoted as g_0. If GDP growth is also g_0, then the situation in the labor market is stable in the sense that any initial unemployment rate (including full employment) will continue unaltered under conditions of such sustainable growth.

Let us assume that the initial productive capital stock in the country under consideration is $K = vY^*$ (where Y^* stands for potential GDP) and ensures enough jobs for the entire workforce. In the less developed countries, the capital stock does not meet that condition. Hence, even at full utilization of existing production capacity (which is by no means automatically assured), full employment is not possible there due to a lack of jobs. Therefore, this type of unemployment is attributable to insufficient production capacity and as such does not fall within the scope of the present discussion. On the other hand, it seems that in developed capitalist countries, the existing capital stock measured (as previously) by the value of production capacity, vY^*, is large enough to enable full employment. However, this capital stock must grow over the subsequent period by g_0 if full employment is to be maintained. This requires private investment adequate to production capacity, which we call after Kalecki capacity adjusted investment,[13] and which is denoted as $IP_U = g_0Y^*$.[14] For instance, if IP_U amounts to 3 percent of the capital stock, K, then that stock will increase by 3 percent, and, at a constant v, productive capacity will also increase at the same rate. If these conditions are met, then economic growth is sustainable in the sense that not only national income and production stock rises at the rate of g_0, but also the prerequisites for full employment are maintained over time.

On the other hand, let us define such private investment, IP_F, which at a given private saving rate, sp, ensures aggregate demand sufficient for full employment GDP, as $Y_F = (IP_F/sp)$. Furthermore, from the previous section it follows that $IP_F = SP_F$. The question now arises as to the relationship between IP_U and IP_F. It seems that most often it is represented by the inequality $IP_U < IP_F$, where $IP_F = SP_F$. It should be kept in mind that in developed capitalist economies real investment tends to fall short of private savings at full employment, SP_F, which is the underlying cause of unemployment according to the Keynes–Kalecki theory. In the past, there were some periods of nearly or completely full employment (e.g., in the 1950s and 1960s), with shortages of labor rather than jobs. This would be impossible if $IP_U > SP_F$, since then the shortage of production capacity would prevent full employment. Finally, it is highly unlikely that the market will spontaneously tend towards the equality $IP_U = SP_F$, in which technological and demographic determinants are in balance with national income distribution and corporate and household propensity to save.

---

[13] See Kalecki (1945 [1990]: 377).

[14] The full formula should be $IP_U = (g_0 + \delta)K$, where δ stands for capital depreciation. However, for the sake of simplicity the depreciation coefficient is left out in this section and for the time being we assume that capital stock does not wear out.

In reality in highly and medium developed economies we observe unemployment caused by insufficient demand rather than any shortage of productive capacity. In this case, the most likely relationship between these economic variables is the inequality $IP_U < SP_F$. In fact, real private investment, IP, does not seem to be too distant from IP_U, since even over longer periods of time these countries do not exhibit a shortage of jobs with respect to the available workforce. Under the circumstances, stimulation of private investment is nonetheless necessary and justified as long as actual private investment is equal to or falls short of the investment necessary to maintain full capacity utilization, or $IP \leq IP_U$. Such stimulation is also beneficial in the sense that it alleviates the cyclical fluctuations in private investment, which are detrimental to the economy as a whole.

The aggregate demand gap has been so far examined in the context of the private propensity to invest lagging behind the private propensity to save, both in the basic model and in the model including government. We have focused on the need to expand private investment as a natural way of bridging the aggregate demand gap with a view to boosting employment. However, we have now reached the conclusion that the stimulation of private investment has a certain limit, which is IP_U. Indeed, filling the remaining demand gap with additional private investment in excess of IP_U would not make sense, as such investment would be superfluous from the point of view of production capacity. After all, the objective of investment is to achieve a production effect in the form of increased production capacity rather than an income effect in the form of higher employment.[15]

A special case of the demand gap is the inequality $IP_U < SP_F$, which corresponds to full employment savings exceeding capacity-adjusted private investment. Here, there are only two ways of closing the gap $(SP_F - IP_U) > 0$. The first one involves outlays financed from the budget deficit and spent on public investments (as long as they do not interfere with the investment opportunities of the private sector) and on other social goals, such as public education, science (especially basic research), collective consumption of the poorer classes, etc. It should be emphasized that this constitutes an additional argument for budget deficits, irrespective of the justification presented in the previous section.

---

[15] A long-term policy stimulating private investment in excess of IP_U would also face other obstacles. At private investment higher than IP_U the rate of growth of production capital would exceed g_0, while national income would continue to grow at a rate of g_0 due to a barrier in the form of a workforce shortage. Also profits equal to private savings (leaving out SW) would grow at a rate of g_0. As a result, the profit rate, equal to the ratio of profit to capital, would decline, as would the degree of production capacity utilization. Both of these factors would also make it difficult to continue such a policy from the point of view of company profitability.

The other way to fill the $(SP_F - IP_U)$ gap involves changes in the distribution of national income aimed at diminishing the share of profits, increasing the share of wages, and obtaining a more egalitarian distribution between households. The objective of such measures is to decrease the private saving rate since the propensity to save out of wages and out of low and medium incomes is smaller than that out of profits or high incomes. This solution narrows the demand gap and is more challenging in political terms, while the previous one fills the gap in a socially useful manner.

5.6 Expansion Driven by Active Fiscal Policy

This section examines the methods and effects of fiscal policy as means of stimulating economic growth in a closed economy. First, let us consider the case of a budget deficit increasing due to higher government spending at a given level of tax revenues, or alternatively due to a tax reduction at a given level of government spending. Further on, we will examine mutually compensating changes of government spending and taxes.

If private investment is insufficient to maintain a satisfactory volume of production and employment, government spending may be used as an instrument of economic expansion. Assuming constant α, sw, tn, and IP, the government spending multiplier is the same as the investment multiplier:

$$\Delta Y = \frac{\Delta G}{(1 - tn)sp + tn} \tag{5.10'}$$

where, as mentioned earlier, $sp = (1 - \alpha) + sw\alpha$.

However, despite the fact that the government spending multiplier defined by (5.10') and the investment multiplier defined by (5.10) are equal, they differ in one important respect. Using the definition of the budget deficit, $D = G - tnY$, we can transform (5.10') as follows:

$$\Delta D = \Delta G - tn\Delta Y$$

$$\Delta D = \Delta G - tn\frac{\Delta G}{(1 - tn)sp + tn}$$

$$\Delta D = \Delta G = \frac{(1 - tn)sp}{(1 - tn)sp + tn} \tag{5.15}$$

which also means that:

$$0 < \Delta D < \Delta G$$

so the budget deficit increases with government spending, but due to higher tax revenues it increases less than that spending.

In turn, given an increase of private investment $\Delta IP > 0$, we obtain from (5.9):

$$\Delta D = -tn\,\Delta Y, \tag{5.16}$$

$$\Delta D = -tn\frac{\Delta IP}{(1 - tn)sp + tn} \tag{5.17}$$

which means that:

$$\Delta D < 0$$

so the budget deficit decreases, because at a given level of spending, government revenues increase. Consequently, the budget deficit decreases when economic expansion is driven by private investment and increases when it is driven by government spending.[16] However, in the latter case the budget deficit increases more slowly than government spending, as in equation (5.15) the term $(1 - tn)sp / [(1 - tn)sp + tn]$ is less than one. This means that part of the increase in government expenditure is automatically financed by the increase in taxation generated by the former. This part depends on the tax rate, tn.

The other fiscal method of driving economic growth is a reduction in taxes at unchanged government spending. A lower tax rate, tn, increases GDP as the denominator of the fraction on the right side of (5.9) declines (see footnote 10). However, thorough analysis requires that we give up the extreme assumption of proportional taxation and distinguish between different tax rates levied on different income groups. Of particular importance is the fact that the propensity to consume varies depending on the type of income. If this propensity is high, a tax reduction will significantly boost consumption, while if it is low, consumption will grow modestly. To take this factor into account, one should at least differentiate between taxation of wages, which are characterized by a high propensity to consume (and a low propensity to save) and profits, which are characterized by a low propensity to consume (and a high propensity to save). For the sake of simplicity, we assume that all profits are saved and all wages are consumed. An in-depth analysis of fiscal stimulation of economic growth by tax reductions in a model distinguishing between taxes on wages and profits is given in Appendix 3. Below, we only present the results of that analysis.

---

[16] However, it should be stressed that despite the different directions of change in budget deficit, D, the increase in profits accompanying a given level of $\Delta IP = \Delta G$ is identical. Since

$$\Delta R = \Delta IP + \Delta G - \Delta TN - \Delta SW, \tag{a}$$

then the increase in profits, ΔR, is identical in both cases. If $\Delta IP > 0$ and $\Delta G = 0$, then:

$$\Delta R = \Delta IP - \Delta TN - \Delta SW, \tag{b}$$

and if $\Delta IP = 0$ and $\Delta G > 0$, then:

$$\Delta R = \Delta G - \Delta TN - \Delta SW, \tag{c}$$

and so (b) = (c), whenever $\Delta IP = \Delta G$.

First, let us consider a tax reduction when government spending does not rise. If the tax on wages is lowered (at $sw = 0$), then all incomes saved thereby will be spent on consumer goods. Due to the multiplier mechanism, the GDP growth generated in this way will be higher than this tax reduction. Obviously, the budget deficit will increase, and so will profits at a given IP.

On the other hand, if the tax on profits is reduced, the money saved by the capitalists will not directly increase aggregate demand. And if demand does not increase, then GDP will also stall. Thus, profits before taxes will remain the same, while profits after taxes will increase by the amount of the tax reduction (which is equal to the increase in the budget deficit). This will certainly improve the investment climate and the propensity to invest. However, the outcomes will not become apparent until the subsequent period. This shows that there is no definitive answer as to the effect of tax reductions on GDP: This effect increases with the spending propensity of the taxpayers benefiting from the tax reduction.

Let us now examine the third variant, with the budget revenues and spending increasing simultaneously, resulting in a zero budget deficit ($\Delta D = 0$). Also in this case we should first investigate the effects of increased wage taxation, then profit taxation, and finally both types of taxation at the same time.

If the increase in government spending is equal to the increase in the tax on wages, GDP will remain unchanged, although its structure may be affected. For instance, the extra government spending may be used to finance the production of cannons, while the higher taxation may force workers to cut down on their consumption of butter. Furthermore, the structure of employment will also be altered as some workers will transfer from the consumer goods sector to the arms sector, but the overall number of jobs will be stable.

In turn, if the increase in government spending is equal to the increase in the tax on profits, the production of consumer goods will not be affected in any way, as according to our assumption all profits are saved. In this case, the higher production of cannons will not diminish the consumption of butter; on the contrary, an increase of employment in the arms industry will trigger a multiplier process as a result of which GDP will grow more than the outlays on armaments financed with the tax on profits. In this case, profits before tax will grow exactly by the amount equivalent to the increase in profit taxation, so profits after tax will remain unchanged. This will be so because profits after tax are equal to private investment plus the budget deficit, and in this case neither changes.

In the short term, such a policy benefits the workers (but the burden of higher taxation of profits must not be passed on to the consumers) and is neutral for the capitalists. However, in the long term, this policy may adversely affect the investment climate as a higher profit tax rate diminishes the net profitability of new investment projects. On the other hand, that climate is going to be boosted by increased utilization of production capacity.

In light of the above, it is impossible to conclusively determine the final outcome of these two contradictory tendencies. Nevertheless, empirical research shows that the sharp increases in government spending and profit taxation of the 1950s and 1960s were accompanied by unprecedented economic growth (which was also stimulated by a range of other factors).

According to the so-called Haavelmo theorem, an identical increase in government revenues and spending yields a multiplier of 1, meaning that GDP grows by the same amount as public spending (and revenues). Our previous discussion seems to contradict this theorem since a simultaneous increase in government revenues and spending results in a multiplier of 0 in the case of increased taxation of wages or a multiplier of more than 1 in the case of increased taxation on profits. Appendix 3 presents a proof showing that the Haavelmo theorem is a special case of our model with a particular ratio of wage taxation to profit taxation; in other words, when wages and profits are taxed uniformly (see equation (A3.7)).

So far, we have examined a simultaneous increase in government revenues and spending. It should be noted that symmetrical conclusions pertain to a concurrent decline of government revenues and spending at a constant budget deficit. A decrease in government spending will not affect GDP if it is fully offset by a reduction of the tax on wages (a decrease in the production of cannons will be compensated by a rise in butter output). In turn, the highest contraction of GDP will occur if the decline in spending is entirely attributable to a reduction of the tax on profits. While this will lead to higher net profitability (after taxation) of new investment projects, the decline of aggregate output caused by such a policy will entail lower utilization of the existing capital stock, and the detrimental effect on investment decisions of the latter is not likely to be canceled out by the former effect of higher profitability after taxation of new investment projects. Generally speaking, the greater the reductions in profit taxation relative to wage taxation, the more severely the GDP will be affected by the decline in government spending.

5.7 Public Debt and the Costs of its Servicing

Theoretically, the budget deficit can be financed either by issuing government securities or by monetization. The latter would involve the state treasury borrowing directly from the central bank. However, that is prohibited by law in most countries to prevent monetary excess. As a result, the government is forced to borrow from private capital markets by issuing securities. It should be noted that although the central bank does not directly provide credit to the government, it does so indirectly in the secondary market by purchasing securities, including government bonds. Since this induces commercial banks and financial institutions to buy government bonds to replace the ones sold to the central bank, such purchases by central banks effectively make private institutions give the government the credit that the central bank cannot give directly. This fact illustrates the difficulty of separating the functions of fiscal and monetary policies, which are in fact highly interdependent. As such, they should be aimed both at price stabilization and maintaining a high employment rate.

Public debt arises from budget deficits. When one person borrows from another, then the debtor is obliged to pay off the debt to the borrower at a certain date and on specified terms. Thus, if the debtor spends more than his income, then in the future, especially around the repayment deadline, his expenses will have to be lower than his income. In this sense, debt is a burden on his future. Indeed, it might seem that this also concerns public debt (specifically the government's debt issued in the national currency), as a burden on the future generations. However, it is not so. In the case of domestic public debt, the creditor and debtor are one and the same entity. Society borrows from itself.

It should be borne in mind that the government may, but does not have to, pay off its debt at the prescribed time. As the state is thought to be an eternal institution, it can issue new securities upon the maturity of previously issued ones, with its debt balance remaining unchanged. Obviously, public debt must be serviced. If the government increases its domestic debt, in the future it will have to pay higher interest, and in this sense its liabilities grow. Thus, one could argue that if the present generation incurs debt, then the cost of servicing the interest on that debt will necessitate higher taxes to be paid by future generations.

However, this line of reasoning is also flawed. The question is: To whom will the interest be paid? Obviously, to the same future generations that will inherit the debt from their progenitors. When discussing government borrowing (in the sense of domestic debt denominated in the national currency), we tend to forget that government securities are purchased by the residents of a given country (for the time being let us leave out foreigners). Thus, if someone says that the average Polish citizen is, e.g., 3,000 euros in debt on account of domestic government debt incurred in the past, it should be remembered that at the same time he holds financial assets amounting to the same 3,000 euros. Thus, the notion of the government incurring debt from the future generation is groundless.[17]

The problem is that the notion of the "average Polish citizen" is misleading. While only certain people purchase government securities, taxes are (or at least should be) paid by everyone. Given that in the future people will have to face extra taxes to pay off the debt incurred in the past, some of them will

---

[17] The situation is different in the case of foreign debt, which is discussed in Chapter 6.

make net profits from debt payments, while others will have net losses, once taxes to service government debt are paid. Nevertheless, these profits and losses necessarily balance out, so any arguments invoking a debt burden on the future generations are laced with demagoguery. Still, a separate question arises whether the resulting income redistribution is desirable or not, but that has nothing to do with the concept that we borrow from the future generations, which might suggest that the government running a budget deficit is akin to a household living beyond its means and handing down to its descendants debt that they will have to, sooner or later, pay off with interest.

We have already mentioned that redistribution of net income in favor of the affluent classes (holding most of the issued government securities) at the expense of the poorer classes (mostly not holding securities) may be problematic, and indeed this is part of the wider problem of income inequalities within society.[18] This problem is caused by the uneven distribution of financial and non-financial wealth, which is outside the scope of the present discussion. However, it should be emphasized that while attempts to discredit the budget deficit and public debt are mere demagogy, the abolition of the budget deficit as an instrument stimulating economic growth under conditions of unemployment and underutilization of production capacity would entail very real and painful losses for the entire society, and especially for the underprivileged classes. Thus, the issue is whether we can afford not to have a budget deficit and squander production opportunities (as a result of unemployment), which would lead to real and irreparable social losses.

Since budget deficits are indispensable and beneficial, as shown above, the next question is what happens to public debt over a longer period of time. The available statistical data for countries around the world show that public debt is always present, but fluctuates over time. As GDP also fluctuates, calculating the ratio of public debt to GDP is a rather complicated issue. It should also be remembered that public debt is a stock variable while GDP is a flow variable, so it would be more appropriate to compare public debt with national wealth, which is another stock variable, but that is rarely done.

First of all, we should examine the conditions under which the public debt-to-GDP ratio tends to a constant value. Appendix 4 gives a detailed analysis of the relationships between the nominal GDP growth rate, g, annual increments of public debt caused by budget deficits, $D = aY$ (where a, $0 < a < 1$, denotes a constant budget deficit-to-GDP ratio), and the stock of nominal public debt, F. The key conclusion from that analysis is that the ratio of nominal public debt to nominal GDP, F/Y, is convergent with the ratio a/g. If GDP grows continually by 5 percent a year with a amounting to 3 percent, then over time public

---

[18] This problem will be addressed further on, when we analyze the case in which the interest on government debt is financed by incurring new debt.

debt will also increase by 5 percent, while the F/Y ratio will tend to $a/g = 0.03/0.05 = 0.6$ which is 60 percent. Let us consider an example in which a country has a GDP of 100 billion euros and a public debt of 60 billion euros, with a budget deficit of $a = 3$ percent GDP. Over one year, that country will add 3 billion euros to its public debt. Given a public debt of 60 billion euros, the increment in debt will be $(3/60) \times 100 = 5$ percent, which is equal to the assumed GDP growth. And since public debt and GDP grow at the same rate, their initial ratio (in this case, 60 percent) will remain unchanged. Therefore, although it is true that a constant budget deficit entails a constant increase in public debt, it should be noted that at a constant GDP growth rate (g) and a constant share of the budget deficit in GDP ($a = D/Y$), the public debt-to-GDP ratio will approach the limit defined by a/g.

It should be noted that for different values of a and g, the F/Y ratio will vary, being particularly sensitive to changes in the growth rate, g. When the latter is high, then the parameter a can be relatively low as the aggregate demand gap will be low as well. On the other hand, when the GDP growth rate is low, then the required value of a will be much larger. This can be easily illustrated using a numerical example: at $g = 6$ percent and $a = 2$ percent the ratio a/g tends to 33 percent. In turn, if g drops to 4 percent and a increases to 3 percent, then the public debt-to-GDP ratio will tend to 75 percent. It is thus no accident that at a time of high economic growth prior to 1975 budget deficits were moderate and debt-to-GDP ratios were on the decline, whereas in the subsequent decades, with generally low GDP growth rates, both a and F/Y rose. As the values of both a and g vary over time, it is little wonder that in different countries and periods of time the F/Y ratio grows or contracts accordingly. Moreover, when the growth rate g is relatively high, then the need for a deficit expressed in the parameter a is lower, so the F/Y ratio decreases. Consequently, one could argue that at a sufficient growth rate an economy can "grow out of debt," as measured by the F/Y ratio, while it will accumulate debt if the growth rate is feeble. The above notwithstanding, there is no theoretical limit to which the F/Y ratio should tend in the long term.

As has already been said, public debt servicing is a major intragenerational rather than intergenerational problem as it leads to income redistribution in favor of the owners of government securities. Public debt servicing influences the volume of aggregate demand at a given level of budget deficit. As a result, it is useful to apply the notion of primary deficit, denoted as $DP = D - zF$, where z stands for the interest on public debt which is paid to the creditors.[19] The

---

[19] The budget deficit, D, was previously defined as the difference between government spending, G, and net taxes, $TN = T - (T_{tr} + zF)$, where T is total tax revenues, T_{tr} stands for money transfers, and zF is the cost of servicing domestic public debt, F, at the interest rate z. Consequently, $D = G - [T - (T_{tr} + zF)]$. Thus, primary deficit, DP, amounts to $D - zF = G - (T - T_{tr})$.

need to separate out the costs of servicing the interest on public debt from other types of government spending is justified by the fact that the recipients of that interest (bond holders) are not likely to increase their spending at all, or will increase it very modestly. Consequently, primary deficit is sometimes called a deficit co-determining aggregate demand.

Once we have introduced the notion of primary debt, we need to examine not only the public debt-to-GDP ratio (F/Y) as before, but also the corresponding ratio of primary deficit to GDP (DP/Y). As we shall see, of paramount importance for this ratio is z, the average interest rate on public debt. Appendix 4 demonstrates that this ratio is expressed by the formula $[1 - (z)/(g)]$.

At a given a, the value of this formula, and even its sign, depends primarily on the ratio of the interest rate, z, to the GDP growth rate, g.[20] This can be most easily illustrated for $z = g$. In this particular case, $DP/Y = 0$ as the term in brackets equals zero. Taking into consideration the definition of primary deficit $(DP = D - zF = 0)$, this gives the equality $D = zF$. As a result, annually issued new debt amounting to $D = aY$ is used solely for servicing public debt, with the primary deficit (equal to 0) not adding to or subtracting from aggregate demand even though the budget deficit is $D > 0$. Moreover, the very idea of interest on public debt as a factor constraining aggregate demand through income redistribution from taxpayers to government bond holders takes on a new meaning. If the cost of servicing debt interest is covered by new debt (rather than taxes), then the rentiers purchasing newly issued government securities finance the rentiers holding previously issued securities. Thus, these capital flows occur within the group of bond holders and as such do not affect aggregate demand.

While this phenomenon is most conspicuous when $z = g$, it is also true for $z < g$, when the interest rate is lower than the GDP growth rate. Then, we have $DP/Y > 0$ and at the same time $DP/Y < a$, which means that after the F/Y ratio stabilizes, primary deficit will expand aggregate demand. This can be best illustrated with another numerical example. Let us assume that $g = 5$ percent and $a = 3$ percent. As we already know, under the assumptions the F/Y ratio tends to $a/g = 60$ percent. Then, at an interest rate of $z = 3$ percent the DP/Y ratio tends to $a[1 - (z/g)] = 0.03(1 - 0.6) = 0.012$, i.e., the ratio of primary deficit to GDP is 1.2 percent, and 1.8 percent GDP has to be spent on servicing public debt. This means that out of the overall debt increment of 3 percent GDP, less than half still contributes to aggregate demand (1.2 percent). Obviously, the lower the interest rate relative to the GDP growth rate, the greater

---

[20] As the GDP growth rate, g, was defined as a nominal value, also z should be understood as a nominal interest rate. One can also use both rates in real terms, i.e., after accounting for inflation.

the proportion of the budget deficit that adds to aggregate demand after subtracting the costs of servicing public debt.

Now, what happens to the part of the budget deficit, D, that is spent on zF, that is, on servicing domestic public debt? Also in this case rentiers purchasing new securities largely finance holders of outstanding bonds, due to which the cost of servicing domestic public debt does not hinder aggregate demand, which would otherwise happen if zF were financed from taxes.

Finally, let us assume that the interest rate is higher than the growth rate ($z > g$). For instance, at $g = 5$ percent let the interest rate, z, be 7 percent. Then, DP/Y tends to $a[1 - (z/g)] = 0.03[(1 - (0.07/0.05)] = 0.03(-0.4) = -0.012$. This means that in this case the rate of primary deficit to GDP amounts to -1.2 percent. Since according to our definition the fiscal deficit is a surplus of government spending over revenues, its opposite counterpart is a surplus of revenues over spending, or a primary budget surplus. In particular, the state increases public debt by 3 percent GDP annually while paying to the holders of government bonds $z(F/Y)$, or $0.07(0.6) = 0.042$, which is 4.2 percent GDP. Consequently, primary deficit amounts to $(0.03 - 0.042) = -1.2$ percent GDP annually, which means that the fiscal policy of the government leads to a reduction in aggregate demand by that amount. Indeed, the rentiers purchasing new government securities worth 3 percent GDP finance the holders of outstanding bonds only up to that volume. In turn, the primary budget surplus (here 1.2 percent GDP) is financed from taxes and adversely affects aggregate demand. As can be seen, the government should strive to keep the interest rate on its securities below the nominal GDP growth rate in order not to reduce the scope for fiscal policy stimulation of aggregate demand, at least in the long term. And keeping the interest rate on government securities below the nominal GDP growth rate is much needed by the economy as a whole, and in particular by the industrial (non-financial) sector as opposed to the financial-speculative sector.

The question here arises as to whether it is possible for the government to accomplish this. In fact, it is both possible and necessary. The state's interference in the economy in the form of a budget deficit is justified by the need to regulate aggregate demand. There is no reason for the government to compete in the capital market with private economic agents. The government borrows in the national currency and sets such interest rates as it deems appropriate. It is noteworthy that these interest rates do not need to be positive (and in reality they often are not). Countries with independent currencies can usually sell their bonds even if the interest rates are below the inflation rate. This is due to the fact that debt denominated in the national currency constitutes an absolutely risk-free investment, which cannot be said of any other securities. The banking system, and especially investment banks, need some solid foundation for their risky operations. And it is government securities that provide it, even though the structures built on them are often made of sand. Therefore, working with the central bank, the government should make sure that the interest on its bonds is lower than the GDP growth rate, or, if need be, even below the inflation rate.

5.8 Myths about the Budget Deficit and Public Finance

5.8.1 *The Budget Deficit and Inflation*

There is a deep-seated belief that the budget deficit gives rise to inflation, and so it should be avoided whenever possible. This is largely a fallacy because, as it has been shown, the budget deficit is only one part of aggregate demand, which in our model predominantly depends on private investment. If all increases in aggregate demand were to be treated as triggers of inflation, this would also apply to the growth of private investment. Since this issue has been analyzed in detail, suffice it to say that under conditions of unemployment and underutilization of production capacity an increment in aggregate demand (including its budget deficit component) leads to a quantity adjustment, while a price adjustment (inflation) happens only when the economy reaches potential GDP, which is a rare occurrence in capitalist countries under normal circumstances; it is more typical of wartime or periods of irresponsible populist rule.

Normally, the capitalist economy is characterized by underutilization of production capacity, so there is no reason why the risk of inflation should be associated in particular with the budget deficit, rather than with private investment or export surplus (this is discussed at length in Chapter 6). Actually, in most cases inflation is not "pulled" by demand, but "pushed" by costs, especially by unit labor costs, and has nothing to do with the budget deficit. Cost-driven inflation is usually due to increases in nominal wages above real productivity growth, resulting in higher unit labor costs and prices, at a given mark-up. Other sources of cost-driven inflation include rising prices of raw materials and energy carriers, and deteriorating terms of trade (the relationship between import and export prices). The effects of these factors are similar to those of declining productivity.

Under some exceptional circumstances, the government may lose control over revenues and spending, and allow the budget deficit to rise without apparent limit. Then, the sum of private investment, balance of trade, and the budget deficit less household savings may exceed the production capacity threshold and trigger demand-driven inflation. If such a situation persists, inflation will accelerate and eventually turn into hyperinflation (defined as a monthly inflation of at least 50 percent lasting for at least three months). Hyperinflation is usually financed by the government borrowing from the central bank. It causes money to lose its purchasing power so fast that people spend it immediately on consumer goods and services. Money no longer fulfills one of its fundamental functions as a store of value, remaining only a medium of payment. When the money circulation rate soars, the inflation rate will be similar to the rate at which the volume of money in circulation increases. Interestingly, it is only under these conditions that the quantity theory of money applies in practice so that prices are determined by the quantity of money. As a result, normal economic activity becomes impossible and other means of exchange are adopted (e.g., the US dollar). Eventually, a reform of the monetary system becomes inevitable. The budget deficit indeed plays a special role in hyperinflation as the banking system stops lending and, at the request of the government, the central bank starts printing money whose value immediately plummets. However, the fact that hyperinflation is impossible without a budget deficit does not imply that the budget deficit is normally responsible for inflation.

5.8.2 The Concept of Crowding out Private Investment

The other myth about public finance is that the budget deficit crowds out private investment. This notion can be interpreted in three ways, all of them founded on erroneous premises. First, some argue that crowding out occurs when production capacity is utilized to the full extent. But then investment would be crowded out not only by the budget deficit, but by all elements of aggregate demand. An increase in consumption would also crowd out private investment, and vice versa. More importantly, in mature capitalist economies full utilization of production capacity is even rarer than full employment.

Second, crowding out may imply a bottleneck linked to private savings. Some claim that in a given period of time the flow of savings is predetermined, with the government and private enterprises competing for them. But it is unclear how a savings flow can be a given if GDP and the factors determining its volume (including private investment and the budget deficit) are not given. As we already know, private savings are generated by private investment without the prerequisite of any initial savings; very much like the budget deficit, private investment finances itself. Furthermore, if savings were given *ex ante*, then not only would the budget deficit crowd out private investment, but no increase in private investment would be possible at all. Indeed, under the circumstances, each investment project would have to crowd out another one. This paradox disappears if, in line with economic reality, we reject the false assumption that the flow of current private savings is determined *ex ante*.

Third, most proponents of crowding out are likely to blame it on insufficient investment lending. This is closely intertwined with the broader issue of the banking system financing the budget deficit and private investment. Both require loans in order for their beneficial effects to fully materialize in the form of increased aggregate demand and GDP growth. This in turn necessitates an accommodating monetary policy with the central bank providing sufficient liquidity to the economy. Indeed, this is the fundamental responsibility of the central bank and its *raison d'être*. In a modern monetary economy, the amount of money in circulation is an endogenous rather than exogenous variable and is co-determined by the demand for credit from companies, households, and the government. If the monetary policy of the central bank interferes with this mechanism even when there exists unused productive capacity, then a higher budget deficit may lead to a rise in the interest rate, which in turn may crowd out some private investment. However, the same can be said of private investment itself. In the absence of lending, each new project would have to crowd out another one.

In reality, in the case of an economic slowdown (and this is the only case in which a budget deficit makes macroeconomic sense), banks suffer from excessive liquidity and underutilize their credit potential. It should be stressed that the cause-and-effect relationship suggested above, which is "an increase in the interest rate caused by a higher budget deficit leads to a decline of private investment" does not have to take place. If investment reacts more weakly to interest rate changes and more strongly to higher utilization of the production stock and GDP growth stimulated by the budget deficit, then the capacity-utilization factor can prevail, with private investment rising as a result of the budget deficit.[21] After all, in effective demand theory, the objective of the budget deficit is to stimulate economic activity, and by the same token, also private investment.

Finally, it should be noted that empirical research is inconclusive as to the exact nature of the relationship between budget deficits and interest rates postulated by the advocates of crowding out. In reality, periods of economic prosperity usually see low budget deficits and high interest rates, while economic downturns typically exhibit high budget deficits and low interest rates.

5.8.3 *The Concept of Twin Deficits*

The concept of twin deficits is related to the notion of crowding out. According to this theory, the budget deficit and current account deficit are closely linked, as epitomized in the famed Treasury View, expressed in the 1930s by representatives of the British Treasury.[22]

---

[21] This phenomenon is sometimes termed the "crowding in" of private investment by the budget deficit, in contrast to crowding out.

[22] When in the 1930s Lloyd George proposed to embark on a program of public works to alleviate unemployment in Great Britain, representatives of the British Treasury replied with what has been since known as the Treasury View: "if the government borrowed £100 million to

Let us rewrite (5.4) in the following form:

$$[(R - IP) + SW] = D + E$$

with the left side representing the private-sector balance, and the right side the sum of balances of the other two sectors.

The twin deficits concept is based on the assumption that at given private investment, the budget deficit will lead to higher interest rates, thus attracting foreign savings financing a surplus of imports. However, in light of the equation given above, it quickly becomes clear that this theory presupposes that the private-sector balance $[(R - IP) + SW] = 0$, as only then will the budget deficit equal the balance of the rest of the world ($D = M - X$). However, there is no theoretical or empirical reason why the balance of the private sector should be always equal to 0. Figure 5.3 shows that the global balance of the private sector has exhibited a constant surplus for the past forty years (mirrored by a constant deficit of the public sector). While there have been some periods in which private savings, SP, were smaller than private investment in individual countries, usually the opposite was true, that is, $(SP - IP) > 0$. As the identity $SP = IP$ is not borne out either theoretically or empirically, the twin deficits concept should be deemed one of the myths of mainstream economics.

5.8.4 *"Expansionary Contraction"*

There is a widespread consensus that stock exchange speculation and the excessive debt burden of the private sector (and especially the household subsector) were the main, but not the only, causes of the financial crisis that broke out in the United States in 2008 and quickly spread across the world. In response to it, many governments took recourse to Keynesian tools (ignored and demeaned by mainstream economists) in the form of massive spending efforts to prevent a downturn in the world's economy. This, together with automatic business-cycle stabilizers, gave rise to unprecedented peacetime budget deficits and soaring sovereign debt. However, the underlying causes of this state of affairs were quickly forgotten and governments embarked on a mission to fight exorbitant debt levels by fiscal tightening, mostly by means of spending cuts, especially in the welfare system. It was claimed that the costs of fiscal tightening would be low and in the long term this policy would remedy the adverse influence of the state on economic activity. An extreme form of this approach is expressed by the term "expansionary contraction," which supposedly does not involve even a short-time

spend on public works, there would be £100 million less for foreign investment. . . . There would be a transfer of employment but no change in the total" (Joan Robinson (1972: 1)).

dip in production. Just on the contrary, the restoration of sound public finance is expected to strengthen the confidence of companies to the extent that a contraction in government spending would trigger such an increase in private investment that would not only offset, but exceed, the former. As a result, fiscal tightening would have expansionary effects also in the short term. Our task here is to expose this myth.

Let us begin by restating the fact that the budget deficit is largely an endogenous phenomenon in the sense that, on the revenue side, it relies on taxes, which are an increasing function of GDP. Thus, an increase in expansionary government spending is partially self-financed by a decline in the budget deficit thanks to higher tax revenues accompanying a GDP increase (see section 4.3 above). A similar, but inverse, relationship occurs in the case of declining government spending, which leads to both lower GDP and tax revenues. The objective of fiscal tightening is to reduce the budget deficit, but the decrease in GDP caused by lower government spending leads to a concomitant decline in tax revenues. As a result, the intended decrease of the budget deficit will be much smaller than the spending cuts.

Let us revisit the equation:

$$\Delta D = \Delta G \frac{(1 - tn)sp}{(1 - tn)sp + tn} \tag{5.15}$$

which represents changes in the budget deficit as a function of government spending. This formula accounts for the multiplier of government spending in the form $\Delta Y = \Delta G / [(1 - tn)sp + tn]$, where the average saving propensity, $sp = [(1 - \alpha) + sw\alpha]$. Using the parameters from the previous example, $\alpha = 0.8$, $sw = 0.1666$, and $tn = 0.25$, $sp = 0.2 + 0.166(0.8) = 0.333$, and so $[(1 - tn) sp + tn] = 0.75(0.333) + 0.25 = 0.5$. The resulting multipliers are $(\Delta Y / \Delta G) = (1/0.5) = 2$ and $(\Delta D / \Delta G) = 0.5$. If in the process of fiscal tightening government spending is reduced by 1 billion euros, then, Y will contract by $2(1) = 2$ billion euros and tax revenues by $0.25(2) = 0.5$ billion euros. Consequently, the budget deficit will decline by 0.5 rather than 1 billion euros. This example can be generalized; for instance in order to reduce the budget deficit, D, from 4 percent GDP to 3 percent GDP, (by 1 percentage point) government spending, G, would have to contract by 2 percentage points. As a result, GDP would shrink by 4 percentage points and net tax revenues TN by 1 percentage point. The objective of bringing the budget deficit down by 1 percentage point would be accomplished (spending and revenues would decline by 2 percentage points and 1 percentage point, respectively), but at the expense of a 4-percentage-point GDP contraction. This is only a numerical example, but it indicates that a decline in government revenues detracts from the effectiveness of a reduction in government spending as a method of lowering the budget deficit. Second, it also becomes evident that the resulting GDP contraction is very severe. If such a policy is implemented under conditions of an economic downturn and high unemployment, it is impossible for it not to aggravate the crisis and incur high social costs.

The question arises as to the origin of the "expansionary fiscal tightening" myth. According to equation (5.9, see p. 62), in the macroeconomic model without international trade, at given *tn* and *sp*, demand is determined by two factors: private investment, *IP*, and government spending on goods and services, *G*. Thus, in the abstract it would still be possible to obtain an increase in *Y* even if *G* decreased, if that decrease were offset and exceeded by an increase in *IP*. But the proponents of the "expansionary contraction" theory claim that *IP* would grow following a decline in *G* as a result of boosting the confidence of companies! This notion is no more convincing than the proposition that consumers will increase their savings with increasing public debt as they predict this will cause higher taxation in the future to pay off that debt. Even though the author of this book is a professional economist, he has never behaved in this way and does not know anyone else who has. And does the reader have a different experience? Indeed, it would seem that "expansionary contraction" is simply a fabrication created by market fundamentalists.

5.8.5 *A Funded Pension System as a Panacea for the Consequences of Population Aging*

In a natural economy, the elderly can survive only if their children provide them with a part of their current production. This principle is valid under any economic system, including the money economy, as individual accumulation of stocks for old age is either entirely impossible (e.g., in the case of perishable goods such as foodstuffs), or very costly and inefficient (e.g., in the case of clothes). Finally, services, which are of particular importance to senior citizens (such as health care) cannot be stored at all. Therefore, workers must have the right to take advantage of future production once they retire. There are two basic retirement systems ensuring that right. One of them, known as the pay-as-you-go system, is part of the public finance sector. Under this system, pensioners receive incomes financed out of contributions from current workers in exchange for the assurance that when these workers retire, they will receive an income from the next working generation. In contrast, the funded system is intermediated through the financial sector. Here, workers save part of their current wages, so when they retire they will have accumulated sufficient capital to purchase goods and services. Thus, both systems are based on the monetary claims of pensioners on future GDP and their claims can be met only to the degree allowed by the GDP volume, as retirees need food, clothing, heating, health care services, etc., rather than money itself. The important conclusion is that irrespective of the pension system, its effectiveness depends on future GDP. Let us then examine the question as to whether the type of pension system influences future GDP, and especially whether it is true that the funded system promotes household saving.

According to effective demand theory, saving primarily relies on investment, so to increase the former one should first expand the latter. There is no reason to believe that investment grows faster in the funded system than in the pay-as-you-go system. Does this mean that economic agents, including households, cannot make decisions about their saving? This is not the case. Each individual household can increase its saving if another household decides to decrease its savings. However, if everyone, or at least the majority, decides to increase their saving at a given level of private investment, this will not result in higher aggregate savings at given GDP, but in lower GDP at given aggregate savings. We already discussed this problem in relation to the paradox of saving (see pp. 41–44). The only thing that society as a whole can do today to better provide for future pensioners is to increase GDP, which will automatically lead to higher corporate and household savings. On the other hand, any attempt to secure future pensions through expanding current savings is not only ineffective, but counterproductive.

The theoretical confusion in this area can be illustrated by the following observation. Calls for a transition to a funded system, motivated by the need to increase savings for securing future pensions, are accompanied by complaints about consumer pessimism, which is, amongst others, generated and fueled by incessant discussions concerning the crisis of the pay-as-you-go system. And in fact consumer pessimism connotes nothing else but increased household savings. The question thus arises: What is really postulated by those who call for higher worker saving today to secure the future and at the same time lower saving today to support their livelihood today? Perhaps individual intuition should not be fully trusted when studying macroeconomic principles, since one needs to take into account effects that are not always considered in individual decisions.

The crisis of the pension system is caused by the fact that the ratio of retirees to workers has been constantly on the rise for the past several years, mostly due to demographic factors, such as longer life expectancy and a lower fertility rate (implying a lower number of workers).[23] Population aging is frequently used as an argument for a transition from a pay-as-you-go system to a funded

---

[23] It should be stressed that the increased ratio of pensioners to workers is also caused by high unemployment levels, due to which part of the workforce remains idle. However, this is beyond the scope of our present discussion and here we assume that the unemployment rate is constant. One should also consider the ratio of non-active persons to workers. The former include not only pensioners, but also children. In a situation of low fertility, the ratio of children to workers declines, and as a result the ratio of non-active persons to workers grows much more slowly than it is suggested by the alarming calculations based solely on the ratio of pensioners to workers. This issue is practically missing from public debate.

system. However, it can be shown that this is yet another fiscal myth. If the funded system could possibly shorten life expectancy (however absurd it may sound) or increase the fertility rate, then it would be economically reasonable to abandon the pay-as-you-go system. However, that is something which has not been claimed even by the staunchest "reformers" of the pension system. Thus, if demographic processes cannot be rectified by altering the pension system, then the discussion concerning the replacement of the pay-as-you-go system with a funded system does not make any sense, as will be shown below. Obviously, the two systems differ in many respects,[24] but we will not go into detail here; our discussion is strictly limited to demonstrating that the manner of financing the pension system has nothing to do either with creating or solving population-aging-related problems. We also show the effects that a reform of the pension system would have on the public sector.

Every system providing for people no longer able to work (pensioners) must meet the very general condition:

$$NEem = PRyb, \qquad (5.18)$$

where NE and em stand for the number of pensioners and the average annual pension, respectively (it is assumed that pensioners do not save). Therefore, the right side of equation (5.18) represents the annual demand of pensioners for consumer goods.[25] PR stands for the number of workers, y is GDP per worker times the share of wages in GDP (y is therefore the average annual worker income; no part of this income is saved), so the product PRy denotes aggregate annual worker compensation. Finally, b represents the sacrifice of current consumption on account of the entitlement rights that workers acquire upon retirement (hereinafter it will be referred to as the sacrifice ratio). Thus, the right side of equation (5.18) gives the annual supply of consumer goods for pensioners that arises thanks to the sacrifice of workers in a given year.

Let us assume that growth is constant in the sense that the productivity increase rate and the distribution of GDP between wages and profits are also constant. Other invariable parameters include the utilization of production capacity and workforce. It should be noted that at a given growth rate and prices, the condition (5.18) must be met. Indeed, if the left side of equation (5.18) were larger than the right side, then pensioners' demand could not be satisfied at constant prices. In turn, if the right side were larger than the left, then some of the consumption given up by workers for the benefit of pensioners would not be marketable. Thus, the consumer goods market is

---

[24] The funded system does not include elements of social solidarity, makes future pensions largely vulnerable to the unpredictable results of stock exchange speculations, and does not protect them from future inflation. Furthermore, this system is very costly (as shown later on).

[25] See Eatwell (2003).

balanced in the sense of equality between demand for and supply of consumer goods only if the condition expressed by (5.18) is met.

Let us then restate (5.18) in the following form:

$$\frac{PR}{NE} = \frac{em}{yb} \tag{5.19}$$

where the quotient PR/NE is the ratio of workers to pensioners (the number of workers per pensioner), and em/yb is the ratio of the average annual pension, em, to the unconsumed part of the average annual worker income, yb. Let us assume that for a given year the variables PR, NE, and y are given, leaving the two remaining variables b and em, undetermined. In this situation we can choose to determine b, thus obtaining em, or vice versa.

Let us illustrate this with a numerical example. If the ratio of workers to pensioners is 4 to 1, then the left side of (5.19) will amount to 4. If the average pension is to be 0.4 (40 percent) of the average wage, then b will equal 0.1 (10 percent), and indeed $0.4/0.1 = 4$. If the average monthly wage is 1,000 euros, then at a sacrifice ratio of $b = 0.1$, or 10 percent, every worker will need to forfeit 100 euros worth of consumption. Thus, four workers will collectively sacrifice 400 euros worth of consumption, which amounts exactly to the value of consumer goods needed to satisfy the average monthly needs of one pensioner. Similarly, it can be shown that at a sacrifice ratio of $b = 0.15$, or 15 percent, every worker will give up 150 euros worth of consumption ($0.15 \times 1,000$), which means that four workers will forfeit 600 euros. At this sacrifice ratio, the average pension will amount to 600 euros, accounting for 0.6, or 60 percent, of the average wage.

There is a simple method of calculating the relationship between b and the ratio of the average pension to the average wage when we know the number of workers per pensioner. If there are four workers per pensioner at a sacrifice ratio of 10 percent, then the combined sacrifice of those four workers corresponds to the average pension (4 times 10 percent, or 40 percent, of the average wage). If the average pension is to equal 50 percent of the average wage, then 50 percent/4 = 12.5 percent, which is the desired sacrifice ratio, b.

The crux of the problem with financing pension systems is that in recent years the number of retirees has been growing faster than that of workers, mostly for demographic reasons. Suppose that the number of workers per pensioner is going to shrink from four to three over the next thirty years. If the initial sacrifice ratio, b, is 12.5 percent, the ratio of the average pension to the average wage is 4×12.5 percent = 50 percent. In thirty years' time, we will face two extreme solutions (along with an infinite number of intermediate ones): We can either maintain the initial sacrifice ratio at 12.5 percent, or maintain the initial ratio of the average pension to the average wage at 50 percent. At $b = 12.5$ percent, the average pension will amount to 3×12.5 percent = 37.5 percent of the average wage. In turn, if we maintain the average pension at 50 percent of the average wage, then the sacrifice ratio, b, can be found by dividing 50 percent by 3, which is 16.6 percent.

Another critical factor that must be taken into consideration is the increase in productivity over the period in question (thirty years). If productivity grows by approximately 2 percent annually, then over thirty years wages will increase by about 80 percent. Thus, if the average monthly wage is now 1,000 euro, then at $b = 12.5$ percent the average pension equals to 500 euros, or 50 percent of the wage (4×12.5 percent). In thirty years' time, the average monthly wage will rise to 1,800 euro. If the sacrifice ratio, b, remains unchanged, then the average pension will amount to 3×12.5 percent, or 37.5 percent of the average wage, or 675 euros. As can be seen, despite a precipitous decline in the ratio of the average pension to the average wage from 50 percent to 37.5 percent (by 12.5 percentage points, or 25 percent), the absolute value of the pension will increase by 175 euros, or by 35 percent. In turn, if the average pension is still to equal 50 percent of the average wage, then the sacrifice ratio, b, must increase from 12.5 percent to 16.6 percent (50 percent divided by 3). In this case, the average pension will amount to 900 euros, in step with wages (a rise of 80 percent). However, the average worker will now give up 300 euros worth of consumption (16.6 percent of the average wage), while at the old b ratio he would have to forfeit only 225 euros worth of consumption (12.5 percent of the average wage); consequently, his sacrifice increases by 75 euros, or 30 percent (75 relative to 225).

So far in our discussion of pension systems we have been using the rather awkward term "sacrifice ratio" for b. This is intentional as we want to show that the choice between a pay-as-you-go or funded system has in fact nothing to do with difficulties in financing pensions. In the pay-as-you-go system, the average pension contribution is denoted by t_E. If in all the previous formulas b is substituted with t_E, then our line of reasoning and conclusions will remain essentially valid. Similarly, if in all the previous formulas b is substituted with s_E, the saving rate under the funded system, then our results will also remain essentially valid. This proves that the difficulties linked to the increase of the (PR/NP) ratio caused by population aging, longer life expectancy, and a lower fertility rate, are completely unrelated to the type of pension financing (whether by tax-like contributions, t_E, or by compulsory individual retirement savings, s_E). In both cases, the right side of equation (5.19) must be adjusted to the left side by changing t_E or s_E, or by changing (em/y). The only major difference is that under the pay-as-you-go system the government must either increase the t_E rate while maintaining the initial (em/y) ratio, or lower em relative to y maintaining the initial t_E rate, or use an intermediate solution. This entails difficult and unpopular political decisions. On the other hand, under the funded system, changes in s_E or (em/y) occur spontaneously, through the market mechanism. To illustrate this, we must now reject our previous assumption about constant prices, as the movement of prices is the main element of this mechanism.

There are many ways in which the market mechanism may meet the condition expressed in (5.19). Let us consider only one of them, assuming that at a given s_E after thirty years pensions to be paid out of the funded system, EM, will be higher than that part of the current production of consumer goods which workers will be ready to give up through retirement contributions. At a given supply of consumer goods, this will give rise to a surplus of demand over supply and prices will increase. Furthermore, at a constant distribution of GDP between wages and profits, nominal wages must also rise in line with the prices of consumer goods for workers to maintain their average real wages at the same level. However, this is not so with pensions. In the funded system, the average pension em is defined in nominal terms. When prices increase, its real value decreases until reaching the level specified in (5.19). This particular case is equivalent to the government's decision, under the pay-as-you-go system, to reduce the average pension relative to the average wage at a given t_E. Of course, one can imagine the extremely unlikely situation that under the circumstances workers decide to increase s_E to increase the supply of consumer goods for retirees at given prices. This would be equivalent to the government's decision to increase the parameter t_E to a level required by (5.19) at a given (em/y) ratio. The only significant difference is of political nature, as under the pay-as-you-go system the government may be forced to make unpopular decisions either worsening the relative position of pensioners or increasing the burden on workers. In the funded system, these decisions are attributable to the spontaneous operation of the market mechanism.[26]

Additionally, the process of transitioning from the pay-as-you-go system to a funded system is fraught with enormous difficulties. At one extreme, all workers could transition to the funded system at once and stop contributing to the existing pay-as-you-go system. But then the government would have to take over all outstanding liabilities of the pay-as-you-go system until they finally expire, which in practice implies a serious strain on the budget. At the other extreme, all workers could transition to the funded system while still

---

[26] Under the pay-as-you-go system pressures to lower retirement age and grant special privileges to certain social groups or professions have political ramifications and are often used as an argument for the superiority of the funded system. Those pressures indeed constitute one of the causes of the relatively low economic activity rate, leading to a higher pension burden on workers. Since under the funded system one's pension depends on the period of saving, no such pressures arise. However, it should be noted that any system of social welfare benefits, including unemployment benefits and free health services, may be abused, and irregularities may occur in the case of all public goods. This should not be taken as an argument for doing away with those goods, but rather for implementing adequate administrative measures to eliminate, or at least considerably reduce, any abuse of the system.

making contributions to the pay-as-you-go system. However, in this case, throughout the lifetime of the members of the old system, workers would have to be doubly burdened, both with the contribution t_E and the saving rate s_E. Many countries that replace the pay-as-you-go system with the funded system choose intermediate solutions, but the dilemma presented above essentially persists. In such situations, governments often introduce incentives for additional pension saving schemes by granting tax breaks, which are mostly taken advantage of by wealthy households, while tax revenues contract.

Actually, it is hard to say why instead of correcting the pay-as-you-go system in line with demographic needs, governments embrace funded systems, whose advantages are a myth. However, as they say, money makes the world go round. The introduction of a funded system gives rise to additional costs (marketing, administration, etc.) without reducing the costs of the pay-as-you-go system throughout the transitional period. This implies high profits of the operators of the funded system at the expense of the accumulated savings. This is also one of the factors which, along with dogmatic reasons, play a major role in adopting funded systems. Yet another equally important issue is channeling new funds to the stock exchange. In the process of transitioning from the pay-as-you-go system to the funded system, the inflow of new capital into the stock market dramatically exceeds outflows, pushing up share prices and giving rise to a speculative bubble, which is bound to burst at some point in the future. The winners are all kinds of speculators, and the losers are pensioners, and especially those who retire during a bear market.

Appendix 3. Stimulating the Economy by Tax Reductions in the Model Distinguishing between Taxes on Wages and Profits

For a closed economy, we have by definition:

$$W + TW + R + TR = CP + IP + G \tag{A3.1}$$

where TW stands for a lump sum tax on wages and TR for a lump sum tax on profits. If we denote profits before tax as:

$$R' = R + TR \tag{A3.2}$$

and assume that profits after tax are fully saved while wages after tax are fully spent on consumer goods, from (A3.1), we obtain:

$$R' = IP + G - TW \tag{A3.3}$$

which means that at given IP profits before tax depend only on G and TW.

If r' is the ratio of R' to Y, then from (A3.3) we obtain:

$$Y = \frac{R'}{r'} = \frac{IP + G - TW}{r'} \tag{A3.4}$$

Furthermore, it should be remembered that:

$$D = G - TW - TR \qquad (A3.5)$$

A.3.1 Tax Reduction at $\Delta G = 0$

At $\Delta TW < 0$ and $\Delta TR = 0$, equations (A3.3), (A3.4), and (A3.5) can be combined to give:

$$\Delta R' = -\Delta TW > 0$$

$$\Delta Y = \frac{-\Delta TW}{r'} > -\Delta TW, \ as \ 0 < r' < 1$$

$$\Delta D = -\Delta TW > 0.$$

At $\Delta TR < 0$ and $\Delta TW = 0$, we additionally take into account (A3.2) and obtain:

$$\Delta R' = \Delta R + \Delta TR = 0,$$

which means that:

$$\Delta R = -\Delta TR$$

$$\Delta Y = 0$$

$$\Delta D = -\Delta TR$$

A.3.2 A Simultaneous Rise in Taxes and Government Spending

At $\Delta G > 0$ and $\Delta TW > 0$, $\Delta G = \Delta TW$, we obtain from (A3.2) to (A3.5):

$$\Delta R' = \Delta G - \Delta TW = 0$$

$$\Delta R' = \Delta R = \Delta Y = \Delta D = 0$$

At $\Delta G > 0$ and $\Delta TR > 0$, $\Delta G = \Delta TR$, if we proceed in a similar way, we arrive at:

$$\Delta R' = \Delta G = \Delta TR$$

$$\Delta Y = \frac{-\Delta G}{r'} > -\Delta G, \ as \ 0 < r' < 1$$

$$\Delta R = \Delta D = 0$$

By combining both cases ($\Delta G = \Delta TW + \Delta TR$) and denoting the ratio $\Delta TW / \Delta TR$ as e, (A3.5) can be transformed to:

$$\Delta D = \Delta G - \Delta TW - \Delta TR = \Delta G - bTR - \Delta TR$$

and:

$$\Delta D = \Delta G - (1 + e)\Delta TR = 0$$

Therefore, $\Delta G = (1 + e)\Delta TR$ and $\Delta TR = \Delta G / (1 + e)$.

Now, from (A3.3) we obtain:

$$\Delta R' = \Delta G - \Delta TW = \Delta TR + \Delta TW - \Delta TW = \Delta TR = \Delta G/(1+e)$$

which, taking into consideration (A3.4), gives:

$$\Delta Y = (\Delta R'/r') = \Delta G/[(1+e)r']. \tag{A3.6}$$

When, in line with the Haavelmo theorem, we assume $\Delta Y = \Delta G = \Delta TW + TR$, then we arrive at:

$$(1+e)r' = 1 \ and \ e = (1-r')/r' \tag{A3.7}$$

Therefore, when the condition (A3.7) is satisfied, the multiplier of a balanced budget is 1, which requires for the ratio of the increase in the tax on wages to the increase in the tax on profits to correspond to the ratio of the share of wages before tax in GDP $(1 - r')$ to the share of profits before tax in GDP (r'). This condition is always met if wages and profits are taxed uniformly, which also satisfies the Haavelmo theorem.

Appendix 4. The Relationship between Public Debt, the Primary Budget Deficit, and GDP

Let us denote the budget deficit (which corresponds to a change in public debt) in year t as $D_t = aY_t$, where a $(0 < a < 1)$ is constant. F_t is outstanding public debt at the beginning of year t. Assuming that there is no initial debt, the volume of F_t may be determined by the following equation:

$$F_t = aY_0 + aY_0(1+g) + aY_0(1+g)^2 + \ldots + aY_0(1+g)^{t-1}$$

where g stands for a constant annual GDP growth rate. Using a formula for the sum of the first t elements in an increasing geometric series, we obtain:

$$F_t = aY_0[1 + (1+g) + (1+g)^2 + \ldots + (1+g)^{t-1}]$$

$$F_t = aY_0 \frac{(1+g)^{t-1} - 1}{g} \tag{A4.1}$$

In the year t, GDP amounts to $Y_t = Y_0(1+g)^{t-1}$. Therefore, the ratio of public debt to GDP in that year can be calculated as follows:

$$F_t/Y_t = aY_0 \frac{[(1+g)^{t-1}]/g}{Y_0(1+g)^{t-1}}$$

$$F_t/Y_t = a\left[1 - \frac{1}{(1+g)^{t-1}}\right]/g \tag{A4.2}$$

The limit of equation (A4.2) for t approaching infinity is:

$$\lim_{t \Rightarrow \infty} (F_t/Y_t) = a/g \tag{A4.3}$$

because with increasing t the term $[1/(1+g)^{t-1}]$ tends to zero.

Primary deficit for year t is expressed as $DP_t = aY_t - zF_t$, where z is the constant interest rate on public debt. Dividing DP_t by $Y_t = Y_0(1+g)^{t-1}$ and using formula (A4.2), we obtain the ratio of primary deficit to GDP for year t:

$$\frac{Dp_t}{Y_t} = \frac{aY_t - zF_t}{Y_t} = a - \frac{zF_t}{Y_t}$$
$$\frac{DP_t}{Y_t} = a - za\left[1 - \frac{1}{(1+g)^{t-1}}\right]/g \tag{A4.4}$$

The limit of equation (A4.4) for t approaching infinity is:

$$\lim_{t \Rightarrow \infty} (DP_t/Y_t) = a[1 - (z/g)] \tag{A4.5}$$

Equation (A4.5) equals 0 for $z=g$, is positive but smaller than a for $z < g$, and is negative for $z > g$.

6

GDP in an open economy model

6.1 International Aspects of Effective Demand

This chapter deals with international trade in so far as it affects the course of macroeconomic processes. In a closed economy without the government sector, the production is determined by private investment and the multiplier mechanism. The government's activity may expand or contract the market. In particular, if the government's acquisitions of goods and services from the private sector exceed the demand-depressing effects of taxation, the resulting budget deficit increases the market. If we incorporate the rest of the world (ROW) in this model, then we need to account for ROW's expenditures, resulting in exports, which add to the domestic market, and ROW's revenues, resulting in imports, which reduce this market. Thus, if ROW's expenditures and revenues are equal, then the domestic market volume remains unchanged. However, if ROW's expenditures are higher than its revenues, then ROW's deficit leads to an expansion of the domestic market. As can be seen, there is a significant similarity between ROW's deficit (the trade surplus of an individual country) and a budget deficit run by the government, but the macroeconomic roles of the government and ROW differ in some important aspects.

Let us begin by recalling that capitalist economies, generally afflicted by insufficient effective demand, are interested in generating export surpluses. Under conditions of unrestrained international competition, the developed countries can achieve such a surplus relatively easily due to their economic strengths. On the other hand, in the same environment, the less developed nations with weaker economies struggle to bring their balance of trade into equilibrium. It is not accidental that the highly developed countries tend to promote free international trade, while the less developed ones often attempt to protect their domestic markets through tariffs, export subsidies, import restrictions, favorable exchange rates, and other protectionist measures. It should be noted that countries such as the United States, which today most ardently advocate free international trade, in the past pursued protectionist policies themselves. The advice offered by those countries to the less developed nations can be then summarized by the slogan "do what we say, do not do what we did."

6.2 Profits and GDP in an Open Economy: The Investment Multiplier and the Export Multiplier

As it has been shown, in a capitalist economy comprising all three sectors, profits and GDP are given by the following equations:

$$R = IP + X + G - Y[m + tn + sw\alpha(1 - tn)] \tag{5.7}$$

$$Y = \frac{IP + X + G}{(1 - tn)[(1 - \alpha) + sw\alpha] + m + tn} \tag{5.8}^1$$

The latter can be further simplified by substituting the previously introduced formula for the average private propensity to save out of disposable income, $sp = (1 - \alpha) + sw\alpha$,

$$Y = \frac{IP + X + G}{(1 - tn)sp + m + tn} \tag{6.1}$$

As can be seen from (5.7) and (6.1), both profits and GDP grow when, all other things being equal, there is an increase in exports, X, leading to an export surplus, $E = X - M$, and they decline when import intensity, m, rises. Let us now take a closer look at this mechanism.

6.2.1 The Investment Multiplier in Closed and Open Economies

Taking (6.1) as a point of departure, let us first examine the investment multiplier, which reflects the response of GDP to changes in investment, ΔIP:

$$\Delta Y = \frac{\Delta IP}{(1 - tn)sp + m + tn} \tag{6.2}$$

The multiplier (6.2) is lower than that for the closed model,

$$\Delta Y = \frac{\Delta IP}{(1 - tn)sp + tn}, \tag{5.10}$$

since in an open economy $m > 0$, with some of the investment-triggered demand impulse "leaking out" in every round of the multiplier process not

---

1 $$Y = \frac{R}{(1 - tn)(1 - \alpha)} = \frac{IP + X + G - Y[m + tn + sw\,\alpha(1 - tn)]}{(1 - tn)(1 - \alpha)}$$
$$\frac{Y[(1 - tn)(1 - \alpha) + m + tn + sw\alpha(1 - tn)]}{(1 - tn)(1 - \alpha)} = \frac{IP + X + G}{(1 - tn)(1 - \alpha)}$$

only in the form of domestic taxes, but also in the form of imports. Indeed, while in a closed model additional demand must be met by an increase in domestic output alone, in an open model some of this additional demand stimulates foreign production at the expense of domestic output.

Let us estimate the increase in GDP for $\Delta IP = 100$ euros, assuming that $\alpha = 0.8$, $r = (1 - \alpha) = 0.2$, and $sw = 0.1$, which gives $sw\alpha = 0.1(0.8) = 0.08$. As a result, $sp = (1 - \alpha) + sw\alpha = 0.28$. If tn is 0.2 and $m = 0.3$, then $(1 - tn)sp + m + tn = 0.8(0.28) + 0.3 + 0.2 = 0.224 + 0.5 = 0.724$. This means that in an open economy the investment multiplier will amount to approximately 1.38, and so GDP growth, $\Delta Y = 100/(0.724)$ will equal approximately 138 euros. It is noteworthy that the rise in disposable income, $\Delta YD = (1 - tn)\Delta Y$, will be approximately $(0.8)138 = 110$ euros, with a wage increase, $\Delta W = \alpha\Delta YD = 0.8(110.40)$, of approximately 88 euros and a profit increase, $\Delta R = r\Delta YD = 0.2(110.40)$, of approximately 22 euros. Consequently, import growth will amount to $\Delta M = mY = 0.3(138) = 41$ euros, leading to a balance of trade change by $\Delta E = -\Delta M = -41$ euros. Also the budget will change due to tax revenues higher by $\Delta TN = tn\Delta Y = 0.2(138) = 27$ euros, which means that $\Delta D = -\Delta TN = -27$ euros. In total, changes in E and D will amount to approximately $-41 - 27 = -68$ euros. Moreover, savings out of wages will increase by $\Delta SW = sw\Delta W = (0.1)88.32 = 8.83$ euros. Thus, consumption will change according to the formula $\Delta C = \Delta W - \Delta SW = 88 - 9 = 79$ euros. Aggregate output growth will be $\Delta IP + \Delta CP = 100 + 79 = 179$ euros, with the national income rising by $\Delta Y = 179 - 41 = 138$ euros, which exactly corresponds to the multiplier specified above.

In turn, in a closed economy under the same set of conditions, $(1 - tn)sp + tn = 0.8(0.28) + 0.2 = 0.22 + 0.2 = 0.42$; the investment multiplier would amount to approximately 2.3 and so at the same investment impulse GDP growth would equal $\Delta Y = (100/0.42) = 236$ euros. As a result, the increase in domestic output of consumer goods ΔCP, would be approximately 136 euros rather than the approximately 79 euros in the open model. This shows that the rest of the world takes advantage of the increase in domestic investment as the country's current account balance deteriorates due to higher imports.

As a result of "import leaks," the multipliers linked to government spending are also lower in an open economy relative to a closed economy. In an open model, an active fiscal policy encounters the same problems as the policy promoting private investment. Therefore, the conclusions concerning the investment multiplier are also applicable to the multipliers associated with government spending in an open economy. Most small and medium-sized countries rely heavily on imports, especially under conditions of globalization, and so their coefficient m tends to be rather high. Thus, in such countries investment growth or an active fiscal policy will lead to a modest improvement of the domestic economy and add to the trade deficit.

The greater the import intensity of the economy, the more severe the problem becomes. It is therefore critical to use the right measures of import intensity in predicting the results of an active fiscal policy and estimating the multipliers linked to government spending. The import intensity coefficient used previously in this book, traditionally defined as $m = (M/Y)$, does not seem to be suitable. In particular, it systematically overestimates the real import intensity, while underestimating the investment and fiscal multipliers in an open economy. This problem is discussed in Appendix 7, which proposes import intensity of final production as a more accurate measure than m.[2]

These international trade difficulties disappear or are greatly diminished if investment grows simultaneously in countries conducting trade exchange or if all of them pursue active fiscal policies. This is true of the EU member states, which taken together may be considered a closed economy (the imports and exports of the European Union as a whole are largely balanced). Thus, in the European Union measures stimulating private investment, along with expansionary government spending, could serve as drivers of economic growth. However, this does not happen because EU policy is focused on containing inflation rather than maintaining high employment.

On the other hand, concerted EU measures can also have some adverse consequences. It has already been mentioned that fiscal tightening is ineffective as a method of mending the public finance of an individual country because it damages its production and employment levels without improving its budget balance. Nevertheless, fiscal tightening usually does cause a temporary improvement in the country's balance of payments, since a decrease in output reduces imports without detriment to exports, as long as foreign demand does not falter. If, however, several EU member states attempt to balance their budgets by fiscal tightening, the declining imports will not bring about even a temporary improvement in the balance of trade and the current account, since exports will decrease accordingly. Since 2008, the European Union's policy has been ignoring these dangerous implications, demanding that member states end persistent budget deficits and balance their budgets, to decrease the public debt-to-GDP ratio. It has now become apparent beyond any doubt that such a policy has a depressing effect on the European Union's economy.

6.2.2 The Relationship between the Export Multiplier and the Investment Multiplier

Equation (4.1) can be used to calculate the export multiplier:

[2] The importance of using adequate measures of import intensity in estimating investment and fiscal multipliers has been highlighted in my many previous publications, see Łaski (2009), Łaski et al. (2010 and 2012).

$$\Delta Y = \frac{\Delta X}{(1 - tn)sp + m + tn} \tag{6.3}$$

It has the same influence on GDP as the investment multiplier (4.2), but its effect on net exports, $E = X - M$, is very different. While it has been demonstrated that an increase in investment, $\Delta IP > 0$ (at $\Delta X = 0$) simply leads to $\Delta E = -\Delta M < 0$, using (4.3) it can be shown that an increase in exports, $\Delta X > 0$ (at $\Delta IP = 0$) gives:

$$\Delta E = \Delta X - m\Delta Y = \Delta X - m\frac{\Delta X}{(1 - tn)sp + m + tn}$$

$$\Delta E = \Delta X \left[1 - \frac{m}{(1 - tn)sp + m + tn} \right]$$

$$\Delta E = \Delta X \frac{(1 - tn)sp + tn}{(1 - tn)sp + m + tn} \tag{6.4}$$

where $0 < \dfrac{(1 - tn)sp + tn}{(1 - tn)sp + m + tn} < 1$.

This means that at $\Delta X > 0$ the balance of trade improves. At the same time, the increase of net exports is lower than that of gross exports because some export revenue is spent on financing additional imports. As it has already been mentioned, GDP growth driven by domestic demand causes the balance of trade to deteriorate. Consequently, individual countries often perceive the promotion of exports as a more attractive method of economic development than the expansion of domestic demand.[3] Unfortunately, such a policy has two fundamental flaws. First, an increase in the net exports of one country automatically implies a decrease in the net exports of its trade partners; hence, economic recovery by export expansion is not a viable option for all countries taken together. Moreover, the growth of output and employment in a country improving its international trade position entails a decline of the output and employment in the countries whose trade position is deteriorating. Therefore, such a policy has been aptly nicknamed "beggar thy neighbor." Second, the measures presented above will not necessarily bring about economic development even in the countries that embrace them because in order to obtain an export surplus they often enhance their competitiveness by slowing down wage increases relative to domestic productivity growth, thus reducing unit labor costs and prices. As a result, domestic demand, which is mostly driven by workers' demand for consumer goods, falters (see pp. 70–71). Given (4.3), this means a higher propensity to save, $sp = (1 - \alpha) + sw\alpha$, because sp increases with

---

[3] This is mostly attained by the depreciation of the domestic currency. The resulting problems will be analyzed further on in this chapter.

a decreasing share of wages in GDP, α. Thus, while the export multiplier does decline, GDP growth slows down or disappears entirely.

6.3 Private Investment in an Open Economy

The profit equation (3.4)

$$R = IP + D + E - SW$$

can be transformed to $\qquad R + SW = IP + D + E$

$$SP = IP + D + E, \tag{6.5}$$

where private savings are represented by $SP = R + SW$ and $SP = sp(1 - tn)Y$. Thus, private savings equal the sum of private investment, budget deficit, and ROW deficit (the country's export surplus), with the components IP, D, and ROW being active factors, and SP being the passive factor. Indeed, in a *closed model*, saving simply means that part of the income generated by households in a given year is not spent within that period of time, but rather turned into potential asset. On the macroeconomic scale, this potential asset may be materialized only if private companies and/or the government incur debt to finance their investments (the former) or expenditures (the latter). In other words, the aggregate financial assets of households arise in line with the liabilities of private companies and the government. In an *open model*, an individual country has yet another potential source of savings in the form of the current account deficit of ROW. As can be seen, savings and deficits are two sides of the same coin. However, contrary to Say's law, they only represent a possibility which can be turned into reality only if a decision to save (not to spend current income) is accompanied by a deficit decision (to spend without a previous income) elsewhere.

The relationship between savings and investment lies at the core of the theory of effective demand, which posits that savings and investment are balanced not through interest rates, as it is claimed by the classical economic theory, but as a result of changes in national income driven by the investment multiplier. In other words, it is not the interest rate, but the volume of national income, that plays a decisive role in adjusting the volume of savings to the volume of investment. However, the mainstream economic theory cherishes a deep-seated belief that domestic savings should be simply added to the world's stock of capital. In this sense, savings can, as it were, "travel" around the world in search of the most profitable use, and it is they that determine the volume of investment, and not vice versa. In particular, if in a given country savings are smaller than investment as a result of a current accounts deficit, $(E - M) < 0$, then that deficit can be conceived of as import of foreign savings. As it will be shown below, it is a misconception that can spawn harmful economic policy recommendations.

The nature of these so-called foreign savings can be best explained using a numerical example. A formal analysis underpinning this example is given in Appendix 5 on "Domestic and Foreign Savings" at the end of this chapter. Let us consider country 1 and country 2, the latter representing the rest of the world. The imports of country 1 and country 2 are defined by the following functions: $M_1 = Ma_1 + m_1 Y_1$ and $M_2 = Ma_2 + m_2 Y_2$, where Ma_1 and Ma_2 are autonomous import volumes, and m_1 and m_2 are marginal import intensity coefficients for countries 1 and 2 respectively. As the two countries taken together represent the world economy as a whole, the term M_1 also denotes the exports of country 2, and M_2 – the exports of country 1. To simplify our analysis, without detriment to the validity of results, we assume that $m_2 = 0$.[4] To make the example even more readily comprehensible, the government sector is ignored.

If country 1 increases private investment by 100 euros, then in a closed model at a saving rate of 0.25 and an investment multiplier of 4, GDP growth will be equal to $\Delta Y_1 = 400$ euros, and the increase in savings will amount to $\Delta S_1 = 0.25 \times 400 = 100$ euros. In an open model, at $m_1 = 0.15$, the multiplier in country 1 will be $1/(0.25 + 0.15) = (1/0.4) = 2.5$. As a result, the GDP of country 1 will grow by $\Delta Y_1 = 250$ euros, and savings will increase by $\Delta S_1 = 0.25 \times 250 = 62.5$ euros. The imports of country 1 will amount to $\Delta M_1 = 0.15 \times 250 = 37.5$ euros. This means that the exports of country 2 (equal to the imports of country 1) will grow by $\Delta X_2 = \Delta M_1 = 37.5$ euros. Let us assume, without detriment to the validity of results, that in country 2 the saving rate is also 0.25, and so the export multiplier also amounts to $(1/0.25) = 4$. GDP growth will then equal $\Delta Y_2 = 4 \times 37.5 = 150$ euros with an increase in savings of $\Delta S_2 = 0.25 \times 150 = 37.5$ euros. It is apparent that the combined increase in the savings of both countries will still add up to 100 euros.

In the closed model, the entire savings increment caused by investment growth remains in country 1, but in the open model, it is split between savings increments in country 1, $\Delta S_1 = 62.5$ euros, and in country 2, $\Delta S_2 = 37.5$ euros, adding up to a total of $\Delta S_1 + \Delta S_2 = 100$ euros. The parameters are selected in such a way that GDP growth in both cases is the same (given an identical saving rate in both countries); at other parameters GDP growth in the open

---

[4] As we already know from previous discussion, investment growth in country 1 adversely affects its balance of trade and promotes an increase in foreign net exports. This situation occurs precisely if the secondary effects of this growth are left out, that is, if we ignore the influence of GDP growth in country 2 on imports from country 1. Given $m_2 > 0$, the increase of net exports in country 2 (driven by investment expansion in country 1) would be smaller and the deterioration of the balance-of-payments position of country 1 (caused by this same expansion) would be lesser, but nevertheless the direction of change would remain unaltered.

model would differ from that in the closed one. Also the allocation of savings between the countries depends on the adopted parameters. However, the basic conclusions hold irrespective of a particular set of variables. If country 1 invests 100 euros, then the increase in savings in the two countries will be $\Delta S = \Delta S_1 + \Delta S_2 = 100$. Importantly, the savings increment ΔS_2 (corresponding to the increase in the imports of country 1 and the exports of country 2), which is known as "import of savings," in fact does not involve importing anything that was created in country 2. Just on the contrary, this so-called "import" is generated by investment in country 1 and accompanied by an outflow of demand from country 1 to country 2. Thus, it makes no sense to call a surplus of domestic investment over domestic savings (which is equivalent to an import surplus) "foreign saving," since those savings actually arise as a result of transferring part of effective demand from the investing country abroad. It is this transfer that enables ROW to achieve an export surplus and a savings increment, and gives ROW a claim to some of the wealth generated in country 1.

Analyzing the mutual relationship between investment and savings, James Meade illustrated the difference between the orthodox theory and the effective demand theory using the metaphor of a dog's tail.[5] In our case, investment growth in country 1 (100 euros) represents a dog. This increase in investment and national income generates savings in country 1 (62.5 euros) as well as imports, inducing an export surplus in country 2 (37.5 euros), which also corresponds to the savings increment in country 2 (the foreign part of the tail). Investment growth in country 1 can be likened to a dog wagging its tail (savings in countries A and B). To say that the savings of country B (foreign savings), along with the savings of country 1, finance investment growth in country 1 would be tantamount to saying that it is the tail that wags the dog.

As was already mentioned, at stake is not so much terminology as the practical ramifications ensuing from this analysis. In the long term, an import surplus is intolerable, especially in small or medium-sized countries. The proponents of the theory that this surplus is attributable to insufficient domestic savings postulate that the latter be raised. Thus, at given investment and exports, they advocate a higher propensity to save. However, that would be detrimental both to countries 1 and 2, leading to lower GDP growth at a given investment impulse. As the imports of country 1 would decrease, the import surplus would decline and domestic savings would rise accordingly (but at the expense of GDP). In turn, country 2 would also suffer: due to the smaller "import leak" from country 1 its GDP growth would also slow down. On the other hand, the volume of savings would remain unchanged in both countries, being determined by the volume of investment. The only thing

---

[5] See Meade (1975: 82).

country 1 would achieve by increasing its saving rate would be a larger share in the global pool of savings, at the cost of country 2.

The real solution to the international trade difficulties of country 1 is to increase its exports rather than domestic savings. This would require not so much higher domestic investment as modification of their structure, with a focus on industries more capable of exporting their products or substituting imports. Such an offensive approach would improve the international competitiveness of domestic production.

6.4 International Competitiveness

The international competitiveness of a country in the strict sense may be evaluated by comparing representative baskets of goods as measures of the competitiveness of the economy as a whole. These baskets contain not only goods and services traded internationally, but also other goods because the prices of the former (e.g., machines) depend to some extent on the prices of the latter (e.g., domestic transportation). Under the circumstances, a broad basket represents the macroeconomic competitiveness of a given country better than one containing internationally traded goods alone. A country's international competitiveness can be measured using the coefficient Q (an abstract number):

$$Q = \frac{qP_F}{P_D} \qquad (6.6)$$

where q stands for the nominal exchange rate of the foreign currency against the currency of country 1 (e.g., in Poland $q = 4$ PLN/euros since 1 euro costs 4 PLN), P_F is the price of a foreign representative basket of goods in the foreign currency (e.g., in euros), and P_D is the price of a domestic representative basket of goods in the domestic currency (e.g., in PLN). For instance, if $P_F = 100$ euros, and $P_D = 250$ PLN, then $Q = 400/250 = 1.6$.

If we require $Q = 1$, then we need to adopt an exchange rate of $q^* = (P_D/P_F) = 250/100 = 2.5$ (PLN/euros). The exchange rate q^*, accompanying a coefficient Q close to one (with respect to the same basket of goods in both countries) represents so-called purchasing power parity (PPP). Indeed, at this exchange rate the residents of either country could purchase more or less the same basket of goods for the same amount in their country (in the domestic currency) and abroad (after converting that currency to euros).

A coefficient Q close to one, or actual exchange rates q close to q^*, are often seen in the highly developed countries, while in the less developed countries that coefficient is usually higher than one, which means that the exchange rate q exceeds purchasing power parity, q^*. For instance, in 2013 in Poland, the exchange rate remained a little above 4 (PLN/euros), so for the sake of simplicity let us assume that $q = 4$ (PLN/euros). It is estimated that the q^* rate corresponding to PPP was approximately 2.5 (PLN/euros).[6] This means that for holders of the złoty, foreign countries are more expensive on average by 60 percent (4/2.5), while for holders of the euro Poland is on average cheaper by approx. 30 percent (2.5/4).

A Q coefficient higher than unity suggests that the economy is competitive. To verify this, however, we must examine its international trade accounts. If its balance of trade, or better still, its current account balance, is zero, then the nominal exchange rate, q, is an equilibrium exchange rate for a given period of time. However, this is often not the case. If a country exhibits a persistent current account deficit and the exchange rate is maintained through a constant inflow of foreign capital or loans (implying continuous accrual of foreign debt), this situation cannot last indefinitely without eventually undermining confidence in the country's solvency.

Also in Poland, the nominal exchange rate q of a little over 4 (PLN/euros) does not automatically ensure a balanced current account, despite the fact that it is higher than q^*, because the current account is also largely affected by other factors determining international competitiveness, as discussed later in this chapter.

If the percentage growth rate of the variable j is denoted by the operator $g(j)$, $j = Q, q, P_F, P_D$, the growth rate of coefficient Q from equation (4.6) is:

$$g(Q) = g(q) + [g(P_F) - g(P_D)] \qquad (6.7)$$

The growth rate of Q depends on two factors: changes in the nominal exchange rate, q, and the difference between foreign inflation, $g(P_F)$, and domestic inflation, $g(P_D)$, which is represented by the term in square brackets. At a given q, competitiveness increases if domestic inflation is lower than foreign inflation. An increase in the nominal exchange rate, q, is called depreciation, while a decrease in this rate is termed appreciation of the foreign currency. Following depreciation, 1 euro might cost, e.g., 5 PLN rather than 4 PLN, and such a change would be favorable for the overall competitiveness of the economy as long as it did not affect domestic prices too heavily. In contrast, following appreciation, 1 euro might cost, e.g., 3 PLN instead of 4 PLN, and such a change would decrease the country's competitiveness accordingly. An increase in q implies a weakening of the domestic currency relative to the foreign currency, while a decrease in q a strengthening (somewhat counterintuitively, this implies that a weaker domestic currency promotes competitiveness, while a stronger currency hinders it).

---

[6] See WIIW Database which is a compilation of data from Eurostat and national statistics; forecasts are also cited after WIIW.

If the domestic and foreign inflation rates are more or less equal, then a change in the nominal exchange rate corresponds to the change in the real exchange rate. If domestic inflation is higher than foreign inflation, then at a given q the national currency appreciates. If the real exchange rate is to be maintained, then under the circumstances the nominal exchange rate of the national currency should be increased in line with the excess of domestic inflation over foreign inflation.

In some special situations, a constant nominal exchange rate may be maintained despite domestic inflation being much higher than foreign inflation. This was the case at the beginning of the transition period in Poland, when a very high nominal złoty–dollar exchange rate was deliberately set and sustained for many months even though domestic inflation greatly exceeded foreign inflation. Thus, the real exchange rate declined and the złoty appreciated, while the inflation rate gradually decreased, which was the main objective of that operation. The rigid nominal exchange rate was an "anchor" for containing domestic inflation, and real appreciation was not harmful since the very high initial nominal exchange rate provided the necessary room for a subsequent appreciation.

Over the past several years, the differences between domestic and foreign inflation have been much smaller in Poland, so changes in nominal exchange rates are closer to changes in real rates. In 1999, the average nominal złoty–euro exchange rate was 4.2. Over the following five years it gradually declined to rebound to 4.5 in 2004. Subsequently, until the end of 2008, the average exchange rate decreased and the złoty substantially appreciated in line with the growth of GDP per capita in Poland, narrowing the gap between this country and the EU average. However, that impaired the competitiveness of Polish companies, especially those which did not make extensive use of import inputs. On the other hand, the large multinationals operating in Poland remained largely unaffected because they obtained some of their intermediate products from their parent or sister companies based in other countries. During the crisis that began in 2008, the nominal złoty–euro exchange rate surged, improving the competitiveness of the Polish economy at that difficult time, and then plateaued at 4.1–4.2 (PLN/euros) in the years 2013–14.

In the past, exchange rates mostly depended on current account balances. The currencies of individual countries were strengthened by current account surpluses and weakened by current account deficits, which was accompanied by corresponding increases (decreases) in foreign reserves. Currently, under conditions of an open capital market, exchange rates depend to a much greater extent on capital flows and interest rates than on the balance of trade or the current account balance.

Let us now elucidate the relationship between exchange and interest rates with i_D and i_F denoting short-term domestic and foreign interest rates, respectively. If a foreign financial investor considers purchasing one-year government bonds (securities with a fixed interest rate), he needs to take into account not only the interest rate, but also the current and expected exchange rates. Let us assume that the investor owns 1,000 euros and compares Polish and foreign treasuries. In order to calculate the profitability of investment in Poland (country 1), he needs to account for the expected change in the nominal exchange rate q:

$$i_D - i_F > E\frac{\Delta q}{q} \tag{6.8}$$

where $E(\Delta q/q)$ stands for the expected change in the nominal exchange rate over one year. For instance, at $i_D = 10$ percent and $i_F = 6$ percent, the investment will be profitable unless the złoty–euro exchange rate increases (the złoty depreciates) by more than 4 percent. Of course, if $E(\Delta q/q) < 0$, that is, the nominal złoty–euro exchange rate decreases (złoty appreciates), the investment will be particularly lucrative as the change in the exchange rate will add to the difference in interest rates, amplifying profits. For instance, the investor may initially exchange euros for złotys at a rate of 4 euros per złoty, and at the end of the year he may purchase euros at a rate of, e.g., 3.8 PLN.

In countries with persistent current account deficits, under conditions of a free market economy and movement of capital, a floating nominal exchange rate, q, will not help balance their current accounts. On the one hand, such countries usually have higher inflation than others, with correspondingly higher interest rates (to ensure positive real interest rates). On the other hand, mainstream economists and international organizations, such as the IMF, recommend increasing interest rates as a method of combating current account deficits by boosting domestic savings, which are supposed to replace "foreign savings." Unfortunately, the resulting high interest rates in the deficit countries are conducive to currency speculation, which artificially strengthens the nominal exchange rate, q, when the inflow of speculation capital exceeds the current account deficit, and may even lead to higher foreign reserves in the central banks of the deficit countries. Under the circumstances, the demand for the domestic currency increases, driving up the exchange rate, q, expanding currency reserves "on credit," and boosting the speculators' confidence until the underlying current account problems of the country become evident. When that eventually happens, an abrupt outflow of foreign capital ensues, triggering a surge in the artificially low exchange rate, q, and throwing the country into a tailspin as a result of difficulties with financing the necessary imports and meeting the debt obligations denominated in foreign currency. There is no easy way out of such a crisis without international cooperation, such as the Bretton Woods system, which was in place until the beginning of the 1970s. The cornerstone of such cooperation is shared responsibility for long-term balancing of current accounts not only in the deficit countries (which strive for it anyway), but also in the surplus countries. In this type of international financial architecture, the accumulation of foreign reserves in some countries at the expense of others would not be tolerated.

6.5 Mercantilist Wage Dumping as an Ineffective Measure to Fight Unemployment

At a given nominal exchange rate, the international competitiveness of a given country primarily depends on the dynamics of domestic versus foreign prices. As it has been shown, prices are predominantly determined by unit labor costs, which are in turn correlated with the growth rates of the average nominal wage and average productivity (measured by GDP growth per worker). Let us assume that in a given year productivity increases by 2 percent, the central bank's inflation target is 3 percent, and nominal wages rise by 5 percent. In this situation, unit labor costs increase by 3 percent $[(1.05/1.02) = 1.03]$ and at a given percentage mark-up prices also rise by 3 percent, meeting the inflation target. Real wages grow in line with productivity at 2 percent per year $(1.05/1.03)$ and, all other things being equal, the market expands sufficiently to absorb the output increase driven by higher productivity. If other countries pursue similar wage and price policies with an identical inflation target, the relationship between domestic and foreign prices will not alter, and at a given nominal exchange rate mutual competitiveness will stay unchanged.

Let us now consider the case of a country afflicted by a high unemployment rate, whose government, persuaded by orthodox economists, embraces the view that unemployment is caused by excessively high wages. Furthermore, the government has convinced the trade unions that restraint in wage demands will both help retain existing jobs and create new ones. In particular, it is assured that at lower wages companies will prefer more labor-intensive production technologies, thus generating more jobs per unit of capital than at higher wages. Continuing our numerical example, if nominal wages grow by 4 percent rather than 5 percent, then at a productivity increase of 3 percent, unit labor costs and prices will rise only by 1 percent $(1.04/1.03)$; thus, prices will increase below the inflation target. Because domestic investment results from decisions made well in advance and can hardly be expected to suddenly expand on the strength of the promised wage rate growth suppression, the market will not be able to absorb the additional output generated thanks to higher productivity. Indeed, domestic demand, which is mostly determined by wages, grows more slowly when the wage rate growth slows down. And if output cannot be sold, production will shrink. Thus, in a closed model without government, this will lead to a situation in which profits (savings) will remain unchanged, but GDP and employment will decline. While profit per unit of good will increase, the quantity of goods produced will decrease to the extent that aggregate profits will stay unchanged. Thus, it appears that attempts to contain unemployment by keeping the nominal wage growth rate below productivity growth in a closed economy are doomed to fail (this mechanism was thoroughly analyzed in Section 4.5 above).

In turn, in an open economy, a decline in domestic prices will enhance the competitiveness of a country pursuing a dumping wage policy. Given sufficient price elasticity of foreign demand, such a country will export more goods and generate a higher volume of foreign currency inflows. Consequently, its current account balance will improve and employment in the export industries and related sectors will increase. However, it is not certain whether this will also enhance GDP and global employment because suppression of the nominal and real wage growth rates not only lowers production costs, but also hampers household consumption. The net outcome of these two mutually contradictory tendencies is unclear. In large countries in which the share of net exports in GDP is by nature limited (as opposed to the share of consumption out of wages) a dumping wage policy is unlikely to stimulate GDP growth and job creation. A far worse outcome can be expected if many countries attempt to take advantage of their international trade partners at the same time. Moreover, the increased net exports of one country are bound to decrease the net exports of another, meaning that higher employment in one place leads to a loss of jobs in another, which sooner or later will backfire. The more countries engage in dumping wage policies, the smaller the likelihood that these policies will promote net exports and the greater the certainty that all those involved will lose due to suppressed consumption out of wages.

6.6 Inflows of Foreign Capital and the Current Account Balance

In order to boost their economic growth, developing countries often need to import goods that they are not able to produce in a sufficient quantity or at an adequate quality. This is even more evident in the case of goods that cannot be produced locally, such as modern technological equipment, raw materials, or energy carriers. Faster growth also requires greater traditional imports, while potentially limiting exports if domestic demand for export goods increases, but their production cannot be scaled up quickly enough (or at all). Thus, it is little wonder that almost all countries that try to achieve a high GDP growth rate face difficulties with balancing their current accounts. It also becomes clear why they need inflows of foreign capital—to bridge the gap between their import needs and the export capacity. At the same time, one should remember that such inflows also generate long-term obligations towards third countries.

In particular, we should address the question of whether a country may indefinitely borrow from foreign creditors to finance its trade deficit. Let this deficit be set at a constant proportion of 3 percent GDP ($f = 0.03$) with GDP growing 5 percent annually ($g = 0.05$). If this situation lasts for a prolonged period of time, then the relationship between foreign debt, FZ, and GDP tends to a constant value $FZ/Y = f/g$, which is $(0.03/0.05) = 0.6$, or 60 percent, similarly as in the case of government debt (see pp. 79–80).

The foreign debt-to-GDP ratio (FZ/Y) will also tend to a constant value when the country borrows both to finance its current account deficit and service the interest on existing debt. This ratio is now defined as $(FZ/Y) = [f/(g - i)]$, where i stands for a constant interest rate on foreign credit and $i < g$.[7]

If $i = 0.03$, or 3 percent, then in our numerical example the ratio FZ/Y tends to a limit of $0.03/(0.05 - 0.03) = 1.5$, or 150 percent of GDP. At this FZ/Y ratio, if GDP amounted to 200 billion euros, then the volume of foreign debt would tend to 300 billion euros. In this situation, a new loan of 15 billion euros would finance a trade deficit of $fY = 0.03(200) = 6$ billion euros and service foreign debt in the amount of $i(FZ) = 0.03(300) = 9$ billion euros. At the same time, the debt would rise by 15/300, or 5 percent, at the same rate as GDP growth, which means that the FZ/Y ratio would remain unchanged.

It should be emphasized that the configuration of parameters adopted in this example is so unlikely to hold in reality that it indirectly proves the impossibility of living "on credit" indefinitely, even if the condition $i < g$, were met (and it usually is not in a situation of persistent foreign debt). In our example, credit is permanently available at the same interest rate, the creditors' trust remains unshaken despite the growing FZ/Y ratio (as it approaches its mathematical limit), the GDP growth rate is constant, etc. In reality, creditors would soon find out that the foreign debt-to-GDP ratio is on the rise and that the country will sooner or later become insolvent. Thus, at a certain point in time the country will have to adjust its imports to its export potential. Let us then assume that over the years the government promoted the country's production potential with a focus on exports, and it finally managed to balance its current account. This means that the coefficient f gradually declined, and eventually reached 0. Does this solve the problem? Not immediately, since the volume of foreign debt continues to grow until the country

---

[7] See Appendix 6.

in question attains an export surplus sufficient for servicing the interest on its debt.[8] Therefore, the country's export surplus should at least prevent a further accumulation of foreign debt, or, better still, enable its gradual reduction.

The current phase of economic globalization is characterized by enormous capital flows, much larger than international trade flows, facilitating the financing of trade and current account deficits in transition economies. Revenues from the privatization of state-owned companies sold to foreign investors also play a major part in financing the deficits. Furthermore, it should be noted that in transition countries interest rates are typically (much) higher than in countries exporting capital.[9] Both of these factors: the inflow of foreign capital in the real sphere and the inflow of foreign speculative capital relaxed the constraints of trade deficits and insufficient foreign capital, which previously hindered growth. They triggered GDP growth that would not be possible otherwise. Capital inflows were so large that they exceeded trade deficits and enabled the accumulation of considerable foreign reserves. However, this situation did not turn out to be a lasting solution because, as has been shown, sooner or later every country must be able to balance its current account.

Inflows of foreign capital include, amongst others, foreign direct investment (FDI). From the point of view of national accounts, investment is defined as the replacement of worn-out capital stock and the creation of new production capacity. FDI falls under this definition only partially, if it is used to establish new businesses or modernize existing companies. On the other hand, some FDI takes the form of acquisition of shares or takeovers (whether through privatization or not), and such portfolio investment does not constitute investment in the sense of national accounts.

The main difference between FDI and foreign borrowing is their effect on foreign debt. In contrast to foreign loans, FDI does not increase the country's debt burden. Whereas the investment projects financed by means of foreign borrowing must be serviced even if they fall short of the expected profits, in FDI it is the foreign investor that runs the risk. It should also be borne in mind that while some FDI profits are reinvested locally, some are transferred abroad as repatriated profits. To be sure, these distinctions are significant, but their macroeconomic implications are not as great as could be expected. Actually, as far as the balance of trade is concerned, the ratio of profits repatriated in a given year to aggregate FDI corresponds to interest payments on foreign debt.

---

[8] Other possible elements of a current account surplus are not considered here.
[9] Interest rates are linked to inflation rates as in order to obtain a positive real interest rate the nominal interest rate should be higher than the inflation rate.

The effect of FDI on the current account balance depends primarily on the strategies of the investors (foreign companies), which can be classified into two groups: those that are looking for new markets for their products and those that are looking for lower unit labor costs to improve their international competitiveness. It is thought that at least half of FDI in the former transition economies of Eastern Europe is made by the first type of companies, especially in the area of infrastructure (energy production, telecommunications, transportation) and services (chain stores, public media, banking, insurance). These companies usually conduct no or only marginal export activity, so the profits they want to repatriate in foreign currency must be generated by the other type of companies if the FDI sector as a whole is to balance its currency account. In reality, this sector often runs a foreign currency deficit which can either be balanced by a trade surplus generated by domestic companies or else added to the trade deficit of the latter.[10] As can be seen, foreign companies do not facilitate the strenuous task of balancing the current account and may even exacerbate it. The belief that an inflow of FDI (which is beneficial from the standpoint of modernizing the economy) will automatically help solve the constraint of the trade deficit on growth is unfounded.

In transition countries, the transformation to a free market economy was accompanied by a complete liberalization of international trade, offering access to the capital markets and at the same time increasing import intensity. The latter was caused by capital flows which enabled wider access to foreign consumer goods, which were often of higher quality and were more effectively marketed than domestic products. Import intensity was further stimulated by foreign investment goods with superior technological standards as FDI often involved modern import inputs. Finally, import intensity was also enhanced by the appreciation of the domestic currency (or the absence of its depreciation despite a current account deficit) attributable to inflows of speculative capital; this appreciation impaired the competitiveness of domestic goods relative to imported goods. Obviously, liberalization also stimulated exports in the transition economies, but not to the same degree as imports, as evidenced by persistent trade and current account deficits over the past decades.

---

[10] Between 1994 and 2005 in Poland foreign companies contributed to the trade deficit more than domestic firms. This changed in 2006 as a result of a considerable increase in the imports of the latter. In 2005, the import-export deficit amounted to $7.5 billion and $4.7 billion for foreign and domestic companies, respectively, whereas in 2006 it amounted to $7.7 billion for foreign businesses and $8.3 billion for Polish firms (see Chojna 2008: 129 – 30). This tendency continued in 2007 and 2008, but recently it has reverted again. In 2011, the net export deficit was $13.2 billion for foreign businesses and $8.2 billion for domestic companies, and in 2012 it was $8.2 billion for foreign businesses and $5.6 billion for Polish companies (see Chojna 2013: 79).

Current account deficits, with the underlying inflows of foreign capital, increase domestic absorption (which is the sum of consumption and investment) relative to total production, or GDP. However, these same factors also reduce the volume of total demand, which is rarely acknowledged. Let us now consider this problem in a more formal manner.

Ignoring the government sector for the sake of simplicity, the formula (6.1) can be rewritten as:

$$Y = \frac{IP + X}{sp + m}$$

where $sp = (1 - \alpha) + sw\alpha$. In the next step, using a simple transformation,[11] we obtain the familiar equation:

$$Y = \frac{IP + E}{sp} \tag{6.9}$$

where $E = X - M$. Thus, at a given private saving rate, sp, we can determine the relationship between Y and private investment, IP, and the balance of trade, E, (which shall also be interpreted as the current account balance, CA). Subsequently, (6.9) can be used to calculate the GDP growth rate:[12]

$$g(Y) = g(IP)a_1 + g(E)(1 - a_1), \tag{6.10}$$

where $g(i)$ stands for the growth rate of the variable i, $i = Y$, IP, E, while $a_1 = (IP/SP)$ and $(1 - a_1) = (E/SP)$ denote appropriate weights. Consequently, the GDP growth rate at a constant sp depends primarily on the growth rates of private investment, IP, and of the current account. When the investment rate in one country increases, then given unchanged demand in the rest of the world (at a constant volume of exports, X) the current account balance will

[11]
$$Y(sp + m) = (IP + X),$$
$$Ysp = IP + X - mY$$
$$Y = \frac{IP + X - M}{sp}.$$

[12] For a constant sp, differentiating (6.9) with respect to time we obtain:

$$\frac{dY}{dt} = \frac{1}{sp}\left(\frac{dIP}{dt} + \frac{dE}{dt}\right)$$
$$\frac{dY}{dt} = \frac{1}{sp}\left(\frac{dIP}{dt} + \frac{dE}{dt}\right)$$

Then, dividing this formula by Y leads to:

$$\frac{1}{Y}\frac{dY}{dt} = \frac{1}{sp}\left[\frac{dIP}{dt}\frac{1}{IP}\frac{IP}{Y} + \frac{dE}{dt}\frac{1}{E}\frac{E}{Y}\right]$$
$$g(Y) = \frac{1}{sp}\left[g(IP)\frac{IP}{Y} + g(E)\frac{E}{Y}\right]$$

deteriorate, adversely affecting E and hindering GDP growth. In turn, if export growth accelerates, then even at a constant $g(IP)$ the current account balance will improve and $g(E)$ will increase, enhancing the GDP growth rate. Finally, if import intensity increases, then at given $g(IP)$ and $g(X)$ the GDP growth rate will decline as imports increase and the current account balance deteriorates. Therefore, these three factors: investment, exports, and import intensity primarily affect the GDP growth rate on the total demand side.

Developing countries that wish to accelerate their growth face some additional constraints, which were discussed above and which are linked to difficulties in balancing foreign deficits. This discussion provides a background for analysis of problems linked to trade liberalization and capital inflows. As far as liberalization and lifting tariffs are concerned, their primary outcome is increased import intensity, causing higher imports and even a trade deficit, which in turn slows down the GDP growth rate as $g(E)$ decreases. This can and should be remedied by depreciating the domestic currency (a higher nominal exchange rate, q). However, if the country permits an inflow of foreign speculative capital and currency speculation driven by exchange rate differences, then the nominal exchange rate may remain too low despite persistent current account deficits. Furthermore, as a result of the continuously increasing debt obligations towards third countries, the servicing of loans denominated in foreign currency will become more difficult when finally the domestic currency begins to depreciate, which is otherwise a desirable phenomenon.

In conclusion, the long-term dependence of a country on inflows of foreign capital (including foreign loans) hampers its economic sovereignty and substantially constrains its monetary and fiscal policies. Taking all of this into consideration, it becomes clear why in the initial period of their development the most advanced economies took recourse to protectionism and why the only countries that have so far managed to narrow the gap between them and the most developed ones are those which did not allow trade liberalization and did not completely waive capital controls (e.g., the "Asian tigers," and especially South Korea). In this way, those countries were able to combine a strong growth of investment (including FDI) with an export expansion and competitive nominal exchange rates, despite running export surpluses. An increase in private investment, $g(IP)$, in conjunction with $g(E)$ dramatically accelerated the GDP growth rate of those countries.

Appendix 5. Domestic and Foreign Savings

Some of the conclusions presented below were already outlined in Section 6.3, where we considered a simple case of countries 1 and 2, with the latter representing the rest of the world. The imports of countries 1 and 2 were defined by the following functions: $M_1 = Ma_1 + m_1 Y_1$ and $M_2 = Ma_2 + m_2 Y_2$, where Ma_1 and Ma_2 stand for independent constant values, while m_1 and m_2 are marginal coefficients of import intensity for countries 1 and 2, respectively. As countries 1 and 2 add up to the entire world, M_1 also denotes the exports of country 2, and M_2 – the exports of country 1. For the sake of simplicity and without any detriment to the validity of results, we also assume that $m_2 = 0$.[13] Additionally, to make the example more readily comprehensible, we ignore the government sector. Note that the variables and parameters used in this appendix may not be the same as those in the main body of text.

Given the above assumptions, the GDP of country 1 is:

$$Y_1 = \frac{I_1 + M_2 - M_1}{s_1}$$

where s_1 denotes the saving rate (S_1/Y_1):

$$Y_1 = \frac{I_1 + Ma_2 - Ma_1 - m_1 Y_1}{s_1}$$

which can be simplified to:

$$Y_1 = \frac{I_1 + Ma_2 - Ma_1}{s_1 + m_1} \tag{A5.1}$$

and the GDP of country 2 is:

$$Y_2 = \frac{I_2 + M_1 - M_2}{s_2}$$

where s_2 denotes the saving rate (S_2/Y_2),
and which can be expressed as:

$$Y_2 = \frac{I_2 + (Ma_1 - Ma_2 + m_1 Y_1)}{s_2} \tag{A5.2}$$

It is assumed that each economy has unused productive capacity and unemployed workers. If in country 1 investment increases by ΔI_1 at constant s_1 and m_1, as a result of which, pursuant to (A5.1), GDP increment in country 1 is:

$$\Delta Y_1 = \frac{\Delta I_1}{s_1 + m_1} \tag{A5.3}$$

while at constant I_2 and s_2, as a result of the increase in the exports of this country amounting to $\Delta M_1 = m_1 \Delta Y_1$, according to (A5.2), the GDP of country 2 rises by:

$$\Delta Y_2 = \frac{m_1 \Delta Y_1}{s_2} = \frac{m_1}{s_2} \frac{\Delta I_1}{s_1 + m_1} \tag{A5.4}$$

The GDP growth of country 2 is exogenous; it is attributable to higher imports from country 2 by country 1 due to increased investment in the latter. The nature of this

---

[13] As already mentioned (see footnote 4), this assumption facilitates analysis and only means that we ignore secondary effects of GDP growth and the resulting increase of imports in country 2 on country 1.

process can be readily elucidated by computing GDP growth for both countries, assuming that they have an identical saving rate of s_1. Under the circumstances, from (A5.3) and (A5.4) we get:

$$\Delta Y = \Delta Y_1 + \Delta Y_2 = \frac{\Delta I_1}{s_1 + m_1} + \frac{m_1}{s_1} \frac{\Delta I_1}{s_1 + m_1}$$

$$\Delta Y = \Delta I_1 \frac{s_1 + m_1}{s_1(s_1 + m_1)} = \frac{\Delta I_1}{s_1} \tag{A5.5}$$

This equation represents GDP growth in country 1 under conditions of a closed economy, in which the investment multiplier process occurs entirely in that country and is controlled by a "savings leak." On the other hand, in an open economy, part of this process also occurs in country 2 (abroad) due to an "import leak," and leads to the same outcomes if the propensity to save is identical in both countries. This is in a way obvious as in the presented example both countries add up to the world's economy, which is closed by definition.

Let us now examine GDP growth in both countries on the assumption of *different saving rates* between the countries. Now, (A5.3) and (A5.4) will give:

$$\Delta Y = \Delta Y_1 + \Delta Y_2 = \frac{\Delta I_1}{s_1 + m_1} + \frac{m_1}{s_2} \frac{\Delta I_1}{s_1 + m_1}$$

$$\Delta Y = \Delta I_1 \frac{s_2 + m_1}{s_2(s_1 + m_1)} \tag{A5.6}$$

At given s_1 and m_1, GDP growth in country 2 increases with decreasing s_2 relative to s_1.

The most important problem involves changes of savings in the two countries triggered by investment growth in country 1. Let us now address this issue. Using the notation adopted in this appendix, $S = I + E$, so an increase in savings can be represented as:

$$\Delta S = \Delta I + \Delta E$$

where E is the difference between exports and imports in the sense of the current account balance.

Based on (A5.3), the increase in savings in country 1 is:

$$\Delta S_1 = \Delta I_1 - \Delta M_1 = \Delta I_1 - m_1 \Delta Y_1$$

$$\Delta S_1 = \Delta I_1 - \frac{m\Delta I_1}{s_1 + m_1}$$

$$\Delta S_1 = \Delta I_1 \frac{s_1}{s_1 + m_1}, \tag{A5.7}$$

while based on (A5.4), that increase in savings in country 2 amounts to:

$$\Delta S_2 = s_2 \Delta Y_2 = \Delta I_1 \frac{m_1}{s_1 + m_1}. \tag{A5.8}$$

Thus, the combined savings increment in the two countries is:

$$\Delta S = \Delta S_1 + \Delta S_2 = \Delta I_1 \frac{s_1}{s_1 + m_1} + \Delta I_1 \frac{m_1}{s_1 + m_1} = \Delta I_1$$

This result corroborates the thesis that "investment finances itself" also with respect to two countries (or the world's economy as a whole). However, the incorporation of "import leaks" implies that the higher the coefficient m_1 at a given s_1, the greater the proportion of the savings increment, ΔI_1, that is transferred to country 2 rather than remain in country 1.[14] Indeed, since $\Delta S = \Delta I_1$, using (A5.7) the ratio of the increase in savings in country 1 to savings in both countries can be expressed using the following formula:

$$h = \frac{\Delta S_1}{\Delta S} = \frac{\Delta S_1}{\Delta I_1} = \frac{\Delta I_1}{\Delta I_1} \frac{s_1}{s_1 + m_1} = \frac{s_1}{s_1 + m_1} \tag{A5.9}$$

where h declines with rising m_1. Furthermore, h is an increasing function of s_1.

Let us now illustrate this analysis with a numerical example, adopting three variants for m_1: the variables will be calculated in three columns according to the above formulas, with the other parameters held constant ($\Delta I_1 = 100$, $s_1 = 0.25$, and $s_2 = 0.2$). As it can be seen, with increasing m_1, the increase in GDP declines in country 1 and increases in country 2, with the combined GDP increment for both countries increasing. Most crucially, the sum of the increment in savings in the two countries is constant and equal to investment increase in country 1. With rising m_1, the proportion of savings increment declines in country 1 and increases in country 2. Thus, savings are not imported from country 2 to country 1; on the contrary, they are generated by the expenditures of country 1 on exports from country 2 to country 1. This means that the term "import of foreign savings" is not only imprecise, but misleading. First, no "foreign savings" are imported, and second, savings in country 2 are generated solely as a result of the increase in total demand in country 1 and the multiplier process induced in country 2 by the former. The larger the "import leak" as measured by m_1, the lower the proportion of the savings increment of country 1 in the aggregate savings of both countries. Table A5.1 presents a simulation of results for ΔY_1, ΔY_2, ΔY and ΔS_1, ΔS_2, ΔS at different levels of m_1, given the parameters adopted above: $\Delta I_1 = 100$, $s_1 = 0.25$ and $s_2 = 0.2$.

The opposite is true if the saving rate, s_1, increases in country 1. Indeed, from equation (A5.9) above, h increases with s_1, that is, with a growing share of the savings increment of country 1 in the aggregate savings increment. As a result of a higher propensity to save in country 1, a greater proportion of savings generated by ΔI_1 will remain there because an increase in s_1 reduces GDP growth in country 1, and consequently also suppresses the "import leak," $m_1 \Delta Y_1$, and ΔS_2, at a given $\Delta S = \Delta I_1$. However, this method of containing the so-called import of foreign savings is costly since it diminishes GDP growth in both countries 1 and 2.

A much more efficient way of improving GDP would be to foster export and reduce import intensity in country 1 in line with investment growth. The point is, that

---

[14] Similar conclusions are drawn by Dalziel and Harcourt (1997).

Table A5.1. Simulation of results for ΔY_1, ΔY_2, ΔY and ΔS_1, ΔS_2, ΔS at different values of m_1

Constant parameters	$m_1 = 0.15$	$m_1 = 0.25$	$m_1 = 0.55$
	($\Delta I_1 = 100$, $s_1 = 0.25$, $s_2 = 0.2$)	($\Delta I_1 = 100$, $s_1 = 0.25$, $s_2 = 0.2$)	($\Delta I_1 = 100$, $s_1 = 0.25$, $s_2 = 0.2$)
$s_1 + m_1$	0.4	0.5	0.8
$\Delta Y_1 = \Delta I_1[1/(s_1 + m_1)]$	250	200	125
$s_2(s_1 + m_1)$	0.08	0.1	0.16
$\Delta Y_2 = \Delta I_1\{m_1/[s_2(s_1 + m_1)]\}$	187.50	250	343.75
$\Delta Y = \Delta Y_1 + \Delta Y_2$	437.50	450	468.75
$\Delta S_1 = s_1 \Delta Y_1$	62.5	50	31.25
$\Delta S_2 = s_2 \Delta Y_2$	37.50	50	68.75
$\Delta S = \Delta S_1 + \Delta S_2$	100	100	100
$\Delta E_1 = -\Delta M_1 = -m_1 \Delta Y_1$	-37.50	-50	-68.75
$\Delta E_2 = \Delta M_2 = m_1 \Delta Y_1$	37.50	50	68.75
$\Delta S_1 = 100 + \Delta E_1$	62.50	50	31.25
$\Delta S_2 = \Delta E_2$	37.50	50	68.75

Source: Own calculations.

investment growth, ΔI_1, should be oriented equally towards the balance of trade and expansion of the production potential to boost exports and replace imports. This implies the adoption of a conscious industrial policy, which is of particular importance today, in the face of extensive internationalization of the financial markets. Due to such internationalization, individual countries quickly run into difficulties when they attempt to boost their GDP growth relative to their trading partners. Being lately a net exporter, the European Union is immune to these problems and is largely independent of the rest of the world in this respect. Unfortunately, it does not take advantage of the opportunities this situation offers.

Appendix 6. The Foreign Debt-to-GDP Ratio

Let us assume that an economy runs a constant trade deficit $E = fY$, $0 < f < 1$, where f is equal to the difference between m and x, which are constant coefficients of import intensity and export performance, respectively, with $m > x$. The trade deficit is financed by foreign debt with a constant annual interest rate, i. As a result, the volume of foreign debt at the end of year t, denoted as $FZ(t)$, is the sum of annual flows of credit obtained in the preceding years, interest included:

$$FZ(t) = fY(t) + fY(t - 1)(1 + i) + fY(t - 2)(1 + i)^2 + \ldots$$
$$+ fY[t - (t - 1)](1 + i)^{t-1} + +fY(0)(1 + i)^t$$

Dividing both sides by $Y(t)$, we obtain:

$$\frac{FZ(t)}{Y(t)} = f + f\frac{Y(t-1)(1+i)}{Y(t)} + f\frac{Y(t-2)(1+i)^2}{Y(t)} + \ldots$$
$$+ \frac{fY[t-(t-1)](1+1)^{t-1}}{Y(t)} + f\frac{Y(0)(1+i)^t}{Y(t)} \qquad (A6.1)$$

It is assumed that GDP grows at a constant rate g, which gives:

$$Y(t) = Y(t-j)(1+g)^j$$

and:

$$\frac{Y(t-j)}{Y(t)} = \frac{1}{(1+g)^j} \qquad (A6.2)$$

Based on equation (A6.2), from the second term on the right side of (A6.1), we obtain for $j = 1$:

$$f\frac{Y(t-1)(1+i)}{Y(t)} = f\frac{1+i}{1+g}$$

Also based on (A6.2), similar transformations for $j = 2, 3, \ldots, (t-1)$ yield:

$$\frac{FZ(t)}{Y(t)} = f + f\left(\frac{1+i}{1+g}\right) + f\left(\frac{1+i}{1+g}\right)^2 + \ldots + f\left(\frac{1+i}{1+g}\right)^{t-1} + f\left(\frac{1+i}{1+g}\right)^t.$$

$$\frac{FZ(t)}{Y(t)} = f\left[1 + \left(\frac{1+i}{1+g}\right) + \left(\frac{1+i}{1+g}\right)^2 + \ldots + \left(\frac{1+i}{1+g}\right)^{t-1} + \left(\frac{1+i}{1+g}\right)^t\right]. \qquad (A6.3)$$

Within the square bracket in (A6.3) there is a geometric series with a quotient of $[(1+i)/(1+g)]$, whose sum for $g > i$ equals:

$$\left[1 - \left(\frac{1+i}{1+g}\right)^{t+1}\right] / \left[1 - \left(\frac{1+i}{1+g}\right)\right]$$

Therefore, from (A6.3) we obtain:

$$\frac{FZ(t)}{Y(t)} = f\left[1 - \left(\frac{1+i}{1+g}\right)^{t+1}\right] / \left(\frac{g-i}{1+g}\right)$$

$$\frac{FZ(t)}{Y(t)(1+g)} = f\left[1 - \left(\frac{1+i}{1+g}\right)^{t+1}\right] / (g-i)$$

$$\frac{FZ(t)}{Y(t+1)} = f\left[1 - \left(\frac{1+i}{1+g}\right)^{t+1}\right] / (g-i). \qquad (A6.4)$$

The formula (A6.4) for $g > i$ tends to a finite limit:

$$\lim_{t \Rightarrow \infty} FZ(t)/Y(t+1) = f/(g-i) \qquad (A6.5)$$

For $g < i$, we obtain:

$$\lim_{t \Rightarrow \infty} FZ(t)/Y(t+1) = +\infty.$$

To illustrate this, let us assume that at $g=0.05$, or 5 percent, we have $f=0.03$, or 3 percent, and i is equal to, 0.02, 0.03, or 0.04, which is 2 percent, 3 percent, or 4 percent, respectively. For an interest rate of 2 percent, the limit is:

$$\frac{FZ(t)}{Y(t+1)} = \frac{0,03}{0,05-0,02} = 1,0, \text{ or } 100 \text{ percent.}$$

For an interest rate of 3 percent, the limit is:

$$\frac{FZ(t)}{Y(t+1)} = \frac{0,03}{0,05-0,03} = 1,5, \text{ or } 150 \text{ percent.}$$

For an interest rate of 4 percent, the limit is:

$$\frac{FZ(t)}{Y(t+1)} = \frac{0,03}{0,05-0,04} = 3,0, \text{ or } 300 \text{ percent.}$$

This example shows how an increase in the interest rate leads to a dramatic surge in the foreign debt-to-GDP ratio. Indeed, at $i=0$, the limit of that ratio amounts to $f/g=0.03/0.05=0.6$, or 60 percent. At $i=2$ percent, $i=3$ percent, and $i=4$ percent, the additional burden arising out of interest payments amounts to 40 percent, 90 percent, and 240 percent of GDP.

Appendix 7. The Effect of Import Intensity on Investment and Fiscal Multipliers in an Open Model

What follows is a summary of my more comprehensive discussion of this question elsewhere.[15] The two sides of the GDP equation are traditionally represented as:

$$W + R + TN = CP + IP + G + X - M$$

which can be transformed to:

$$R = IP + G + X - M - TN - SW$$

where:

$$Y = \frac{R}{(1-\alpha)(1-tn)}.$$

Maintaining the assumption $SW = (1 - \alpha)(1 - tn)Y$, the average import intensity of final production is defined as mf:

---

[15] See Łaski (2009) and Łaski et al. (2010).

$$mf = \frac{M}{(IP + G + X + CP)} \tag{A7.1}$$

where $(IP + G + X + CP) = FG$ is the volume of final production FG. This is so because imported goods serve (indirectly or directly) as inputs to final production, but they are not inputs to imports. However, this is the case if import intensity is measured as m:

$$m = \frac{M}{Y} = \frac{M}{FG - M} = \frac{M/FG}{1 - (M/FG)} = \frac{mf}{1 - mf} \tag{A7.2}$$

Consequently,

$$mf = m(1 - mf)$$
$$mf(1 + m) = m \tag{A7.2'}$$
$$mf = \frac{m}{1 + m}$$

and hence:

$$mf < m, \text{ as } m > 0.^{[*]}$$

* In what follows, in the original Polish text of Appendix 7, there is a mistake that was overlooked by the author and the editor of the book. The value of national income multiplier given by his equation (6.1) makes it a function of national income leakages: sp, tn, and m. Appendix 7 attempts to express this relation in terms of a new parameter, i.e., import intensity of final output, mf, rather than m, which represents the ratio of imports, M to national income, Y. However, his equation (D.7.3 in the Polish edition of the book) is incorrect because when transforming the equation $Y = R/[(1 - \alpha)(1 - tn)]$ the component $mfCP$—i.e., import intensity of private consumption—was lost. This mistake invalidates the subsequent equations derived from his (D7.3) as well as his numerical example given at the end of the Appendix). Therefore the remaining part of the Polish edition of Appendix 7 is omitted here.

7

Endogenous money

7.1 Preliminary Remarks

The capitalist economy is most of all a money economy. Hence money has featured repeatedly in these lectures. However, the question remains as to the nature of the money currently used in capitalist countries. How is it created and destroyed? Is it exogenous, a limited resource like gold, or is it endogenous, emerging from processes of production and distribution? How is credit generated and what is the relationship between credit and savings? These are some of the issues that the present chapter addresses, without delving into the history of money, the development of the theory of money, or the problems of contemporary finance, which would require a much broader approach than that afforded by this book.

Generally, money is said to fulfill three basic functions as a medium of exchange (or, more broadly, a medium of payment, e.g., in the context of taxes, contributions, etc.), a store of value, and a unit of account. From the point of view of endogenous money, its primary role is to serve as a medium of payment, with its most important measure being *M1* (the quantity of transaction money that determines the volume of company and household expenditures). There are also other measures of money involving assets that are less liquid than *M1* but can still be relatively quickly converted into transaction money.

The point of departure in our analysis is the production of goods rather than their exchange, which is traditionally associated with the creation and use of money. In the case of exchange, of foremost importance is the function of money as a medium of exchange, a function that helps overcome the difficulties inherent in a moneyless economy. Indeed, in the case of a direct exchange of good A (e.g., shoes) for good B (e.g., trousers), the owner of the shoes would have to find an owner of trousers who would be willing to trade them for shoes. In this context, money is a medium facilitating exchange akin to a lubricant reducing friction in a machine and enabling its operation.

The medium-of-exchange approach is typical of the traditional quantity theory of money. It is usually represented in the form of the Fisher Equation:

$$MV = PT \tag{7.1}$$

where M denotes the quantity of money,[1] V the velocity of circulation, P the general price level, and T the volume of transactions within a given period. It should be noted that in formula (7.1) the symbol of money supply, M, refers to a stock (measured at a point in time), while the symbol of transactions, T, refers to a flow (measured over a period of time). As a result, at given M we can get different results for T and V depending on the selected period (e.g., month, year, etc.).

By definition formula (7.1) is always true. Indeed, if we take empirical data concerning M, P, and T, then we will always find a V which makes the equation "true." However, for formula (7.1) to become a piece of economic theory, it should be defined more precisely, which is non-trivial. The very notion of the volume of transactions is problematic: Does it refer to sales transactions concerning goods and services produced during a certain period, or to all transactions including financial ones? It should be borne in mind that nowadays the number of transactions involving traditional goods and services constitutes only a small fraction of financial transitions. Despite that, it is often assumed that the volume of GDP is related to the volume of transactions, T, and so (7.1) is often given in the form of:

$$MV = PY \tag{7.1'}$$

where PY denotes nominal GDP or national income.

The most important element in formula (7.1') is the velocity of circulation of money. In all versions of the quantity theory of money, it is assumed that it is a (relatively) constant parameter, which would imply a correlation between the quantity (supply) of money, M, and the flow of monetary income, PY. The short conclusion that can be drawn here is that a rise in prices, or inflation, always results from an increase in the volume of money in circulation. However, it is usually not specified what amount of money is meant. In typical situations, researchers seek such a measure of money which is consistent from the standpoint of formula (7.1').

In response to the financial crisis, which began in the United States in 2007/8, almost all central banks started to increase money supply by means of an operation euphemistically called quantitative easing (QE). In the process, enormous quantities of money have been injected into the economies of the most developed countries by central banks purchasing government bonds and private securities. At the same time, almost all of those countries face

---

[1] In this chapter the symbol M always denotes money rather than imports.

deflation rather than inflation tendencies. Do we then need better proof that the volume of money in circulation is poorly correlated with prices? As mainstream economists continue to scare the public with an invisible threat of inflation, they turn a blind eye to the already present, and much more dangerous, danger of deflation.

According to the quantity theory of money, the independent variable in formula (7.1') is the volume of money in circulation, M, while the dependent variable is the general price level, P. However, as Joan Robinson aptly remarked, it would make more sense to treat PY as an independent variable, with M being a dependent variable given a more or less constant V.[2] Indeed, this is the case if money is treated as an endogenous factor, and its supply is conceived of as the end point rather than the starting point of the monetary circuit.

7.2 Endogenous Money and the Monetary Circuit

Let us begin with an outline of the balance sheet of a typical commercial bank in a closed economy (see Table 7.1 below). The assets of such a bank primarily include the loans it has extended to companies and households, the securities it holds, and its reserves. The bank also owns other assets, including gross real wealth. Its liabilities mostly consist of the customers' demand and term deposits (savings), as well as other liabilities, and finally the bottom line— the bank's net wealth.

Bank money consists of *demand and term deposits* owned by the bank's clients. Bank money can be converted into cash (banknotes) either immediately (demand deposits) or with a certain delay (term deposits). However, most bank money is used directly as a medium of exchange or payment in interbank dealings because banks mutually recognize their liabilities. *Bank reserves* are made up mostly of deposits held at the central bank, as well as a small amount of actual cash.

The above considerations provide a background for analysis of the monetary circuit in which the creation and destruction of money is primarily

Table 7.1. Outline of a bank's balance sheet

Assets	Liabilities
Loans	Demand deposits
Securities	Term deposits
Reserves	3. Other liabilities
Other assets including gross real estate	4. Net wealth

[2] See Joan Robinson (1971: 77–8).

determined by the process of production. A very good introduction to this discussion was given by Kalecki in his 1935 paper: "Let us assume that as a result of some important invention there is an increase in investment associated with its spreading. Now, is it possible for the capitalists to step up their investment, even though their profits have not increased ... and they have not curtailed their consumption ... ? The financing of additional investment is effected by the so-called *creation* of purchasing power."[3] Kalecki went on to say: "By making use ... of additional purchasing power, they set in motion the mechanism of the upswing. This case is very close to that of government anti-slump intervention. In order to pass from the former to the latter, it suffices to substitute for the entrepreneurs induced to invest by the new invention the government taking up investment, which is financed likewise by means of additional purchasing power, in order to break the deadlock of the slump." (Kalecki 1935: 193). This thesis of Kalecki provides an answer to the still topical question of how to obtain money for active fiscal policy of the state, should such a policy be necessary.

7.2.1 *The Monetary Circuit in a System with Commercial Banks*

A systematic account of the process of creation of purchasing power was given, amongst others, by Marc Lavoie.[4] The example presented herein follows a similar pattern, with commercial banks as a point of departure. We use the previously described two-sector model, but with certain modifications. First, households will now be receiving not only wages, but also dividends (distributed profits) and interest. As a result, in equation (4.1) above (see p. 32), R will now denote only the undistributed (retained) part of corporate profits. Furthermore, a third sector will be added to the production and household sectors, namely, an integrated sector of commercial banks which, at the beginning of a production period, extend loans to companies, households, and possibly other entities, as well as play the role of intermediaries in financial transactions between households and companies.

As it was defined before, the production sector is divided into two internally integrated subsectors: subsector 1 manufacturing investment goods, *IP*, and subsector 2, manufacturing consumer goods, *CP*. The production sector directly or indirectly (through banks) pays to households wages on account of labor, and profits on account of ownership: distributed profits (dividends) and interest on loans. Household income in this sense will be denoted as Q_i, with the subscript indicating the subsector with which this income is associated. It is assumed that companies do not have any working capital at the beginning

---

[3] Kalecki (1935 [1990]: 190); emphasis added by K. Ł.   [4] See Lavoie (1992: 149–69).

of the production period, so they need to take out loans, denoted as Q_1 or Q_2, to pay for the current production costs and other expenses in both sectors. The banks extend those loans by the creation of appropriate entries in their balance sheets, on the assets and liabilities sides at the same time (see Table 7.2).[5]

Money, in the strict sense of means of payment, appears on the deposit side, which includes banks' liabilities to companies, used for conducting transactions. Money also appears on the asset side in the form of corporate loans that may be used as means of payment. It should also be noted that banks create credit money *ex nihilo*, merely by means of an accounting operation, and we may assume that this money enjoys sufficient public confidence to be accepted as means of payment. It is also assumed that companies take out loans only when they need to make payments, since holding idle deposits would be costly (the interest on debt is usually much higher than that on deposits). Therefore, companies relatively quickly transfer their deposits to households in the form of incomes of the latter, amounting to $Q_1 + Q_2$, with the balance sheet of banks as shown in Table 7.3.

The situation presented in Table 7.3 will last slightly longer than that given in Table 7.2, but it will also soon change. Households are going to spend most of their income on consumer goods, and save some of it. As a result, the disbursements of households will feature as the revenues and deposits of companies, while household savings, S_H, will remain as bank deposits, as shown in Table 7.4.

This situation will not last very long, either, since companies use their deposits to reduce their debt to the banking sector. By paying off loans, companies destroy the money created at the beginning, which is again done

Table 7.2. Changes in the balance sheet of a commercial bank: Corporate loans and deposits

Assets	Liabilities
New loans to companies $Q_1 + Q_2$	New deposits from companies $Q_1 + Q_2$

Table 7.3. Balance sheet of commercial banks: Corporate loans and household deposits

Assets	Liabilities
New loans to companies: $Q_1 + Q_2$	New deposits from households: $Q_1 + Q_2$

[5] Table 7.2 and subsequent tables in this chapter leave out the balance sheet entries "gross real wealth" and "net wealth of the banks."

Table 7.4. Balance sheet of commercial banks: Corporate loans and corporate and household deposits

Assets	Liabilities
New loans to companies: $Q_1 + Q_2$	New deposits from companies: $Q_1 + Q_2 - S_H$ New deposits from households: S_H

Table 7.5. Balance sheet of commercial banks: Increase in corporate debt and household deposits

Assets	Liabilities
Increase in company debt, S_H	New deposits from households, S_H

Table 7.6. Closing balance sheet of commercial banks

Assets	Liabilities
Increase in company debt: M_H	Increase in deposits from households: $M_H = S_H - F_H$

by means of another accounting operation by banks, with the outcome presented in Table 7.5.

In the last step, we need to acknowledge the fact that households will not hold all their savings in the form of low-interest-bearing bank deposits. Let us then assume that they purchase some financial assets (shares) issued by the production sector, for an amount of F_H, thanks to which companies will be able to further reduce their debt to the banks. The remaining part of household savings will still be held as bank deposits; let us define it as $M_H = S_H - F_H$, where M_H is the increase in the volume of money at the end of the examined monetary circuit. The closing balance sheet of commercial banks is given in Table 7.6.

This model of the monetary circuit may be illustrated with a numerical example, with the production sector obtaining 3,000 euros in loans from the banking sector and expending it all. Households spend 2,500 euros on consumer goods and services and save 500 euros, out of which 300 euros in the form of shares and 200 euros in liquid form (bank deposits). Household deposits are mirrored by the increase of corporate debt to the banking sector, also amounting to 200 euros. Indeed, out of the 3,000 euros borrowed from the banks, companies paid off 2,800 euros obtained from households: 2,500 euros from the sale of goods and services and 300 euros from the sale of securities.

Companies will not be able to pay off the part of debt amounting to M_H due to the fact that households keep some of their savings in the form of bank deposits. Lavoie observed that it is only at this stage that the banking sector acts as a financial intermediary between households and companies. This intermediation would be unnecessary if households invested all their savings in the form of non-liquid financial assets, F_H. Thus, from the point of view of the monetary circuit, what matters is not the volume of S_H, but its structure in the sense of the degree of liquidity of household assets.

So far, we have dealt exclusively with monetary circuit from the viewpoint of trade in consumer goods between the household sector and the production sector as a whole. Consequently, can Table 7.6 be treated as the final result? This is the case if we assume that the production sector as a whole also takes out loans from the banking sector to purchase investment goods produced in the subsector 1 (these transactions take place within the corporate sector). If some companies incur additional debt to purchase investment goods amounting to IP then, following the purchase, exactly the same amount will appear in the form of deposits in other companies (producing investment goods), which will make it possible to pay off the debt of the production sector as a whole. Thus, Table 7.6 indeed presents the final results of one complete monetary circuit, also if we account for investment loans.

So far, we have ignored the internal problems of the banking sector, and in particular its potential profits and losses. It is possible that some debtors will not be able to meet their obligations and will default on their loans. Moreover, banks, just as all other companies, have overheads and payroll costs. Finally, they should also bring profits for their owners. For these reasons, the interest rate on loans, i_B, must be higher than that on deposits, i_D ($i_B > i_D$). If loans and deposits at the beginning of the year are denoted B and DEP with $B = DEP$, at the end of the year we obtain $B(1 + i_B)$ for loans and $DEP(1 + i_D)$ for deposits (these amounts consist of the principal and interest). This gives rise to the profits of banks equal to $B(i_B - i_D)$. Let us assume that all of these profits are distributed between bank owners and spent just like other incomes of households as discussed before. As a result, Table 7.6 remains valid if we take into account costs and profits in the banking sector. Furthermore, we need to bear in mind that in addition to loans $Q_1 + Q_2$, banks also transfer to households their wages and profits, which are subsequently disbursed by those households. If, however, those profits of the banking sector are not distributed among the bank shareholders, they increase the banks' equity.

So far it has not been explained what types of money are used by companies and households. These may include money transfers within one large bank and cheques raised by deposit owners. Nowadays, there is a universal system of automatic telling machines and credit cards, which have largely replaced the checking system.

Lavoie's model is extremely simplified: it does not contain a central bank, the government sector, or the rest of the world. However, this should be considered its strength rather than weakness, since it allows us to present very complex problems and draw conclusions which, as it turns out, remain valid also in more realistic models. These conclusions primarily concern the relationship between credit and money as well as the position of companies in a money economy.

In this model, the increase in the volume of money in circulation is identical to the increase in corporate debt, both at the beginning and end of the monetary circuit. Loans generate money deposits, and household savings in the form of M_H are the end result of the initial loans $Q_1 + Q_2$. Thus, household savings *are not a prerequisite* for loans, but rather *their consequence*. The very process of extending loans is merely an accounting operation in the banking sector; as shown above, banks create additional purchasing power out of nothing as long as there is demand for credit on the part of trustworthy economic agents with collateral.

It should be noted that in the model presented, the role of the interest rate imposed by banks on deposits is limited, but it does influence the distribution of household savings into liquid deposits, M_H, and illiquid financial assets, F_H, depending on the relative magnitudes of the interest rate and the yield on securities. In this sense, the interest rate is exogenous with respect to the endogenous volume of money.

The most important conclusions from the above argument concern company debt in a money economy. At the end of the monetary circuit, companies cannot receive more money than they spent at the beginning. However, they often receive less if households increase their bank deposits. This means that the production sector is permanently indebted and that its debt increases unless household deposits are reduced. This also implies that the working capital of companies is part of their debt, because it cannot be raised otherwise. This also explains the assumption that in the model under consideration companies operate without their own working capital from the very beginning.[6] Companies' debt to the banking sector should be offset with investment-generated continuous growth of their fixed assets, thanks to which they remain reliable debtors.

---

[6] Let us imagine that at the beginning of a production cycle companies own sufficient working capital, amounting to $Q_1 + Q_2$. Following our analysis, if households save $M_H = S_H - F_H$ in the form of deposits (where F_H is the volume of household savings kept in financial assets purchased from the real economy sector, and M_H is the increase in the volume of money at the end of the examined monetary circuit, see p. 129), then at the end of the production cycle companies taken collectively will find that their working capital has diminished by M_H. Therefore, in the next production cycle the volume of output will be smaller than in the previous one, unless the banking sector starts creating money *ex nihilo*.

In reality, the processes discussed above are not synchronized with one another: when some companies commence the monetary circuit, others are in the process of continuing it, while still others are finishing. Households do not spend or save money in a concerted fashion, either. When some loans are being paid off, others are being granted. Companies take out both working capital loans and investment loans, and the Lavoie model makes it possible to comprehend the generally obscure relationships between economic events and their motivations and to reveal their significant characteristics with a focus on the endogenous nature of money and the independence of credit from savings.

These characteristics are also useful for a better understanding of Kalecki's famous thesis that investment finances itself. Remembering that Q_1 and Q_2 represent credit income spent on consumption and investment respectively, and S_H represents household saving, the consumer goods market analyzed in the model can be given by the following equation:

$$Q_1 + Q_2 - S_H = Q_2 + R_2,$$

with the left and right sides representing demand and supply in that market, respectively. By eliminating the term Q_2 on both sides, we obtain the previously introduced formula defining R_2, or profits in subsector 2:

$$R_2 = Q_1 - S_H \tag{7.2}$$

This equation represents the fundamental condition of internal consistency between the consumer and investment goods subsectors. The left side of (7.2) is the surplus of the consumer goods subsector (which cannot be sold within subsector 2), while the right side represents the external demand for that surplus.[7]

Profits in subsector 1, denoted as R_1, are equal to company spending on investment goods, IP, less household incomes from that sector, Q_1:

$$R_1 = IP - Q_1 \tag{7.3}$$

According to (7.2) and (7.3), the sum of profits in both subsectors amounts to:

$$R = R_1 + R_2$$
$$R = IP - S_H \tag{7.4}$$

The formula (7.4) is of paramount importance to an understanding of the relationship between investment and household savings. If we take into account the inevitable delay between investment decisions (actual investment plans) and investment itself, then IP is essentially given in the short term.

---

[7] Obviously, this is the same condition that was stipulated when household income was defined as consisting only of wages (see, e.g., pp. 34–5).

Consequently, at a given volume of investment, profits, R (understood here as internal savings of companies), decreases with increasing savings, S_H. It should also be noted that R represents gross profits in the sense that they are inclusive of depreciation; at given depreciation every increase in S_H reduces the net profits of the production sector, thus undermining the fundamental motivation of business activity in the capitalist economy. From the macroeconomic perspective, household savings hinder growth exactly because they decrease profits at a given volume of investment. However, from the standpoint of households, the situation is quite different. As the future is uncertain and unpredictable, saving makes perfect sense and is inevitable, also in the long term as workers strive to provide for their old age. These conflicting perspectives on household savings constitute a dilemma which should be taken into account by economic policymakers. Mainstream economics evades this problem by adopting the untenable assumption that household savings finance the investment expenditures of companies, whether directly or indirectly (through banks).

Figure 7.1, borrowed from Lavoie (1992), illustrates the financial aspects of the relationship between the two production subsectors. The two identical rectangles at the top, denoted as Q_2, represent household incomes in subsector 2. The two identical rectangles at the bottom, denoted as R_1, represent profits in subsector 1. The middle rectangle on the left-hand side shows household incomes from subsector 1, Q_1. The corresponding middle rectangle on the right-hand side (the sum $R_2 + S_H$) also amounts to Q_1. Indeed, as $R_2 = Q_1 - S_H$, then $R_2 + S_H = Q_1$. The formula $Q_1 = R_2$ graphically represents equality between the demand for consumer goods from subsector 2 (Q_1) and the surplus of consumer goods in subsector 2 (R_2) in the absence of household savings.

Naturally, the discussion of the monetary circuit involves nominal values. Hence, the volume of consumption, $CP = p_C x_C$, is the product of the price of

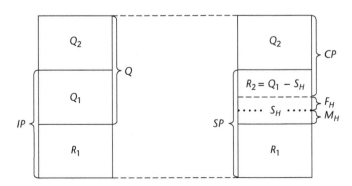

Figure 7.1. Profits and investment in a two-sector model
Source: See Lavoie (1992: 158).

the basket of consumer goods, p_C, and the quantity of those baskets, x_C. In turn, the volume of private investment, $IP = p_I x_I$, is the product of the price of the basket of investment goods, p_I, and the number of those baskets x_I. It should be stressed that the amount of realized profits depends on whether the produced goods were actually sold and at what prices. However, this mostly concerns consumer goods, since investment goods are mostly made to order at predefined prices. Thus, the profits realized in subsector 2 will suffer if some of the goods remain unsold or are sold at lower prices than expected. Nevertheless, irrespective of whether companies' expectations are met or not, according to Kalecki investment finances itself. "[T]he profits, to put it paradoxically, are invested even before they come into being. Profits that are not invested cannot be retained, because they are annihilated by the ensuing fall in production and prices."[8]

A similar summary is given by Lavoie: "Circuit theory demonstrates that savings play no role when production starts off at the beginning of the period, while sufficient savings are always forthcoming at the end of the period, without any necessary adjustment in interest rates. The causal elements are rather the production plans of firms and the bank loans which make these production plans possible and effective. Within this vision, the investment plans of firms are the causal element."[9]

7.2.2 The Monetary Circuit Model Incorporating the Central Bank

Our model can now be extended to incorporate a fourth element, that is, the central bank, CB. As we know, nowadays this institution has a monopoly on the emission of banknotes, known as base money, high-powered money, or cash, which constitute the legal tender used for settling all monetary obligations. This paper money derives its value from the government, whose revenues (taxes) and expenditures are disregarded for the time being. The inclusion of CB in our model has two consequences. First, at any point in time households can demand their deposits from commercial banks in cash, and so the banks have to hold sufficient reserves to meet such demands on pain of losing the confidence of their clients. Second, CB imposes on commercial banks the obligation to maintain required reserves at CB, amounting to a certain small percentage of deposits, λ_R.

Commercial banks can meet the reserve requirements only by borrowing from CB, since base money is created exclusively by the latter. As we temporarily disregard the existence of government securities, commercial banks can offer commercial securities (e.g., private bonds) in the way of collateral.

---

[8] Kalecki (1935 [1990]: 191). [9] Lavoie (1992: 160).

Required reserves are available at the so-called discount window of the central bank. Commercial banks' demand for cash can be defined as $\lambda_H M_H$, where λ_H denotes the percentage of cash held by households plus reserve requirements equal to $\lambda_R(1 - \lambda_H)M_H$. Thus, total credit extended by CB to commercial banks amounts to $\lambda_H M_H + \lambda_R(1 - \lambda_H)M_H$; this sum will be found as a liability in the balance sheet of commercial banks and as an asset in the balance sheet of CB (see Table 7.7).

Continuing the previous numerical example, let us assume that the volume of cash in households is 50 percent of their money resources of 200 euros, which amounts to 100 euros ($\lambda_H = 0.5$). As a result, household deposits in commercial banks decrease from 200 to 100 euros. In addition, let us assume that the required reserve rate is 10 percent ($\lambda_R = 0.1$). Now the assets of commercial banks include company debt, 200 euros, plus required reserves (calculated relative to household deposits), 10 euros, adding up to a total of 210 euros. The liabilities of the banks consist of household deposits, 100 euros, plus credit from BC, 110 euros, again adding up to 210 euros.

The situation presented in Table 7.7 means that companies borrow from commercial banks, while commercial banks borrow from the central bank; this was aptly labeled by Hicks an "overdraft economy" (Hicks 1974: 54). In this model, commercial banks continue to create credit for trustworthy companies, but are to some extent constrained in their activity by the reserve requirements, which they cannot generate on their own. To obtain them, they are forced to adjust the structure of their financial portfolios by decreasing the proportion of securities (used as collateral for CB credit) and increasing the proportion of cash (borrowed from CB). Given that the above conditions are met, commercial banks can continue to create credit for companies and CB

Table 7.7. Balance sheet of commercial banks and the central bank

Balance sheet of commercial banks	
Assets	Liabilities
Loans extended to companies: M_H	Deposits from households: $(1 - \lambda_H)M_H$
Reserves: $\lambda_R(1 - \lambda_H)M_H$	Loans from CB: $\lambda_R(1 - \lambda_H)M_H + \lambda_H M_H$

Balance sheet of the central bank	
Assets	Liabilities
Loans extended to commercial banks: $\lambda_R(1 - \lambda_H)M_H + \lambda_H M_H$	Deposits from commercial banks: $\lambda_R(1 - \lambda_H)M_H$
	Cash in households: $\lambda_H M_H$

has no control over the volume of reserve requirements. Indeed, at a given required reserve rate and assuming that commercial banks are solvent, CB cannot refuse to extend the loans necessary to cover the reserves, as CB is their sole source.

Although it is CB that sets the required reserve rate, it does not control the volume of reserves because commercial banks can extend loans on their own discretion and CB has to adjust reserves to a given credit supply (and not vice versa) if it wants to keep the rate of interest stable. However, CB can determine the price at which reserves are available for commercial banks by setting the discount rate to best address both economic and political goals. The major economic factors include the inflation rate, the national balance of payments, as well as, implicitly or explicitly, the country's overall economic situation and unemployment. Indeed, the discount rate is the most critical factor determining the interest on commercial loans and bank deposits.

It should also be noted that daily interbank transactions usually give rise to some surpluses or deficits. At the end of the day, banks specialized in working with firms (F Banks) will find that the volume of deposits they hold is smaller than the volume of the loans they have extended, which means that they are indebted to banks servicing households (H Banks). Similarly, by the end of the day, H Banks will find their deposits to be higher than loans, implying that they owe money to F Banks. These disproportions give rise to the interbank market, in which commercial banks exchange their surpluses and deficits on a daily basis.

However, the banks need to find an interest rate that would be attractive to both groups of banks, which is known as the interbank interest rate. It is somewhere in between the low interest rate that H Banks pay to their depositors and the high interest rate demanded by F Banks from their debtors, and is strongly influenced by the CB discount rate.

Crucially, the "overdraft economy" model clearly shows that CB does not have the monetary policy instruments necessary to adjust the volume of money in circulation. The reserve requirements imposed on commercial banks imply that the latter have the right to obtain the cash reserves needed to meet them since they are not allowed to create it themselves. This means that CB must unconditionally satisfy the borrowing needs of creditworthy commercial banks that can supply sufficient collateral in the form of securities. Under the circumstances, similarly as in the basic model, the essential elements are the companies' credit needs and the creation of that credit *ex nihilo* by commercial banks. Commercial banks' borrowing from the central bank constitutes the starting point of the monetary circuit. The volume of money generated at the end of that circuit, M_H, represents both company debt and household savings, S_H, whether in the form of deposits held at commercial banks, $(1 - \lambda_H)M_H$, or in the form of cash directly held by households,

$\lambda_H M_H$. Thus, the amount of money, M_H, is a residual from the primary flow of bank loans. The role of the CB discount rate, affecting all other interest rates, is significant, but limited. First, it is one of the factors that have an indirect influence on companies' initial demand for loans (especially of the investment type). Second, it may modify the structure of the financial portfolios held by households, that is, the ratio of cash to private securities. However, in this model CB cannot control money supply by adjusting the discount rate or reserve requirements. This conclusion remains valid also in a more complex model incorporating the government budget.

7.2.3 The Monetary Circuit in the Model with Government

Finally, let us introduce to our model the government and its budget. Nowadays, government spending typically accounts for more than a third of national income (or more than a fourth if money transfers are disregarded). Therefore, without it analysis of the monetary circuit would be incomplete even if budgets were as a rule balanced. However, governments usually run a budget deficit, which is macroeconomically justified as an instrument filling the gap in total demand and helping attain a desirable employment level (see section 5.4 above).

Furthermore, a budget deficit is also useful from the standpoint of the financial sphere. Of particular importance among financial assets are government bonds with different maturities. Commercial banks tend to invest their financial surpluses in these bonds even if the interest rate they carry is lower than that of other securities, since government obligations are regarded as a perfectly safe investment. They offer their owners a firm ground in a murky field of financial dealings, especially of speculative type. Government bonds also constitute an important element of CB operations in the open market aimed at influencing short-term interest rates in the interbank market. In the absence of a budget deficit (or in the presence of a budget surplus), this element would be increasingly missed in the relative sense (with respect to other financial assets) or even in the absolute sense if public debt were to be eliminated altogether.

Let us now consider the conclusions that follow from the theory of the monetary circuit for a situation in which the government runs a budget deficit, D, but is not allowed to borrow directly from the central bank. If we disregard companies and households for the sake of simplicity, in the closed economy model the government can borrow only from commercial banks, similarly as the previously discussed production sector. The only difference is that the government does not take out loans, but sells bonds, which the banks purchase as assets and pay for them by creating the government's deposits as liabilities. Also here commercial banks create money *ex nihilo*, this time for the government.

The government can dispose of these deposits in accordance to its spending schedule. To make things simpler, let us assume that all government expenditures are disbursed directly to households in the form of unemployment benefits. Thus, at the beginning of the monetary circuit, the deposits of households include not only the previously defined sum $Q_1 + Q_2$, but also the amount of the budget deficit, D, and so after subtracting their saving, S_H, households hold the amount $Q_1 + Q_2 + D - S_H$, to be spent on consumer goods in subsector 2. After it is expended, this sum will appear on the deposit accounts of companies, and so at the end of the monetary circuit the debt of companies will amount to $(Q_1 + Q_2) - (Q_1 + Q_2 + D - S_H) = S_H - D$.[10] After households purchase company securities, F_H, this debt will decrease to $S_H - F_H - D$ and $M_H - D$ if we recognize that the volume of money at the end of the monetary circuit, M_H, corresponds to the difference $S_H - F_H$.

The balance sheet of commercial banks towards the end of the monetary circuit (disregarding banknotes) can be represented using a scheme similar to Table 7.7, with now a major difference. In the previous case, households' deposits were offset with loans to companies, while now they are offset with both loans to companies and government bonds. The basic question arises as to whether the purchase of government bonds hinders the commercial banks' capacity to lend to companies (whether the latter is squeezed out by the former)? This is certainly not so as in both cases commercial banks create money *ex nihilo* (see Table 7.8).

This conclusion is corroborated by analysis of profits in both subsectors. Those in the production of consumption goods in subsector 2 are equal to the difference between sales and costs, and amount to:

$$R_2 = (Q_1 + Q_2 + D - S_H) - Q_2 = Q_1 + D - S_H \qquad (7.5)$$

A comparison of this formula with (7.2) shows that in the case of a budget deficit, profits, R_2, would remain unchanged relative to a balanced budget only if $\Delta S_H > 0$ equaled $\Delta D > 0$. Lavoie rightly observes that such a situation is

Table 7.8. Balance sheet of commercial banks

Assets	Liabilities
Company debt: $M_H - D$ Government bonds: D	Deposits from households: M_H

[10] It is assumed that $S_H > D$; this assumption is empirically justified since S_H typically accounts for approximately 10 percent of GDP, while D can reach such a magnitude only exceptionally.

implied by the 'Ricardo equivalence' proposition, that households increase their savings in step with the budget deficit.[11] However, this has not been reflected either in the behavior of households, most of which do not have any information about the current budget deficit, or in empirical data. Consequently, the budget deficit increases profits in subsector 2, and, taking (7.3) into consideration, also the sum of profits of the two subsectors:

$$R = R_1 + R_2 = IP + D - S_H \qquad (7.6)$$

The rise in revenues triggered by the budget deficit, which was previously discussed (see pp. 58–60) implies that the budget deficit does not squeeze out investment. On the contrary, the budget deficit reduces the investment-related increase of company debt. This is in fact inevitable: when the government runs a deficit, then, in the absence of the foreign sector, the private sector has to exhibit a surplus.

In the last step of our analysis, let us account for the cash kept by households and the government bonds held by commercial banks. Once again taking Table 7.8 as a point of departure, we now recognize that households keep some of their monetary resources, M_H in the form of cash (λ_H). In terms of liabilities, this results in a reduction of household deposits by $\lambda_H M_H$, which is represented as the entry $(1 - \lambda_H)M_H$ in the commercial bank balance sheet in Table 7.9.

Furthermore, the portfolios of commercial banks contain some government bonds which fall in the category of excess reserves. Due to these assets, the

Table 7.9. Balance sheets of commercial banks and the central bank incorporating government bonds

Balance sheet of commercial banks	
Assets	Liabilities
Company debt: $M_H - D$	Deposits from households: $(1 - \lambda_H)M_H$
Government bonds: $D - \lambda_R(1 - \lambda_H)M_H + \lambda_R M_H$	
Reserves: $\lambda_R(1 - \lambda_H)M_H$	

Balance sheet of the central bank	
Assets	Liabilities
Government bonds: $\lambda_R(1 - \lambda_H)M_H + \lambda_H M_H$	Deposits from commercial banks: $\lambda_R(1 - \lambda_H)M_H$
	Cash held by households: $\lambda_H M_H$

[11] See Lavoie (1992: 167).

banks do not necessarily have to borrow from the central bank when they need base money; instead, they can obtain it by selling those bonds to CB. It should be borne in mind that commercial banks' demand for base money consists of two elements: required reserves calculated in proportion to household deposits, $\lambda_R(1 - \lambda_H)M_H$, and cash held by households, $\lambda_H M_H$. The total demand for base money from commercial banks is $\lambda_R(1 - \lambda_H)M_H + \lambda_H M_H$, and they obtain it by selling government bonds amounting to that sum. In Table 7.9, the entry "Government bonds" is given with a negative sign as the stock of government bonds is reduced by this amount, while the presence of deficit, D, means an increase in their stock. As far as the central bank's balance sheet is concerned, the only difference with respect to Table 7.7 is that the entry "Loans extended to commercial banks" has been replaced with "Government bonds."

Consequently, the conclusions previously drawn remain valid. Money is created by commercial banks in line with demand for credit on the part of creditworthy companies. In commercial banks, deposits are used as the main medium of payment in transactions between companies as well as between companies and households. Some of these deposits are held in the form of banknotes as required reserves. These reserves, as well as the cash held by households, must be provided by the central bank. There are two basic ways of supplying the economy with banknotes, or base money. The first one involves the operations of the central bank in the open market, when it purchases or sells government bonds with different maturities; in this case it is the central bank that is the active agent. The other one consists of the central bank's discount window used by commercial banks to borrow base money against government bonds (here, initiative rests with commercial banks). The central bank cannot refuse to supply base money to commercial banks, but it can and does set the discount rate on the money it lends. As a result, the central bank controls the interest rate, but not the volume of money in circulation, the latter being a residual value rather than a goal adopted by the central bank.

7.3 The Supply of Endogenous and Exogenous Money: The Horizontalists and the Verticalists

The discussion concerning endogenous money may be summarized as follows: Companies apply for loans from commercial banks pursuant to their production and sales plans. Their demand for credit creates debt, whose volume more or less corresponds to the monetary income flow. Households decide how to divide their portfolios between securities, deposits, and cash. The central bank has to ensure an adequate supply of base money (banknotes) at an interest rate it sets itself. Under these circumstances, the money supply is

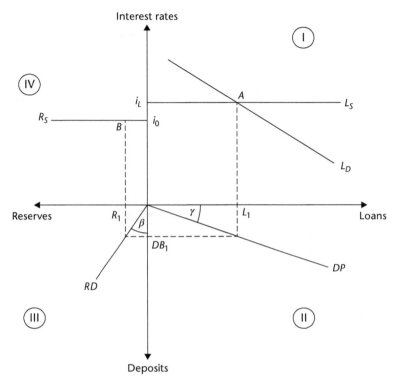

Interest rates

Figure 7.2. Scheme of endogenous money supply

endogenous in the sense that it is determined by demand for money, which in turn depends on the volume of output, prices, and interest rates.

Since money is a credit-based phenomenon with loans giving rise to bank deposits and deposits to reserves, demand for money and money supply are interdependent. The controlling instrument of the central bank is not the volume of money but rather the discount rate. These relationships are shown in graphical form in Figure 7.2.

Quadrant I represents the process of extending loans to companies (or households) by commercial banks, which is the initial step in the monetary circuit. The banks are ready to grant loans to creditworthy clients at a nominal interest rate, i_L, which is determined by a percentage mark-up, m, on the central bank's discount rate, i_0:

$$i_L = (1+m)i_0 \tag{7.7}$$

Thus, the segment AL_S represents a perfectly elastic supply of credit, which runs at a distance of i_L from the horizontal axis. Demand for credit corresponds to the segment AL_D and is usually a decreasing function of the interest rate, i_L. L_1, the abscissa of point A, represents the volume of loans extended at that interest rate. The position of the segment AL_D depends on the expectations of companies: if they are optimistic about sales prospects, L_D moves to the right together with point A. Then, the resulting higher demand for credit will be met by the increased volume of money at a given interest rate, i_L.

Quadrants II and III show the two processes that follow the granting of loans amounting to L_1. In quadrant II, loans, which are recognized as bank assets, generate deposits, which are the liabilities of banks towards their clients. Assuming a preference for debtor liquidity, expressed by the slope of the radius, DP, loans amounting to L_1 give rise to bank deposits amounting to DB_1.

Quadrant III illustrates the demand of commercial banks for money reserves (base money), which those banks need in order to satisfy the cash demands of the owners of deposits. The minimum level of money reserves is usually set by the central bank. Since the reserve requirements (the ratio of reserves, R, to deposits, DB) are reflected by the slope of radius RD, deposits DB_1 are accompanied at least by reserves R_1, with $(R_1/DB_1) = \tan \beta$ being the required reserve rate.

Finally, quadrant IV shows the process in which CB supplies commercial banks with the necessary reserves. The segment R_S is the reserve supply curve. This supply is perfectly elastic because at a given interest rate, i_0, the central bank has to meet every demand of solvent commercial banks. This is necessary to prevent a bank run that might otherwise ensue and spread to the entire system if any of the banks were found to be illiquid. The very fact that the central bank is a lender of last resort prevents speculation against the limited liquidity of individual banks. In the case under consideration, point B indicates that commercial banks meet the minimum reserve requirements, R_1, at an interest rate i_0.

The proponents of the endogenous theory of money are called "horizontalists" as the line representing money supply in Figure 7.2. is horizontal.[12] In turn, the advocates of the orthodox theory of exogenous money are called "verticalists" as their model of money supply is represented by a vertical money supply line. The proponents of the orthodox theory assume that the amount of credit extended by the banking system depends on the reserves controlled by the central bank, as shown by the following equation:

$$M = h_m H \tag{7.8}$$

where M is still the volume of money in circulation, while h_m and H stand for the money multiplier and the supply of base money, respectively. In terms of causality, this equation should be read from right to left: H is the independent variable controlled by the central bank, while M is the dependent variable

---

[12] The distinction between "horizontalists" and "verticalists" was made by Moore (1988); see also Palley (2013).

at a more or less constant money multiplier, h_m (with a corresponding required reserve rate $1/h_m = H/M$). If the money multiplier, h_m, is 4, then the required reserve rate is $(1/h_m) = \frac{1}{4} = 25$ percent, and vice versa.

When a bank holds reserves amounting to, e.g., 1000 euros, then it can extend a loan of 750 euros and the remaining 250 euros must be retained in the form of required reserves. This loan of 750 euros will sooner or later become deposited with another bank and enable a further loan of 0.75 (750) = 562.5 euros, with 107.5 euros again retained due to the reserve requirements. The geometric series of loans:

$$750 \quad 562.5 \quad 421.8 \quad 316.4 \quad 237.3 \quad 177.9 \quad 133.4\dots$$

quickly decreases, with its sum tending to a limit of $750(4) = 3,000$ euros. At the same time, the series of the required reserves:

$$250 \quad 187.5 \quad 140.6 \quad 105.4 \quad 79.1 \quad 59.3 \quad 44.5\dots$$

decreases at a corresponding rate, with its sum tending to a limit of $250(1/4) = 1,000$ euros. In this way, an initial rise in the monetary base by 1,000 euros leads to a rise in the volume of money in circulation by 4,000 euros, including a 3,000-euro increase in lending and a 1,000-euro increase in required reserves. Of critical importance to this process are the tacit assumptions that there are always some creditworthy companies willing to take out loans, and that banking activity is in fact constrained by insufficient reserves.

In Figure 7.3, the segment $0A$ represents the stock of banknotes H, and $0B$ the volume of money in circulation, $M = h_m H$. Indeed, $\tan \beta = 0A/0B = H/M = (1/h_m)$, where $(1/h_m)$ stands for the ratio of the monetary base to the volume of money (the required reserve rate). As a result, money supply M is represented by the vertical segment BC, derived from the monetary base

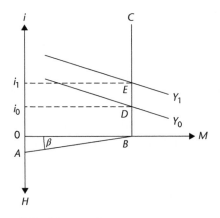

Figure 7.3. Scheme of exogenous money supply

$H = A0$, controlled by the central bank. This theory is explicitly or implicitly linked to the older 'currency' tradition in which the central bank can control the monetary base and money circulation through the gold reserves it holds.

In the traditional Keynesian approach, it is assumed that in addition to the transaction demand for money linked to the volume of national income, there also exists some speculation-driven demand. Speculative cash balances do not bring an income: the higher the interest rate, the higher the costs of maintaining them. Thus, the volume of speculative cash is a decreasing function of the interest rate. As a result, at a given volume of money supply ($M = OB$), the ratio of transaction to speculative cash will increase when the interest rate rises, e.g., from i_0 to i_1. In other words, a given volume of money can be used to service a greater number of transactions, as required by a larger national income, $Y_1 > Y_0$. Thus, Figure 7.3 explains why higher output and employment volumes imply a higher interest rate. These are the main inferences drawn from analysis of the traditional *LM* curve.

7.4 Central Bank Policy

In the 1960s, monetarism became the dominant element of mainstream economics with the two central theses: 1) the money supply can and should be controlled by the central bank and 2) monetary policy, in contrast to fiscal policy, is the only effective component of macroeconomic policy. Pursuant to the first tenet, Milton Friedman claimed that to maintain economic stability central banks should be guided by a simple rule: the money supply should be increased at a constant rate, with the exact magnitude of that rate being of secondary importance. In the 1970s some central banks made efforts to implement this rule, but it turned out to be impracticable, leading to increased volatility of interest rates. As a result, central banks embraced the discount rate in the belief that it can be used to control money supply, even if indirectly. Central banks and mainstream economics also continue to profess the superiority of monetary policy over fiscal policy.

The endogenous money approach developed in opposition to monetarism both in the sense of macroeconomic theory and monetary policy guidelines. In recent years, monetary policies have been largely based on the so-called Taylor rule, founded on the belief in the existence of an equilibrium interest rate. At that rate, the inflation target would be attained at optimum utilization of the production capacity with a non-accelerating inflation rate of unemployment (NAIRU), i.e., a rate below which inflation does not rise. When inflation is above the target, production capacity is thought to be overutilized (aggregate demand is purportedly too high) as the unemployment rate is lower than NAIRU. In this situation, central banks are advised to raise their discount rates in order to lower production capacity utilization (to reduce the "excessive" aggregate demand) by bringing the real unemployment rate closer to NAIRU. Once again, this approach is grounded in the assumption that there exists a natural equilibrium interest rate at which savings and investment are brought into balance at a national income corresponding to optimum utilization of production capacity and workforce after accounting for "natural unemployment."

Obviously, the above is inconsistent with the theory of effective demand. High levels of employment and production capacity utilization at a moderate inflation rate require an explicit policy of demand management, and cannot be attained merely by the operation of market forces augmented with the central bank's decisions based on the Taylor rule. As our lectures have shown, such objectives can be achieved only by concerted efforts involving monetary, fiscal, and wage policies. Within the fiscal policy framework, the total demand gap, which is characteristic of the capitalist economy, should be filled in by means of an adequate tax system and the necessary budget deficit, increasing the utilization of production potential and employment levels. In turn, wage policy should ensure that real wages increase in step with productivity, and especially that the average nominal wage increases in step with productivity plus the inflation target. Such a wage policy calls for cooperation between strong trade unions and strong associations of employers and should lead to a moderate increase in prices corresponding to the inflation target without any cynical disempowerment of employees by creating an army of unemployed workers (known as NAIRU in mainstream economics and as the reserve army of labor in Marxism).

Under the circumstances, the role of monetary policy and central banks is very important, but limited. Of essence is their influence on private investment and currency exchange rates. The relationship between interest rate policy and the exchange rates, and the need for international cooperation in this respect has already been discussed and is not reiterated here (see pp. 108–110). As far as private investment is concerned, what is critical is the availability of credit whenever it is needed as a result of satisfactory utilization of production factors or due to innovations.

One should also bear in mind that the effectiveness of monetary policy varies depending on whether it is used to stimulate or inhibit investment activity. When the goal is to curtail excessive demand, e.g., with a view to improving the country's balance of payments, an appropriate increase in the interest rate should be effective. On the other hand, when demand is insufficient, interest rate cuts will not encourage new investment if the existing production stock is already underutilized. While pulling the reins may stop a galloping horse, slackening those reins will not make the horse run again if it does not want to.

Finally, it should be noted that central banks can use some quantitative restraints when interest rate adjustment is insufficient. Credit rationing may be particularly useful in the face of speculation bubbles. For instance, minimum down payment requirements may be set for mortgage loans to prevent banks from recklessly fueling housing speculation.

On the other hand, there are some doubts as to whether the central bank should be responsible for the inflation rate and for meeting the inflation target, which is in itself a very useful and, indeed, indispensable instrument. However, it seems that it should be set by the government in consultation with employers and workers. Indeed, except for periods of hyperinflation, inflation is not a monetary phenomenon, but is rather closely linked to changes in unit labor costs. As a result, the fight against inflation, or rather the efforts to contain it within desirable limits, should be conducted in the field in which the main determinants of unit labor costs are decided. Ideally, this should involve central bargaining between strong and responsible nationwide trade unions and employer associations in line with the golden wage rule, according to which the average nominal wage rate follows the real increase in productivity (accounting for changes in terms of trade) plus the inflation target.

Arguably the inflation target should be set somewhere between 2 – 3 percent annually and accompanied by measures preventing prices from rising above or below the target. The dangers of accelerating inflation are obvious, especially if it becomes a bargaining element in negotiating nominal wage growth. However, excessively low inflation is also risky and may lead to deflation. When prices decline, the business outlook is poor at least for two reasons. In the capitalist economy, companies are as a rule indebted (as are the majority of households). As loans and interests are by necessity expressed in nominal terms, then declining prices increase the debt burden. The other factor is postponing purchases: if a price decrease is expected, then people will delay buying major consumer goods, thus increasing the deflationary recession pressure.

It should be noted that deflation may occur even before inflation reaches zero. Let us imagine that the economy exhibits a high unemployment rate and the central bank is ready to institute temporarily a negative real discount rate to stimulate economic activity, and especially private investment. As the real interest rate is the difference between the nominal rate (which is, or at least should be, non-negative) and the inflation rate, then at an inflation rate of 3 percent, the central bank can obtain a real interest rate of, e.g., -1 percent (at a nominal interest rate of 2 percent) or -2 percent (at a nominal interest rate of 1 percent). Under the same assumptions, at an inflation rate of 2 percent and a nominal interest rate of 1 percent, the real interest rate will be -1 percent.

Entrusting the central bank with attaining the inflation target results in an unemployment rate that disempowers the trade unions in their struggle to maintain a share of wages in national income that would be, even remotely, consistent with the golden wage rule. This not only threatens social cohesion, but also does macroeconomic harm by undermining domestic demand and perpetuating or aggravating unemployment. Indeed, the central bank should be co-responsible for meeting the inflation target only if the government, pursuing a clearly defined fiscal policy and in consultation with social partners, is unable to arrive at a solution satisfactory from the standpoint of the overarching social interest.

Last but not least, the central bank should cooperate with the institution responsible for public finance and they both ought to strive for high employment levels. The implications for the government's budget have been discussed elsewhere and there is no need to reiterate them here. However, it is worth stressing that, as a rule, the central bank should make every effort to maintain the interest rates on government bonds below the GDP growth rate. Furthermore, the central bank should act as a lender of last resort, also for the government. The opponents of this view often bring up the argument of moral hazard, which is a major problem concerning the political responsibility of government, and all political decisions in general. Nonetheless, double standards must not be applied in this context. During the financial crisis that began in 2008 many banks were bailed out since their default could have had serious consequences for the entire system (they were considered "too big to fail"). However, those who warn against the moral hazard of the central bank acting as a lender of last resort to the government fail to see the same moral hazard with respect to private banks. Indeed, in both cases a specialized institution should be tasked with mitigating the moral hazard problem involving liquidity guarantees extended to banks as well as the government.

7.5 Commercial and Investment Banks

Business decisions are made in the face of an unknown future, their profitability is by nature uncertain and thus they inevitably contain an element of risk. This in particular pertains to investment decisions. In an economy founded on private property, risk is borne by the capitalists who contribute their own capital and either win or lose. However, as we know from the previous discussion, their capital is generally insufficient and a continuous inflow of credit (with a concomitant increase in company debt) is needed to expand private investment and the capital stock. We also know that this inflow of credit is provided by the banking system. The question then arises as to which companies and with what collateral should credit be granted and which ones do not deserve it? Such decisions are mostly made by commercial banks, which is their basic role in the capitalist economy.

Due to their special role, commercial banks have direct access to the central bank and can meet their financial needs at privileged interest rates. These banks make a profit by setting a higher interest rate on loans than on deposits. However, there is a risk that some debtors will default on their loans and the banks will face losses or even insolvency, as distinct from illiquidity (the latter implies transient difficulties in meeting the current demand for cash withdrawals and may occur when the bank's financial standing is stable, but the prices of the securities it holds have dropped, perhaps temporarily, so that the bank is reluctant to sell them).

The illiquidity risk is linked to high leverage in the banking system. A bank's own capital typically finances approximately 5 percent of its assets only, which means that the remaining 95 percent of its assets is financed by the bank's other liabilities. This is so because banks often finance their assets by borrowing from each other. Such a high degree of leverage would not be possible without special safeguards, including access to the central bank's money and the government's guarantee of deposits (up to a certain threshold). With these safeguards in place, a bank run, which could ruin any financial system, is unlikely to occur, and, if it does, can be quickly contained.

The access of commercial banks to base money from the central bank at privileged interest rates is justified by the special role they play in the market mechanism. However, there is no justification for conferring the same privilege on investment banks, which, contrary to what their name implies, do not finance real investment, but conduct speculation-oriented financial operations often conflicting with the social interest. In the case of speculation, as in any other game of chance, it is the speculator who should be liable for his losses. However, those investment banks that have direct access to the central bank enjoy all the privileges, while the costs of their failures are often borne by the taxpayers in the event of a crisis. This means the privatization of gains from financial speculation and the socialization of losses. For many years following the Great Depression of the 1930s, a strict distinction between commercial and investment banks was maintained for the benefit of the entire economy. Unfortunately, over time this approach was gradually undermined, which largely contributed to the outbreak of the world's financial crisis in 2008. The distinction between commercial and investment banking has yet to be fully restored.

8

Economic growth and the growth of effective demand

8.1 Introduction

Previous chapters essentially assumed constant production capacity. While we did take into account investment, and, implicitly, also its production aspect in the form of increases in the capital stock, in the short run its effect on production capacity was treated as negligible, especially since that capacity was presumed to be underutilized. However, analysis of economic growth no longer permits such an approach. Investment is a necessary element of economic growth and its fundamental prerequisite. Indeed, in the presence of an adequately skilled workforce and a sufficient supply of raw materials and energy, it is investment that enables GDP and employment growth. However, this growth is only potential and for it to materialize effective demand has to expand in step with production capacity. Therefore, the issue of effective demand is of utmost importance also in the theory of growth of the capitalist economy. In contrast, the orthodox theory disregards this problem, assuming that if it exists at all, it only affects cyclical fluctuations, while long-term economic growth depends solely on supply-side factors. As we shall see, this leads to grave errors in economic research and policymaking, and also in economic education.

The supply-side elements of the model presented in this chapter are known in Poland from Michał Kalecki's works on the theory of growth of the socialist economy. That theory ignored total demand, which is irrelevant in a centrally planned economy (but crucial to the capitalist one). Indeed, in an economy characterized by a seller's market, a scarcity of goods, long lines of shoppers, and an insufficient workforce, total demand never fell short, so it was consciously disregarded by Kalecki. Due to the fundamental differences between capitalist and command economies, the model needs to be modified to make it adequate for the former.

8.2 General Growth Model

We assume after Steindl (1979, 1990: 108–14) that real GDP, denoted as Y, accounts for a certain proportion of maximum production capacity Y^*:

$$Y = uY^*, \quad Y \leq Y^*, \tag{8.1}$$

where the coefficient u ($0 < u \leq 1$) stands for the degree of utilization of that capacity. Hence:

$$\Delta Y = u\Delta Y^* + Y^*\Delta u. \tag{8.2}$$

The gross private investment necessary to expand production capacity by ΔY^* amounts to:

$$IP = v\Delta Y^* + \delta vY^*, \tag{8.3}$$

where v is a constant, technologically determined ratio of capital to production capacity (i.e., the capital-output ratio), while δ is the rate of depreciation expressed as the proportion of the productive capital stock, vY^* that is needed to provide only for the replacement of the oldest equipment actually retired in a given year.[1] From (8.3), we obtain:

$$\Delta Y^* = \frac{IP}{v} - \delta Y^* \tag{8.3'}$$

and substituting ΔY^* from (8.3') in (8.2), we arrive at:

$$\Delta Y = u\frac{IP}{v} - u\delta Y^* + Y^*\Delta u$$

If both sides are divided by Y, then:

$$\frac{\Delta Y}{Y} = u\frac{IP}{Y}\frac{1}{v} - u\,\delta\frac{Y^*}{Y} + \Delta\,u\frac{Y^*}{Y}$$

$$\frac{\Delta Y}{Y} = \frac{sp}{v/u} - \delta + \frac{\Delta u}{u} \tag{8.4}$$

because in a closed economy without the government sector it is true *ex post* that private saving, SP, must equal private investment, IP, and so $IP/Y = SP/Y = sp$ (in addition, $Y^*/Y = 1/u$).

Formula (8.4) differs from the Kaleckian equation for the centrally planned economy in that capital intensity, v, is corrected by u, or the degree of utilization of production capacity. Steindl emphasizes, in line with Harrod's theory, that a distinction should be made between the two factors as v is a technologically determined element, while u is dependent on the volume of

---

[1] See Bhaduri (1972).

total demand.[2] The formula $\Delta u/u$ reflects changes in the degree of utilization of production capacity, and its value can be either positive or negative, amplifying or obliterating the effect of the parameter $u(sp/v)$.[3]

8.3 Sustainable Growth and its Instability

In the case of sustainable growth, formula (8.4) is substantially modified by the assumption that u is constant, which eliminates the $(\Delta u/u)$ factor. A major prerequisite for such growth is the alignment of the production and income effects of investment. The production effect arises upon the completion of an investment project, while the income effect persists throughout the period in which investment goods are manufactured and disappears after the project has been completed. To ensure adequate utilization of the implemented investment, new investment projects, of sufficient magnitude, must be commenced.

Let us denote the investment projects carried out in the *previous* period as *IP*. When they are completed and commissioned in a given period, the increment in production capacity, at a constant rate of utilization, u, increases by:

$$\Delta Y = \frac{IP}{v/u} \tag{8.5}$$

if we disregard depreciation of existing production capacity for the sake of clarity. In turn, on the demand side, GDP growth results from the increase of investment *within* a given period. As total demand is determined by $Y = (IP/sp)$, then at a constant sp the increment of total demand amounts to:

$$\Delta Y = \frac{\Delta IP}{sp}. \tag{8.6}$$

The equality of the increase in total supply, derived from (8.5) to total demand, derived from (8.6) leads to:

$$\frac{\Delta IP}{IP} = \frac{sp}{v/u} \tag{8.7}$$

Thus, according to (8.7), sustainable development is possible if investment increases at a pace equal to the ratio of the propensity to save to the capital

---

[2] See Steindl, (1979 [1990]: 109).

[3] It should be noted that the theory of growth of the centrally planned economy also includes a parameter expressing non-investment factors of growth, defined as the coefficient of improvements attributable to progress in organization, worker skills, etc. In Kalecki's equation, this coefficient is represented by a small positive fraction of a constant magnitude. While the factor u depends on effective demand, the Kaleckian coefficient of improvements is determined by organizational advancement, and as such is a supply side factor (see Kalecki, 1970 [1993]: 116).

intensity coefficient corrected for the degree of production capacity utiliz-ation. If, for instance, the propensity to save, $sp = 0.2$, capacity utilization, $u = 0.8$, and the capital-output ratio, $v = 3.2$, then $(v/u) = (3.2/0.8) = 4$.[4] These parameters result in a sustainable growth rate of $[(sp/(v/u)] = 0.2/4 = 0.05$, or 5 percent (disregarding the depreciation of fixed assets). Let the productive capital stock, vY^*, maximum output Y^*, and actual output $Y = uY^*$, and private investment, IP in the period $(t = 1)$ amount to 800, 250, 200, and 40 euros, respectively. These figures are given in Table 8.1, illustrating a sustainable growth example.

In the first part of Table 8.1, all values grow at a rate of 5 percent annually, with total supply and total demand increments being aligned as a result of satisfying condition (8.7): ΔIP is 2 in the period $(t = 1)$, while IP is 40 in the period $(t = 0)$. Their ratio is $(2/40) = 0.05$, or 5 percent, which corresponds to the assumed ratio $[sp/(v/u)] = [0.2/(3.2/0.8)] = (0.2/4) = 0.05$. Consequently, the *production* effect IP in the period $(t = 1)$ emerges in the period $(t = 1)$ as $\Delta Y^* = (40/3.2) = 12.50$. In turn, the *income* effect in this period results from $\Delta IP = 2$ in the period $(t = 1)$ and $sp = 0.2$, due to which $\Delta Y^0 = (2/0.2) = 10$. The income effect ΔY is then equal to the production effect ΔY^* at a constant capital stock utilization rate of $u = 0.8$. Table 8.1 also shows the parameters in question for periods $(t = 2)$ and $(t = 3)$, which are relevant to our subsequent discussion.

The interpretation of Table 8.1 first of all requires an understanding of the way investment decisions are made in Harrod's model, since those

Table 8.1. Numerical example of sustainable growth

Period	vY^*	Y^*	ΔY^*	Y	ΔY	ΔY^e	IP	ΔIP	u
$t = 0$	800	250		200			40		0.8
$t = 1$	840	262.50	12.50	210	10	10	42	2	0.8
$t = 2$	882	275.62	13.125	220.5	10.5	10.5	44.1	2.1	0.8
$t = 3$	926.1	289.40	13.7812	231.52	11.02	11.025	46.30	2.2	0.8
$t = 4$						11.5762			
Variant A									
$t = 2$	882	275.62	13.125	220.5	10.5	10.5	44.1	2.1	0.8
$t = 3$	926.1	289.40	13.7812	220	−0.5	11.025	44	0.1	0.76
$t = 4$						11			
Variant B									
$t = 2$	882	275.625	13.125	220.5	10.5	10.5	44.1	2.1	0.8
$t = 3$	926.1	289.40	13.7812	240	19.5	11.025	48	3.9	0.83
$t = 4$						12			

[4] If technological capital intensity, v, is 3.2, then real capital intensity, (v/u), will equal $(3.2/0.8) = 4$ at a capital stock utilization of 80 percent, $(3.2/0.66) = 4.8$ at a capital stock utilization of 66.6 percent, etc. Real capital intensity at given technological stock increases with decreasing real equipment utilization.

decisions are the fundamental element of any growth model. Let us adopt the perspective of companies in the period $(t = 0)$. Investment projects amounting to $IP = 40$ are in the process of being implemented and will be commissioned at the beginning of the period $(t = 1)$. However, the volume of investment in the period $(t = 1)$ remains an open question because it depends on decisions made in the period $(t = 0)$. According to the accelerator principle, these decisions are meant to prepare production capacity for the expected increase in sales in the period $(t = 2)$. If private investment in the period $(t = 1)$ is denoted as IP_1, and the expected increase in national income in the period $(t = 2)$ as ΔY^e_2, then investment decisions in the period $(t = 0)$ at given (v/u) will amount to $IP_1 = \Delta Y^e_2(v/u)$, which is $42 = 10.5 \times 4$.

Similarly, decisions made in the period $(t = 1)$ concern investment IP_2 (44.1) and are affected by the expected sales growth represented by ΔY^e_3 (11.025) at a capital intensity coefficient of $(v/u) = 4$, etc. If the real increase in national income, ΔY, corresponds to the expected increase, ΔY^e, then companies' expectations will be met and, at the typical capital stock utilization rate, u, they will be able to sell their output. Under the circumstances, they are likely to continue the decision-making process outlined above, ensuring further sustainable growth.

However, economic reality is not free from mistakes, random occurrences, parameter changes, etc. Stability therefore emerges as the basic criterion of explanatory usefulness of any model. Thus, the question arises as to whether in the case of error (e.g., in predicted sales levels) the presented method of investment decision-making will eventually return to the path of sustainable growth, or perhaps progressively deviate from it.

In variant A, in the period $(t = 2)$ companies make investment-related decisions concerning $(t = 3)$, expecting an increase in national income of $\Delta Y^e_4 = 11$ (rather than 11.57625). Accordingly, $IP_3 = 4 \times 11 = 44$ and $Y_3 = (44/sp) = (44/0.2) = 220$. IP decreases by 0.1 relative to $(t = 2)$, and so Y declines by $(0.1/02) = 0.5$. It should be noted that in the period $(t = 3)$ the productive capital stock and production capacity are not affected by investment made in that period, but rather by previous investment; hence, $Y^*_3 = 289.4$ and the degree of production capacity utilization now amounts to $(220/289.4) = 0.76$ (76 percent rather than 80 percent). This result is surprising: since companies were too cautious in their foresight and did not make sufficient investment, the market feedback tells them that their production capacity is excessive as its utilization has declined. Therefore, in the next period they need to estimate the sales increase even more cautiously, which will lead to a further drop in the u coefficient, etc. Thus, the growth rate will increasingly fall short of $g = 0.05$, or 5 percent.

Variant B leads to similar conclusions, but in this case the expected increase in national income is too high: $\Delta Y^e_4 = 12$ (instead of 11.57625), which gives

$IP_3 = 48$ and $Y_3 = 240$, with production potential utilization rising to $(240/289.4) = 0.83$ (from 80 percent to 83 percent). Although the predictions were already too high, they now appear underestimated—in the next period companies should make even bolder predictions and growth will accelerate. As can be seen, a growth model based on a simple combination of the investment multiplier and the accelerator principle is extremely unstable because the slightest deviation from the sustainable course leads either to depression or inflation.[5] That is why, the Harrod growth model has been rightly termed a "razor edge" growth model, which cannot be used reliably to describe and understand real economic dynamics.

8.4 Kalecki's Model of Cyclical Fluctuations

The Kaleckian model of economic dynamics combines analysis of cyclical fluctuations and long-term growth trends. The separate treatment of these two elements of economic dynamics in these lectures, is simpler, although less accurate. Let us begin with a model of business-cycle fluctuations attributable to changes in private investment.

Let us first recall the crucial distinction that Kalecki made between investment decisions and investment itself. Investment cannot be compared to the purchase of consumer goods, routinely made by households, sometimes on impulse. Investment projects are irrevocable undertakings which tie up considerable resources for a long time, and are financed not only with the investors' own capital, but usually also with bank loans. Thus, investment is not made on the spur of the moment, but rather as a result of in-depth studies, analyses, and calculations. Moreover, investment decisions, once made, cannot be implemented immediately; this in particular concerns construction projects, which have to be designed, the site has to be cleared, etc. It also takes some time to purchase and install the necessary equipment and machines, which are often manufactured (or even developed) to order. To reiterate Kalecki's distinction—an investment decision is not an investment. The investment implemented in a given year usually results from decisions made the previous year, while this year's decisions will turn into investment the following year.

The difference between investment and investment decisions is of critical importance also because it reveals the role of time as a factor contributing to

---

[5] Changes in the saving rate would lead to similar effects, e.g., if it increased on a one-off basis, the model would show a constant decrease in output, while if *sp* declined on a one-off basis, the model would show a constant acceleration of output.

economic dynamics.[6] Investment is by nature changeable and unpredictable because no-one knows the future. Thus, it is little wonder that investment fluctuates over time. At times entrepreneurs are more optimistic and ready to take risks, while at other times they tend to be more wary. Furthermore, there is a tendency towards a cumulative movement of investment. Pessimism, like optimism, is contagious; hence, the growth or decline of investment is likely to accelerate rapidly.

As a result, the investment function understood as a formula containing the factors determining investment volume is extremely complex. The adoption of the interest rate as the main, or indeed the only, argument of this function, would be a risky simplification of reality. Obviously, the interest rate does play a role. But of even greater importance is how capitalists perceive the future in terms of sales and profit prospects. For these reasons, the investment function is one of the most difficult elements of economic theory and actually there seems to be no agreement as to its most vital constituents. Nevertheless, one could argue that two factors are particularly critical in decision-making. These are the volume and change of profits and the volume and change of the utilization of productive equipment. The first factor determines the benefits gained or the losses sustained, and the second one shows whether new investment is needed or not. Both are crucial to Kalecki's theory of economic dynamics. They shall be presented in a general manner, first the automatic business cycle and then long-term growth trends (a more formalized presentation of the determinants of investment outlays on fixed capital is given in Appendix 8).

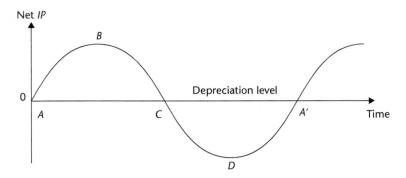

Figure 8.1. Hypothetical curve of investment over time

---

[6] Joan Robinson liked to interpret Bergson suggesting that the only reason for time in economics is so that everything does not happen at once. Unfortunately, many economic discussions disregard the importance of time. In the course of our subsequent lectures this factor shall be shown to play a major role in economic dynamics.

It should be remembered that private investment with its fluctuations is the principal determinant of profits, and thus the driver of the capitalist economy, in which profits invariably remain the prime objective. In turn, profits, at a given distribution between labor and capital, also influence GDP. As a result, fluctuations in investment are accompanied by changes in output and employment. Figure 8.1 presents regular fluctuations of net investment (gross investment less depreciation of fixed capital).

Of greatest interest are points A, B, C, and D. First, let us examine the curve between points A and B, where net investment is positive and increasing. This implies a rise in net profits and fixed capital up to a maximum around point B. In turn, the B–C segment of the curve represents net investment which is still positive, but decreasing, with shrinking net profits. Fixed capital continues to grow, but more and more slowly. In the neighborhood of point C, the volume of fixed capital reaches an equilibrium as investment equals depreciation. In the C–D segment, net investment is negative and decreasing. Net profits are still on the decline, as is fixed capital, because negative net investment implies a level of gross investment that does not offset depreciation. In the neighborhood of point D, net investment and net profits reach a minimum. In the D–A' segment, net investment continues to be negative, but it is increasing, which means that losses in net profits and productive equipment are diminishing. In the neighborhood of point A', net investment equals zero, indicating that the volume of gross investment has reached that of depreciation, and so the fixed capital stock no longer contracts.

Let us analyze in greater detail what is happening at the four critical points of the business cycle. In the neighborhood of point A, the investment curve intersects the depreciation level, which means that at that point gross investment is equal to depreciation and the fixed capital stock remains unchanged. It should be remembered, however, that the curve crosses the abscissa from below, indicating growth of net investment, as well as an increment in profits and output. The (very low) profit rate rises and production capacity utilization (also low) improves. Due to these factors, investment does not remain constant, but intersects point A and moves towards point B.

In the neighborhood of point B, net investment and profits reach the highest levels: it is the maximum of the business cycle with high employment and output on the one hand, and high rates of profit and productive equipment utilization on the other hand. Around point B, investment volume is constant, which means that the increase in investment, profits, and production equals zero, while the fixed capital stock rises rapidly as net investment is very high relative to depreciation. This means that the high profit rate begins to decline in line with productive equipment utilization. Due to these two factors, net investment begins to contract as it has stopped expanding.

This downward movement of net investment continues throughout the segment *B–C*. In the neighborhood of point *C*, net investment reaches zero as the volume of gross investment is only sufficient to offset depreciation. However, net investment and net profits decrease, which implies that the profits-to-fixed capital ratio deteriorates, still pulling investment down. This is also compounded by the shrinking productive potential utilization, as around point *C* output wanes while fixed capital does not change. This process continues up to point *D*.

The bottom of the business cycle occurs in the neighborhood of point *D*: net investment and net profits stabilize at the lowest level. This means that output and employment levels are also very low, but they no longer decrease, in contrast to the fixed capital stock, which still declines as net investment is negative. As a result, the profit rate begins to rebound with improving utilization of the productive equipment. Signs of the growth of profits, output, and employment emerge. Net investment begins to increase as it has stopped contracting. Now, investment and the economy are moving towards point *A'*, initiating a new business cycle.

8.5 Long-term Growth of the Capitalist Economy

The model of business cycle fluctuations presented above alone cannot explain the growth trend, and especially investment in the fixed capital stock, which is the fundamental driver of the capitalist economy. Indeed, in this model gross investment as a whole is equal to depreciation within the business cycle. This is so for two reasons: first, the entire amount of gross savings, equal to gross investment, returns to companies and can be reinvested. Second, at the end of the business cycle, the fixed capital stock is the same as at the beginning since the sum of net investment throughout the cycle is zero. Under the circumstances, random disturbances and shocks may affect the character of the business cycle, and especially the amplitude of fluctuations (constant, explosive, or dampened cycles), but cannot explain the long-term growth trend, in which gross investment exceeds depreciation. This trend is primarily driven by technological progress in the form of *innovation*. On the other hand, it is dampened by savings external to profits, which shall be termed *rentier savings*. Both of these factors were disregarded in the pure business cycle model, since in that model investment motivations included only routine gradual technological developments and profits were identified with internal company savings.

As already mentioned, investment decisions are fraught with risk linked to unpredictable future conditions, such as future costs and selling prices, affecting profitability. However, entrepreneurs continue to make such risky decisions in the hope of achieving high profits, which arise when they gain a competitive edge as a result of innovation. Therefore, innovations constitute a very important motivation, creating new investment opportunities. Of course, if the lagging competitors want to stay in the market and catch up with the innovative entrepreneurs who have outpaced them, they also need to make innovation-related investment over time.

Innovation involves not only improving the production of existing goods and services, but, most importantly, developing new goods and services. A similar role is played by discoveries of new sources of known raw materials, new substitutes for old materials, as well as inventions in the area of communications, health care, environmental protection, etc. The more intensive the flow of discoveries and inventions (largely dependent on research and development efforts, and to some degree on luck), the larger the flow of private investment and the larger the growth rate of that flow. Importantly, the less advanced countries can imitate the technological solutions developed abroad and in this way bridge the gap to the more advanced ones.

At a given intensity of technological progress, the number of investment opportunities is also in a sense a given value. Under the circumstances, the greater the volume of investment projects that are under way, the fewer are the remaining investment opportunities. In this context, investment leads to contradictory effects. On the one hand, its growth increases profits and induces further investment, but on the other hand it saturates the market and decreases the remaining pool of investment opportunities. This contradiction was observed by Kalecki, who noted that investment is not only produced (increasing effective demand at given supply), but also contributes to production (increasing supply at given effective demand): "The tragedy of investment is that it calls forth the crisis because it is useful. I do not wonder that many people consider this theory paradoxical. But it is not the theory which is paradoxical but its subject—the capitalist economy."[7]

The investment-related contradictions are mitigated in the case of high innovation intensity, which leads to a higher rate of investment and the growth of national income. On the other hand, lower innovation intensity magnifies the contradictions, slowing down growth.

In this context, rentier savings play an opposite role to innovations. They have been defined as (mostly) external savings, in contrast to internal company savings. Their nature can be most readily shown upon the assumption that gross investment equals depreciation. In this situation, the volumes of depreciation and gross savings are equivalent. As a result, "company savings plus rentier savings equal depreciation," which means that company savings amount to depreciation less rentier savings. Here,

---

[7] Kalecki, (1937 [1990]: s. 318).

investment spending does not return to the companies in the form of savings, and their equity declines or their debts rise.[8] This factor would actually introduce a negative trend to the system, standing in opposition to the positive trend of innovations.

At given innovation levels, mostly dependent on technological advances, private investment growth is also determined by another major factor, which is the volume of shareholders' equity (the capital "owned" by the company): the larger it is, the greater the volume of investment that the company can finance using its own capital. Moreover, the ability to obtain additional funds from the financial markets also relies on equity levels.

Shareholders' equity affects the willingness to initiate investment in yet another way, because the amount of shareholders' equity influences the degree of risk that can be taken by the company. A failed investment decision of a given magnitude may imply the bankruptcy of a small company, but may be only a passing problem in a large one. As a consequence, whatever promotes the growth of shareholders' equity is also conducive to making private investment decisions.

The increase in shareholders' equity depends on company savings, which have been so far identified with profits. However, since some profits are distributed, only their retained portion constitutes company savings. In contrast, external savings include both worker savings and savings arising out of distributed profits. The latter are so predominant that one can quite accurately interpret external savings as rentier savings. Indeed, these savings diminish the internal savings of companies, slowing down the build-up of shareholders' equity, which is an important determinant of investment decisions.

Rentier savings are often employed for stock market speculation and divert resources from the real sphere to the sphere of speculative financial operations, which carry the promise of fast and easy profits. Their allure attracts even some non-financial companies, which engage in speculation rather than carry out real investment projects, to the detriment of their core activity. The savings of non-financial companies increase shareholders' equity, thus facilitating the making of new investment decisions. But this process is more and more often disturbed by stock market speculation. When the dynamics of stock market capitalization is many times higher than the dynamics of GDP and of the output of private-sector companies, long-term economic growth must be unstable. Indeed, today Keynes's admonition sounds almost prophetic: "Speculators may do no harm as bubbles on a

---

[8] As it was already explained (see pp. 132–3), companies take out loans for investment also if gross investment is higher than depreciation, but as fixed capital increases this does not present a threat to the creditors. However, in a stationary economy, increasing debts at constant fixed capital would engender instability.

steady stream of enterprise. But the situation is serious when enterprise becomes the bubble on a whirlpool of speculation. When the capital development of a country becomes a by-product of the activities of a casino, the job is likely to be ill-done."[9] The ongoing economic crisis is yet another example showing that the unbridled pursuit of speculative gain by a small group of high-income individuals combined with deregulation of the financial sector must lead to financial bubbles which sooner or later burst, precipitating downturns whose costs are borne by everybody.

In summary, the factors determining the long-term investment trend, and thus the economic growth rate, are innovations and rentier savings. This trend will be positive only if the effect of the former outweighs that of the latter. Moreover, a decline in innovation intensity or a rise in rentier savings relative to the capital stock will have an adverse effect on the trend and slow down economic growth.

Appendix 8. Determinants of Investment in Fixed Capital in the Kaleckian Model

Let us denote private investment in fixed capital during the period $(t+1)$ and investment decisions during the period t as IP_{t+1} and $D(IP)_t$, respectively. In his analysis of investment decisions, Kalecki examines changes over the period t in three domains: a) gross company savings derived from undistributed gross profits, b) gross profits, and c) changes in fixed capital stock. Factors b) and c) taken together determine changes in the rate of profit understood as a profit-to-fixed capital ratio.

The relationship between investment decisions and gross savings is obvious, as the latter are a source of financing of the former. Moreover, gross savings also increase shareholders' equity, which facilitates access to the capital market and countervails the "principle of increasing risk." Gross company savings can be considered equivalent to private savings if household savings are disregarded. In addition, given our assumption that capitalists do not consume, gross savings are equal to gross profits; hence, investment decisions are an increasing function of gross saving (profits).

Changes in gross profits imply that investment projects which previously were not attractive enough, now become the subject matter of investment decisions, the latter being an increasing function of profits. Finally, the growth of fixed capital at given profits adversely affects the rate of profit. As a result, investment decisions are a decreasing function of fixed capital.

Assuming a linear relationship between the arguments and the investment decision function, we arrive at:

$$D(IP)_t = aSP_t + b\frac{\Delta P_t}{\Delta t} - c\frac{\Delta K_t}{\Delta t} + d \qquad (A8.1)$$

---

[9] Keynes, (1936 [1967]: 159).

This means that investment decisions in the period t are an increasing function of savings, SP_t, an increasing function of the profit increase, $(\Delta P_t/\Delta t)$, and a decreasing function of the fixed capital increase, $(\Delta K_t/\Delta t)$ in that period, with the coefficients a, b, and c being positive, and c being relatively small. Formula (A8.1) also contains a constant parameter, d, which represents long-term variation. Given that $IP_{t+1} = D(IP)_t$, formula (A8.1) can be transformed to:

$$IP_{t+1} = aSP + b\frac{\Delta P_t}{\Delta t} - c\frac{\Delta K_t}{\Delta t} + d \qquad (A8.1')$$

Changes in capital can be represented as the difference between gross investment and depreciation, δ

$$(\Delta K_t/\Delta t) = IP_t - \delta,$$

which leads to:

$$IP_{t+1} = aSP_t + b\frac{\Delta P_t}{\Delta t} - c(IP_t - \delta) + d$$

$$IP_{t+1} = aSP_t + b\frac{\Delta P_t}{\Delta t} - cIP_t + c\delta + d$$

$$IP_{t+1} + cIP_t = aSP_t + b\frac{\Delta P_t}{\Delta t} + c\delta + d$$

Dividing both sides by $(1 + c)$, we obtain:

$$IP_{t+\tau} = \frac{a}{1+c}IP_t + b'\frac{\Delta IP_t}{\Delta t} + d' \qquad (A8.2)$$

where $IP_{t+\tau}$ is defined by Kalecki as gross investment in the period $(t + \tau)$ with a delay of τ close to 1,

$$b' = b/(1+c),$$
$$d' = (c\delta + d)/(1+c),$$

and $IP_t = SP_t$, gross investment is identical to gross savings in a closed economy without the government sector, and $\Delta IP_t = \Delta P_t$, changes in gross savings and profits are identical if household savings are disregarded.

In a stationary state, gross investment equals depreciation, $IP = \delta$, and so (A8.2) can be transformed to:

$$\delta = \frac{a}{1+c}\delta + d', \qquad (A8.3)$$

since in a stationary economy profits are constant.

Subtracting (A8.3) from (A8.2), Kalecki arrives at:

$$IP_{t+\tau} - \delta = \frac{a}{1+c}(IP - \delta) + b'\frac{\Delta IP_t}{\Delta t} \qquad (A8.4)$$

where: $(IP_{t+\tau} - \delta)$ and $(IP_t - \delta)$ denote net investment and the difference between gross investment and depreciation in the periods $(t - \tau)$ and t, and $(\Delta IP_t/\Delta t)$ stands for the change in investment in the period t. Formula (A8.4) can be used to interpret the change in net investment in a given period as a function of profits and changes of profits in the preceding period.

9

Stylized features of economic growth after World War II

9.1 The Capitalist World Following World War II: From the Golden Age to the Global Financial Crisis

In the period since World War II, the advanced capitalist world, in Europe and North America, has evolved through three stages of development. The 1950s and 1960s saw unprecedented economic growth rates that can only partially be explained by post-war recovery. In the second stage, economic development slowed down to varying degrees in different countries. The third stage began with the financial crisis in 2008.

It is not very difficult to identify the historical factors that contributed to fast GDP growth in the first stage, at a time of post-war reconstruction and the Cold War. In Europe, investment was stimulated by the flow of innovations from the United States and facilitated by the Marshall Plan. The ideology of full employment and government responsibility for the economy was almost universally acclaimed and memories of the Great Depression of the 1930s were too vivid and horrifying to have been forgotten. Rivalry with the socialist bloc prevented the policymakers from condoning mass unemployment. The capitalist system successfully proved its economic superiority, also under conditions of full employment, to the extent that Western Europe became an importer of workforce from southern European countries as well as other nations (mostly Turkey). The welfare state, in which the public sector played a major role in the economy, turned out to be a winning alternative to the rigid system in the centrally planned economies. Thus, the years following the end of World War II have come to be known as the Golden Age of the capitalist economy.[1]

---

[1] See Maddison (2001).

The oil crisis of the 1970s marked the beginning of a new era. But the seeds of change had been sown even before that. The stream of imported American innovations gradually dried up as imitations were developed. As Cold War tensions eased the internal unity of the capitalist bloc eroded. This was reflected in a departure from the Bretton Woods agreement, which had been the foundation of the international monetary system. Inflation started to accelerate, fueled by the indexation of wages. Indeed, if the wage policy is based on indexation rather than a common inflation target, then inflation can be triggered even by a one-off increase in prices. And that is what happened when oil prices rose sharply in 1974. The unfavorable terms of trade for net oil importers led to lower productivity in the developed countries. The resulting losses had to be distributed between labor and capital. Due to disagreement on how to tackle this issue, inflation soared under conditions of an economic slowdown. Finally, stagflation (a combination of stagnation and inflation) settled in. This was used as a decisive argument to do away with Keynesianism.

What was actually at stake was the undoing of the full employment policy, which had previously strengthened the working class and trade unions. In 1943, Kalecki presciently observed:

> Indeed, under a regime of permanent full employment, the "sack" would cease to play its role as a disciplinary measure ... It is true that profits would be higher under a regime of full employment than they are on the average under laissez-faire ... But "discipline in the factories" and "political stability" are more appreciated than profits by business leaders. Their class instinct tells them that lasting full employment is unsound from their point of view, and that unemployment is an integral part of the "normal" capitalist system.[2]

Little did Kalecki know that, in the future, academic economics would justify the inevitability of unemployment by invoking a "natural rate of unemployment," which is nothing else but a neutral scholarly name given to the "reserve army of labor" theorized by Marx and scorned by mainstream economists.

The second stage of development spanned the years from the mid-1970s to the outbreak of the 2008 financial crisis. This stage was characterized by a much slower rate of economic growth and much wider income inequalities resulting from the return of economic policy to orthodoxy derived from mainstream economic theory and founded on three pillars.

The first one is the belief that a "free" market economy—free from the harmful influence of the state—is essentially stable and fosters the welfare of society under conditions of advanced privatization of the public sector and deregulation ensuring completely free markets for goods, services, capital, and

---

[2] Kalecki (1943 [1990]: 351).

labor. These are purported to create spontaneously a high rate of production growth and employment.

The second pillar, which became widespread in Europe, is the postulate that macroeconomic policy should be restricted to promoting suitable growth conditions through a combination of stable prices and "sound public finance." The fight with inflation, whether actual or potential, should be the principal, or indeed the sole, aim of the European Central Bank. According to this theory, monetary policy can only affect nominal quantities, and especially prices, but has no effect on real volumes of production or employment levels. "Sound public finance" is supposed to be brought about by the Stability and Growth Pact (agreed in Europe in 1997, with subsequent modifications and restrictions), which in the medium term calls for a balanced or surplus budget to pay off public debt, which is always considered excessive.

Third, unemployment is thought to result primarily from labor market failure rather than insufficient total demand. Therefore, increased flexibility of that market, and especially of wages, is recommended as the main instrument of containing joblessness.

The economic crisis in Europe and North America that marked the beginning of the third stage, inflicted damage similar to that caused by the Great Depression of the 1930s and, with no end in sight, has already lasted longer than that Depression. Within the European Union, and especially within the Monetary Union, it has led to tensions that not only threaten the integrity of individual countries, but also present a challenge to the very existence of the Union.

Table 9.1 presents average annual GDP growth rates for the years 1961–2008. In the EU-15, the slowdown was initially more pronounced than in the United States, but in the last decade the difference almost disappeared. In Japan, growth slowed down even more than in the EU-15.

In all countries, the economic slow-down was accompanied by increased joblessness, as evidenced in Table 9.2, showing average annual unemployment rates for the years 1961–2010, for the same countries. In this case too, the negative trend was much less severe in the United States as compared to

Table 9.1. Average annual GDP growth rates in 1961–2010 (at constant 2000 prices, in percent)

Country	1961–70	1971–80	1981–90	1991–2000	2001–10
EU-15	4.8	3.1	2.4	2.3	0.8
Germany	4.4	2.9	2.3	1.9	0.7
United States	4.2	3.2	3.3	3.5	1.5
Japan	10.1	4.4	4.6	1.1	0.8

Source: Statistical Annex of EU, Autumn 2013.

Table 9.2. Average annual unemployment rates in 1961–2010 (in percent)

Country	1961–70	1971–80	1981–90	1991–2000	2001–10
EU-15	2.2	4.0	8.5	9.2	8.1
Germany	0.6	2.2	6.0	7.8	8.9
United States	4.8	6.4	7.1	5.6	6.1
Japan	1.3	1.8	2.5	3.3	4.7

Source: Statistical Annex of European Union, Autumn 2013.

Table 9.3. Differences between the real wage growth rate and the productivity growth rate in the years 1961–2010 (in percentage points)

Country	1961–70	1971–80	1981–90	1991–2000	2001–10
EU-15	0.0	0.3	−0.9	−0.6	−0.3
Germany	0.4	0.4	−0.8	−0.1	−1.0
United States	0.1	−0.2	−0.2	0.1	−0.5
Japan	−1.3	1.3	−1.3	−0.1	−1.3

Source: Statistical Annex of European Union, Autumn 2013.

the EU-15 or Germany. In the EU-15 and Japan, the unemployment rate grew almost incessantly and in the last two decades it was approximately twice as high as in the 1970s, while in Germany it was four times as high.

The strong correlation between unemployment rates and GDP growth rates suggests that it is the latter, rather than wage rates, that exert the most pronounced effect on the labor market. Indeed, at a given trend of productivity growth (which varies between countries), only a GDP growth rate exceeding that trend enables an increase in employment and a decline in joblessness. Hence, a high GDP growth rate lies at the core of a full (or high) employment policy.

For such a policy to work properly, the income of households must rise in step with the increase in supply. The best indicator that this is the case is the small difference between the growth rate of real wages compared to that of labor productivity. If this difference is zero, then income distribution between wages and profits remains constant; if it is positive, the distribution is skewed towards wages, and if it is negative, then the distribution is skewed towards profits (see Table 9.3).

Until the end of the 1980s, this difference was usually larger than zero and for the two decades as a whole it was close to zero (in Germany it was slightly on the positive side). During that period, the share of wages in GDP was relatively constant, or even grew slightly. On the other hand, in the following periods, the difference between the real wage and productivity growth rates was almost never positive, meaning that the share of wages in GDP gradually declined.

After the year 1980, the decrease in the share of wages in GDP was accompanied by rising income inequality among households in favor of wealthy and extremely wealthy households. The median household income divides households into two groups: one receiving incomes higher than the median, and an equal number of households receiving incomes lower than the median. If the median income follows productivity, income inequality remains constant in the sense that the incomes of the poorer and wealthier households grow at a similar rate. However, if the income median lags behind productivity growth or stagnates, then the incomes of the poorest households do not grow perceptibly, while the benefits of economic growth are entirely appropriated by the wealthy and extremely wealthy ones. Figure 9.1 presents detailed data on this measure of income distribution in the United States.

Up to the year 1980, both productivity and median income doubled, which means that the benefits arising from expanding output were enjoyed by all households. This changed after 1980: over the following three decades productivity again doubled, but this time the poorer households gained very little, with the lion's share of this growth being reaped by those households that lived off profits or received high and very high salaries.

In Europe, the trend was similar, but less extreme. The richest 10 percent of households in the United States received almost 35 percent of aggregate profits before taxes in 1980, and almost 45 percent in 2010. In Europe, the corresponding figures were 30 percent and 35 percent (Piketty and Saez 2014).

The data shown above illustrate the problem which emerged after 1980. Changes in the distribution of income in favor of profits and high salaries were thought to accelerate growth, but in reality they led to a slowdown as the

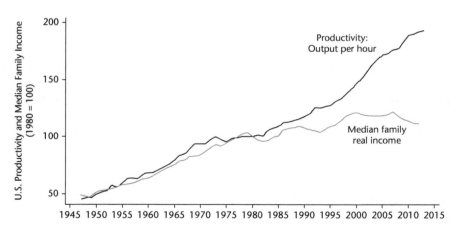

Figure 9.1. Output per labor hour and median family real income in the United States, 1947–2013 (1980 = 100 percent)

Source: "The Most Important Economic Chart," *Economist's View*, March 18, 2014.

meagre wage increases experienced by the majority of households hindered the growth of domestic demand and output.

Let us now consider the arguments purportedly justifying the policy of income redistribution in favor of profits. One of the main motivations behind investment decisions is the profit rate, which is the ratio of profits, R, to the capital stock, K. The ratio can be expressed as follows:

$$\frac{R}{K} = \frac{R}{Y}\frac{Y}{Y^*}\frac{Y^*}{K} \tag{9.1}$$

where the right side of (9.1) is obtained by multiplying the numerator and the denominator by Y (GDP) and Y^* (potential GDP). In this formula, at a constant rate of production capacity utilization (Y/Y^*) and a constant technological capital-output ratio (Y^*/K), the rate of profit depends on the profit-to-GDP ratio, (R/Y).[3] Under the circumstances, a growing share of profits in GDP, (R/Y), is accompanied by an increasing rate of profit, (R/K), which should stimulate investment decisions and actual investment. The resulting economic growth is supposed to benefit everybody, including those who initially sustained losses due to the lower share of wages in GDP.

However, the problem is that in the economy, just like in life, everything does not happen at once. A decrease in the share of wages in national income immediately precipitates a drop in demand for consumer goods, leading to lower utilization of production capacity (Y/Y^*). Indeed, if investment is given, because it is dependent on decisions made in the past, profits are also given, and so the left side of (9.1), representing the rate of profit (R/K), is predetermined in the short term as well. As a result, the first consequence of increased profits per unit of output is a decline in output and in the degree of utilization of production capacity, that is a fundamental determinant of investment decisions. Capitalists will not undertake new investment when the utilization of the existing plant and equipment is reduced. An increase in the share of profits would be an effective tool for economic growth if changes in the distribution of income entailed higher private investment. However, if one takes into account the lag between investment decisions and actual investment, such a reaction is simply impossible. And if private investment does not rise right away, it will not do so in the future either, since, at a given rate of profit, the equipment utilization rate will continue to decline. However, it should be noted that a decrease in the share of wages in national income does lead to lower unit labor costs and higher international competitiveness of companies. This factor has an immediate effect and to some extent countervails the above line of argument. In practice, however, the decrease in domestic

---

[3] See Chapter 8, which discusses these factors.

demand due to lower wages outweighs the increase in foreign demand due to greater export competitiveness.

9.2 Household Indebtedness and Economic Growth Sustainability

Can an increase in household debt provide a stable foundation for economic growth? To address this issue, let us begin with analysis of selected statistical data concerning the growth of GDP and its components in the United States in the years 1960–80 and 1980–2007 (see Table 9.4).

The most pertinent inferences that can be drawn from Table 9.4 are as follows:

1. Private investment grew faster than GDP in the first period and more slowly in the second one (at slightly lower GDP growth rates).
2. Private consumption expanded in step with national income in the first period and faster than national income in the second period.
3. The increase in imports was greater than that in exports, especially in the second period.
4. Net taxes lagged behind government spending on goods and services, especially in the second period.

What is particularly striking is the behavior of private consumption. As noted above, between 1980 and 2010 there was a significant decline in the share of wages in national income, with a simultaneous rise in income disparities, and especially in the share of the wealthiest households in national income. While the low- and middle-earners generally exhibit a much higher

Table 9.4. United States: Rates of growth of GDP and its components, 1960–2007 (in percent p.a.)

Indicator	1960–80	1980–2007
Y = GDP	3.5	3.0
C = consumption	3.5	3.3
CP = private consumption	3.5	3.4
CG = public consumption	3.4	2.9
I = domestic investment	3.8	2.9
IP = private investment	4.2	3.0
IG = public investment	2.7	2.6
X = exports	6.9	3.6
M = imports	8.0	4.8
G = government spending	3.2	2.8
TN = net taxes	2.8	2.8

Source: AMECO.

propensity to consume than the high- and highest-earners, the share of the former group in GDP contracted. This wage-rates polarization, compounded by the waning overall share of wages in GDP, should have resulted in mass consumption lagging behind aggregate income growth. However, this is not reflected in empirical data. Let us try to explain this discrepancy beginning with examination of a chart presenting private savings (see Figure 9.2).

In the United States, the private savings-to-GDP ratio was higher before 1980 than in the following period. However, a major downward tendency occurred only on the side of household savings, *SH*, rather than company savings, or undistributed profits, *RN*. At a more or less constant share of private investment in GDP (see Figure 9.3.), the share of private savings after 1980 decreased; hence, the difference between private savings and private investment, (*SP* − *IP*), was lower in the second period than in the first one, becoming even negative in some years.

This can be seen from Figure 9.4, which shows the trajectory over time of the balances of all the three sectors. The balance of the private sector is by definition the sum of the balances of the government sector, *D*, and the international trade sector, *E*.

For more in-depth analysis of the processes illustrated by the financial balances of the various sectors we need to recall the already discussed Kaleckian profit equation. In our previous models, it was assumed that capitalists do not consume, and so profits were defined as undistributed profits (internal

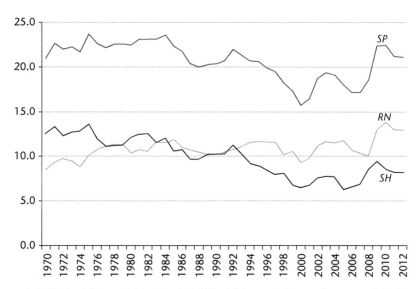

Figure 9.2. United States: Private saving (*SP*) and its constituent elements, firms' saving (*RN*) and household saving (*SH*) 1970–2012 (in percent GDP)
Source: AMECO.

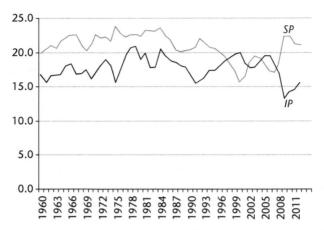

Figure 9.3. United States: Private-sector saving (*SP*) and investment (*IP*), 1970–2012 (in percent GDP)
Source: AMECO.

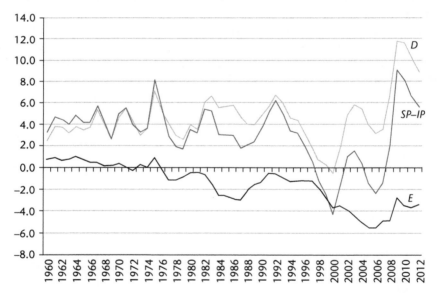

Figure 9.4. United States: Balances of private sector (*SP − IP*), the government sector (*D*), and the foreign sector (*E*), 1960–2012 (in percent GDP)
Source: AMECO.

savings of companies). However, when we turn to examining statistical data, this simplifying assumption has to be dismissed. Nevertheless, our formulas shall remain essentially unchanged once wages are replaced with total incomes of households from the corporate sector (including distributed profits, ownership-related incomes, interest, etc.). At the same time, *SH* shall be interpreted as household or external savings, consisting of the small savings of blue-collar workers and the large savings of white collar-workers (especially those in high-level positions) and capitalists. Hence, for undistributed profits, we arrive at the following formula:[4]

$$RN = (IP - SH) + D + E \tag{9.2}$$

This form of Kalecki's equation shows that profits, *RN*, are derived from three sources: private investment (less household savings), the budget deficit, and the balance of trade. When spending exceeds income, this implies a budget deficit ($D > 0$), and a deficit of the rest of the world (when $E > 0$). To better understand these relationships, equation (9.2) can be written as:

$$SH = (IP - RN) + D + E \tag{9.3}$$

In this form, the equation shows that the flow of household savings, *SH*, must be counterbalanced by an increase in company obligations to households ($IP - RN$), government debt, *D*, or debt of the rest of the world, *E* (assuming that they are all positive). As can be seen from the subsequent discussion, usually it is private investment that is the principal source of profits, while private savings, *SH*, are typically balanced by an increase in company debt.

Growing company debt and financial assets of households, *SH*, constitute a stable combination since it is not only the debt of companies that rises, but also their real productive capital, which is used both as a collateral and for securing payable installments.[5] The increment in the financial assets of households can be supplemented by government debt resulting from budget deficits, which are incurred to increase profits. This combination of company liabilities to households and company profits is stable because a country issuing a sovereign currency will always be able to service its domestic debt. On the other hand, increasing household debt, which would be accompanied by a decline in *SH*, would not generate sustainable growth.

Up to 1980, the US balance of trade was in equilibrium, and subsequently it became negative. However, US budget deficits were generally larger than the trade deficit. It should be noted that an imports surplus leads to market contraction, while a budget deficit results in its expansion. Since the latter factor prevailed in the United States, the adverse effects of trade deficits on output and employment in that country were usually more than offset by the positive effects of budget deficits in the years 1980–2000. In turn, between 2000 and 2008 the contraction of aggregate demand attributable to import surpluses was higher than budget deficit stimulation. Under this constellation

---

[4] This interpretation was used in Chapter 7.   [5] See Flassbeck and Spiecker (2013).

of sector balances, economic growth was ever more dependent on the balance of the private sector and its changes.

As can be seen from Figure 9.4, the private-sector surplus ($SP - IP$) oscillated around 4 percent GDP up to the end of the 1980s. Between the beginning of the 1990s and 2008, this difference shrunk from 7 percent to approximately 2 percent, i.e., by 5 percentage points. Since the volume of private investment was more or less constant, changes occurred mostly in SP (see Figure 9.4), and within private savings mostly in SH (see Figure 9.3).

According to (9.2), profits are affected positively by private investment, IP, and adversely by household saving, SH. When SH is on the decline, the effects of these two factors converge. In other words, decreasing SH adds to private investment, which is the most important determinant of profits. And this largely explains why a slower increase in IP only moderately affected the economic growth rate after 1980 and why US private consumption rose faster than national income in that period.

Between 1970 and 1980, household savings (approximately 12 percent of GDP) were mostly offset by company and government debt (see equation 9.3). Indeed, the surplus of private investment, IP, over undistributed profits, RN, amounted to approximately 8 percent of GDP, while government debt arising from budget deficits (which were larger than trade deficits) was approximately 4 percent of GDP. Still, household debt caused by a spectacular decline in SH may conceal a major economic problem. It should be noted that shifts in income distribution in favor of the wealthiest households (which generally exhibit a higher propensity to save) should have led to higher SH levels. Thus, the cause of the precipitous drop in SH should be sought elsewhere—in the propensity to save of the middle- and low-income households, which constitute the most numerous household category. It seems that in those households the saving rate diminished, amongst others, as a result of the demonstration effect exerted by the luxury consumption of the wealthy ones. However, even more importantly, the less wealthy households did not accumulate net savings and were on the whole indebted. As their debt-to-income ratio rose, then, according to the statistical data, their saving rate declined. Indeed, SH is the difference between disposable income and consumer spending. For instance, if the income of middle- and low-income households decreases or stagnates, then to maintain their previous consumption standards (or to imitate those of the affluent part of society), they must incur debt. Then, the saving rate declines as the consumption-to-income ratio increases.

In the United States, the largest contributor to household debt was mortgage lending. In principle, mortgages should be granted only to households meeting certain criteria, such as income, downpayment, collateral, etc., in order to ensure that the loans can be repaid and to prevent mass defaults.

However, the banking system increasingly relaxed those rules, both legally and illegally. At a certain point in time, financial speculation in the United States dramatically proliferated, to the extent that mortgages were granted not only to borrowers that may have failed on a specific criterion, but to those who did not meet any criteria at all. The banks extending mortgages were only interested in charging fees on them, as those worthless loans were subsequently repackaged and bundled into financial products traded around the world as low-risk financial instruments. This process was sustained for a long time by an upward trend in real estate prices, which, however, could not last indefinitely, while the increasing debt of households implied higher costs of servicing it. Before 1980, household debt grew slowly and reached 48 percent of GDP in 1981 as compared to 41 percent of GDP in 1960. After 1980 household debt accelerated dramatically and reached 100 percent of GDP in 2007. At the same time, despite declining interest rates, the costs of servicing household debt rose from approximately11 percent to 14 percent of disposable income.[6]

When real estate prices began to fall towards the end of the second period, in many cases the outstanding debt exceeded the current value of properties, technically putting the mortgages in default. As a result, the pyramid of financial instruments based on those mortgages crumbled, triggering a widespread financial crisis. This was the inevitable end of the practice of stimulating economic growth through household debt, which had been thought to eliminate the need for household incomes to rise in line with productivity.

The pattern described above had previously occurred in Japan, leading to the 1990 downturn, more than fifteen years prior to the onset of the financial crisis in the United States. In Great Britain and Ireland, the build-up of speculation and its unraveling were similar to the United States. Similar phenomena were observed in countries such as Spain and Greece, but they did not emerge with full force until the crisis in the European Monetary Union.

9.3 Foreign Debt and Economic Growth Sustainability

The question arises as to whether foreign debt may constitute a stable foundation for economic development. Germany attempted to supplement the unsatisfactory growth of the domestic market caused by the insufficient income of the majority of households in a way different from that used in the United States, but it also contributed to the global financial crisis. First, let us examine selected quantitative indicators of economic growth in Germany, given in Table 9.5.

---

[6] See Palley (2012: 41).

Table 9.5. Germany: Rates of growth of GDP and its selected components, 1960–2007 (in percent p.a.)

Indicators	1960–80	1980–2007
$Y = $ GDP	3.5	2.2
$C = $ consumption	4.0	2.1
$CP = $ private consumption	3.6	2.1
$CG = $ public consumption	5.6	1.9
$I = $ domestic investment	2.6	1.5
$IP = $ private investment	2.4	1.8
$IG = $ public investment	4.0	− 0.8
$X = $ exports	5.1	4.4
$M = $ imports	5.9	3.8
$G = $ government spending	5.3	1.6
$TN = $ net taxes	2.8*	2.0
Absorption $= C + I$	3.6	1.9

Note: *1970–80. Source: AMECO.

The most important conclusions that can be drawn from Table 9.5 are as follows:

1. In contrast to the previous period, after 1980, aggregate consumption, C, and especially public consumption, CP, lagged significantly behind national income growth.

2. The growth of domestic investment, I, slowed down considerably, from 2.6 percent to 1.5 percent after 1980. The decrease of public investment was on average 0.8 percent annually.

3. Before 1980, exports grew more slowly than imports. But after 1980, the trend reversed (export growth doubled relative to national income growth).

4. Absorption, the sum of consumption and investment, which had been slightly ahead of GDP prior to 1980, substantially lagged behind after 1980.

It should be noted that these tendencies were observed in every decade following 1980. In particular, the average annual growth of private investment, IP, the most important component of total demand, was only 0.9 percent in the years 1991–2000, and became negative, at − 0.4 percent, in the years 2000–7. Hence, Table 9.5 seems to suggest that since 1980 Germany has consistently pursued a policy of fiscal tightening and export surpluses. Let us examine this conclusion by analyzing the balances of the individual sectors (see Figure 9.5).

First, let us explore changes in private savings in Germany, as shown in Figure 9.5 below. Disregarding the data discontinuity due to the 1991 unification of Germany, the curves representing both private saving, SP, and its

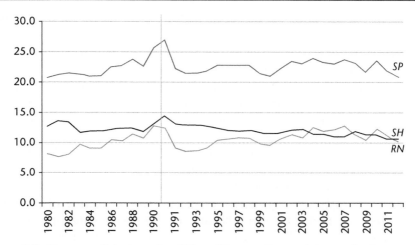

Figure 9.5. Germany: Private saving (*SP*) and its constituent elements, business saving (*RN*) and household saving (*SH*), 1980–2012 (in percent GDP)
Source: AMECO.

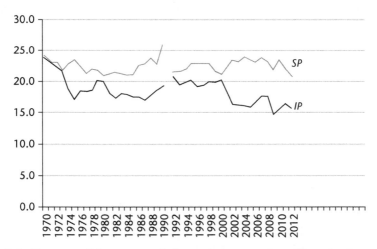

Figure 9.6. Germany: Private-sector balance (private saving, *SP*, and private investment, *IP*), 1970–2012 (in percent GDP)
Source: AMECO.

constituents (undistributed profits, *RN*, and household saving, *SH*), are all relatively stable. Private investment, which is the most important determinant of changes in economic growth, behaved differently before and after 1991, as shown in Figure 9.6, illustrating the time-pattern of private saving and investment. In the first period, the share of *IP* in GDP fluctuated around

20 percent, while after 1991 it oscillated around a declining trend from approximately 20 percent to 15 percent.

Figure 9.7 represents the balances of the three sectors and their interrelationships arising from the identity of the private-sector surplus $(SP - IP)$ and the sum of the fiscal deficit and the external surplus $(D + E)$. On closer inspection, it becomes apparent that after 1980 the budget deficit, D, symmetrically reflected the balance $(SP - IP)$, while the deficit of the rest of the world, E, followed that balance. As private investment grew, the difference $(SP - IP)$ decreased, and when IP contracted, the private-sector surplus $(SP - IP)$ rose. Private savings, SP, obviously also changed, but at a different rate. During periods of economic prosperity, the trade balance typically deteriorates with increasing imports. The opposite tends to be true at a time of economic slowdown. As a result, the trade balance usually follows the private-sector balance, in contrast to the government-sector balance: taxes follow the business cycle, which means that the deficit shrinks during an economic upswing and expands during a downturn.

As in most other countries, Germany also exhibits a long-term tendency for a surplus of private savings, SP, over private investment, IP, of 2–4 percent GDP. However, in contrast to most countries where this surplus is primarily compensated by a budget deficit, in Germany it is largely offset by the export surplus, as it seems that in that country budget deficits are perceived as a

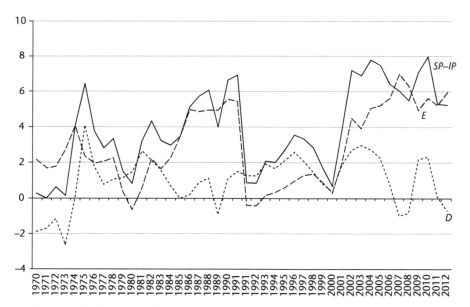

Figure 9.7. Germany: Balances of three sectors, 1970–2012 (in percent GDP)
Source: AMECO.

morally reprehensible phenomenon. In turn, export surpluses and the related appreciation of the domestic currency seem to be treated as a virtue of more than economic nature. Probably due to this, in the mid-1990s the trade unions cooperated with the government in bringing down the growth of real wages to almost zero, despite constantly increasing labor productivity. This exercise in restraint was supposed to stimulate investment and reduce unemployment. Obviously, those goals could not have been achieved by those means since a reduction in real wages relative to productivity leads to an immediate slowdown in consumption growth and, as a result, a decrease in the utilization of production capacity. In turn this causes private investment to decline rather than rise. However, as a side effect, unit costs of labor decrease, improving the international competitiveness of the country through this kind of wage dumping. Indeed, as can be seen from Figure 9.7, Germany's trade surplus increased to 7 percent of GDP in 2007. Nevertheless, even such a massive trade surplus cannot make up for insufficient private investment and fiscal tightening. Consequently, Germany did not benefit from this policy, while its neighbors, especially in southern Europe, suffered as a result of contracting demand abroad and mounting foreign debt.

The increasing trade surpluses attained by Germany are a manifestation of a mercantilist tendency which seems to be deeply rooted in that country. The outcomes of that policy are noteworthy since, in a sense, they represent the results of a historic experiment. Generally, such a policy cannot be maintained in the long term under conditions of a floating exchange rate, because the currency of a country with persistent trade surpluses tends to appreciate, while the currencies of countries with persistent trade deficits tend to depreciate. After some time, a combination of these factors brings both types of countries back to the starting point, triggering deflationary tendencies on both sides. The mercantilist country will continue its wage-dumping policy in order to maintain its competitive advantage in terms of unit labor costs, while the countries with import surpluses will be forced to restrict the growth of total demand. Such a situation was prevalent in Europe, as well as within the European Union, prior to the Monetary Union. Germany would periodically gain a competitive advantage and then lose it as a result of the depreciation of the Italian lira, French franc, British pound, etc. Upon the introduction of the common currency, countries losing their outlet markets to Germany were no longer able to defend their interests in this way.

Essentially, it was assumed that those countries would no longer have to protect their markets because with all eurozone countries pursuing a common inflationary target, their relative competitiveness would stay the same. That was generally expected of the member states which adopted the common currency. However, it turned out that the golden wage rule, according to which nominal wages should increase in line with real productivity growth plus the inflationary target, was not adhered to by some countries, with some exceeding it and others lagging behind (the latter was the case in Germany, in line with its mercantilist tradition). Within the Monetary Union, the former group of countries were no longer able to protect themselves by depreciating their currencies, so Germany's export surpluses grew substantially, especially towards the end of the period under study. Naturally, under the circumstances, countries with compromised international competitiveness ran import surpluses and incurred more debt. Due to the fact that their debt was accumulated in the common currency, for some time the financial markets considered all members of the EMU to be equal, much to the liking of governments in its less wealthy members (which sought to gain the confidence of the financial markets).

The weakness of this system did not fully emerge until after the onset of the 2008 financial crisis. Actually, the euro has become a sovereign currency without a sovereign, as in a sense it is foreign to individual EMU members, and especially those with vulnerable economies. Here, we cannot delve further into the matter, and indeed there is no need to; suffice it to say that economic growth based on accumulation of foreign rather than domestic debt is not only unstable, but dangerous; primarily for the debtor countries, but in the long run also for the creditors. Economies with import surpluses will be able to repay their obligations only if they are able to generate export surpluses in the future. This implies that at a certain point in time countries such as Germany will have to accept import surpluses, leading to a loss of jobs that were previously created. Thus, the question arises as to whether this policy should be pursued in the first place? Would it not be wiser to maintain the balance of trade in equilibrium from the very beginning and base the employment policy on company debt arising from investment outlays and on government debt arising from budget deficits?

The above analysis of the German economy also applies to countries such as the Netherlands, Austria, etc. It demonstrates that economic growth founded on foreign or household debt is unsustainable. At a constant household share in increasing productivity, economic growth must be financed through corporate debt, and if that is insufficient, the government should have recourse to a budget deficit. This is the conclusion that the reader should reach upon completing this section.

9.4 The Economic and Political Ramifications of Growing Income Inequalities

In keeping with the scope of this book, the present chapter examined the economic consequences of dramatically increasing disparities in the distribution of national income between wages and profits, as well as between low- and high-income households. However, one can hardly fail to mention other ramifications of this adverse tendency.

There exists a fundamental tension between two principles of equity: one lying at the heart of the capitalist system and one underpinning democracy. While the market-capitalist system embraces the rule "one euro, one vote," the democratic system professes the principle of "one citizen, one vote." However, due to the inherently unequal distribution of income and wealth, the voice of the wealthy is louder than that of the less rich. While this cannot be entirely avoided, of essence is the scale of inequality; it is a matter of no small concern whether the median income amounts to, e.g., 1/10 or 1/1,000 of the highest incomes. The ability of the affluent groups to influence public opinion, the mass media, parliament, government, and the social elites increases with income disparities.

This can be best shown by considering income redistribution between social classes and groups in a "welfare state" or the "social market economy." The genetic makeup of children and their gifts are not determined by the economic status of their parents; physical and mental capacities are rather randomly distributed across the various social groups. Hence, it makes sense for education and health care to be provided independently of one's wealth, on equal terms to the entire society. This means that in practice these services must be financed by taxes, which should be progressive to achieve this goal.

In a situation where the inevitable discrepancies in income distribution widen while the tax system becomes less progressive (as a result of income tax cuts, shifts from direct to indirect taxes, inheritance taxation reduction, and, importantly, tax evasion due to legal loopholes or tolerated tax havens), the government is no longer able to finance a welfare state, even though it could do so half a century ago, when labor productivity was much lower than today. In addition, the commercialization of public services deepens inequalities, further undermining the democratic principle in favor of the market paradigm. Society is already breaking up into discrete communities living in different districts and using different schools and hospitals, and sometimes also private security services. Is this a goal worth pursuing by modern society?

The conclusion that should be drawn from the above analysis is that we should strive to uphold the European welfare state system. It is not only economically effective, ensuring high employment free from unstable forms of debt, but also cares for all citizens, providing them with a minimum of social security from cradle to grave. As a result, this system also provides political stability.

Concluding remarks

The true significance and usefulness of economic theory becomes apparent primarily in situations of crisis, when there is a sudden breakdown of the economy. Since 2008, the most advanced capitalist countries have suffered financial instability and mass unemployment, often likened to the catastrophic Great Depression of the 1930s. This gives rise to the following questions: Which economic theory can better explain the root causes of the crisis? Which theory underpins the practical measures that can be designed and implemented by governments to contain the crisis? Which theory provides better guidance to prevent such crises in the future?

In the closing section of the small book that the reader holds in his or her hands, it is impossible to provide exhaustive answers. However, among the issues addressed and conclusions formulated so far, there are some examples particularly relevant to an understanding of what we are witnessing these days.

1. The limits of potential GDP are defined by supply factors—the available labor force and productive capital equipment. However, in a capitalist economy, the volume of GDP, understood as products and services sold, is determined by aggregate effective demand, which primarily depends on investment. Is the theory of effective demand vindicated by the developments of recent years with declining GDP growth rates and increasing unemployment, and by the outbreak of the 2008 economic crisis? Or do those events support academic economics, which has long advanced the supply-side paradigm? After all, in 2008 and 2009, production capacity not only did not contract, but it expanded as gross private investment certainly exceeded the volume of output produced by the aging equipment that was being retired. Was it the case that workers' readiness to work declined and their preference for living off social security benefits increased? A parallel decrease in GDP and employment combined with growing production capacity and human capital cannot be explained without reference to demand-side economics.

2. Private investment is an extremely volatile and changeable phenomenon dependent on a number of highly unpredictable determinants because the future is always unknown. As a result, expectations based on intuition and a climate of trust or its absence have a distinct effect on investment decisions, which are also influenced by present levels of profitability and production capacity utilization. Since current developments heavily affect expectations of the future, the capitalist economy is particularly vulnerable to cumulative changes: growth often leads to the economy overheating, while contraction may result in a crisis. The imperfections inherent in the market mechanism give rise both to its advantages and shortcomings. Therefore, this mechanism requires regulation and economic policy intervention if the excesses of speculative euphorias and depressions are to be prevented from periodically shaking the very foundations of the capitalist economy, placing the greatest burden on the weakest individuals, who are in no measure responsible for those excesses.

Does this picture provide a better explanation of the present situation, or perhaps it is more plausibly explained by mainstream economics, based on the principle of rational expectations and the belief in market self-regulation? Should central banks focus solely on containing inflation, or should monetary policy be also given an equal-priority task of maintaining the highest possible employment? Is the efficiency of monetary policy overestimated, especially at a time of crisis, when other economic policy instruments (especially of fiscal nature) would be effective?

3. Neoliberal myths concerning fiscal policy lack theoretical foundations. It is not true that the budget deficit (due to any resulting increase in the interest rate) crowds out private investment, preventing the growth of effective demand; that it places a burden on future generations through government debt; that it causes inflation; that the minister of finance should act as a prudent housewife who adjusts her expenses to her income. At the beginning of the current crisis, the vast majority of the proponents of those myths kept silent, at least for a time, while economic policymakers on both sides of the ocean embraced fiscal expansion and budget deficits as the main tools for containing the financial and economic downturn, devoting enormous resources to that end, measures that would have been previously considered extravagant. At the same time, despite the very expansionary monetary policy currently pursued, the risk of deflation greatly outweighs that of inflation.

4. Problems with the pension system are attributable to demographic factors rather than the financing method. At the end of the day, at a given ratio of working to non-working population, what the retirees will get depends not on stock market speculation, but on GDP volume. The funded system is not only costly, but less efficient than the pay-as-you-go one; it is also capricious, being affected by stock market volatility. Investment funds may default overnight, and the pension plans that have been offered for many decades

by mega-corporations may shrink or disappear altogether should those organizations crumble. Is the state pay-as-you-go system not a more stable and trustworthy foundation for pension provision?

5. Recent exchange rate stability has been maintained by capital flows, despite growing trade imbalances. But a country's international balance of payments cannot be indefinitely sustained in equilibrium by the inflow of foreign capital; what is needed is a long-term strategy of coping with trade deficits, especially in terms of the current account of the balance of payments. It is predicted that in the future the inflow of foreign capital to the emerging markets, including those within the European Union, will be greatly reduced. Under the circumstances, modern industrial policy instruments, which proved effective in many Asian economies, can no longer be ignored. A country's development should be largely based on internal factors, especially in those countries which, for historical reasons, are still working their way up in the process of industrial catching up.

6. Many beliefs about money are relics of the quantitative theory. Today, we have to do with fiat money which is backed by the state rather than by gold or other precious metals. An endogenous element is created by the banking system in response to the credit needs of trustworthy companies and households. The processes of granting loans and increasing the amount of money do not require any previous savings. The concept of a money multiplier which could be used by the central bank to control the volume of money in circulation is a myth. A sovereign currency is an important tool enabling coordination of the monetary and fiscal policies with a view to attaining desirable rates of inflation as well as employment.

7. Policymakers have failed to address the actual root causes of the ongoing crisis, such as unbridled speculation in the financial markets and deepening income inequality; indeed, they have embraced fiscal tightening rather than fostering aggregate demand. Fiscal tightening has not put an end to the crisis. Instead, it has led to stagnation and threatened the existence of the European Monetary Union, and as a result, the survival of the European Union itself.

8. Finally, the question arises: How did the 2008 crisis catch the economic sciences and public opinion completely off guard? How were the lessons of the Great Depression, which came at such an excruciating cost, almost entirely forgotten? In the case of Kalecki's theory, it is not even a matter of deficient memory since one can forget only what one previously learned or knew. With some small exceptions, Kalecki remains unknown and ignored. This is not accidental. In contrast to Keynes, Kalecki could not be "domesticated" in free market capitalism. The academic background of this self-taught theorist was too foreign to the economic establishment; his conclusions were too acute, his theory too coherent, and his belief in the political will of capitalist governments to pursue a full employment policy (whose capabilities and limitations

he scrutinized) too feeble. As a result, outside his students, who admired him, and a handful of scholars who recognized the importance of his theory, he simply went unnoticed. Kalecki's name is not to be found in any academic textbook of mainstream economics.

It was not so with Keynes. An eminent member of Cambridge academia, he was well versed in the economic theories of the day and in fact had serious difficulty revising them in an attempt to explain the Great Depression of the 1930s. Of particular importance were Say's law and the principle of strict corporate profit maximization. While Keynes rejected Say's law, he adhered to the latter, although he did demote it. According to the profit maximization principle, the volume of the marginal product of labour must equal the nominal wage rate. However, in Keynes's theory, employment depends not on the wage rate, but on aggregate effective demand, and nominal wages become adjusted to the marginal product of labor only after the employment level is determined.[1] Over time, the ramifications of this concession turned out to be negative, even though initially it may have facilitated the acceptance of Keynesian economics in a community embracing the principle of profit maximization as one of the fundamental axioms of academic economics.

Despite this and other major deficiencies, Keynes's theory became an integral part of academic teaching and gradually found its way into common knowledge, as did the related belief in state intervention aimed at alleviating business-cycle fluctuations and ensuring high employment. However, the resistance of a major part of the economic establishment did not disappear, but only temporarily subsided, lying in wait for a suitable opportunity to commence counterreformation.

Such an opportunity presented itself at the beginning of the 1970s, with the onset of the oil crisis. Accelerating fuel prices triggered inflation that was aggravated by the fact that neither workers nor businesses were ready to bear the brunt of the resulting losses. This inflation combined with stagnation in economic activity paved the way for a frontal attack on Keynesian economics, which was accused of having caused the stagflation. While neither Keynes's theory nor the theory of effective demand were responsible for inflation, it was blamed on government intervention in the economy, which would have purportedly returned to equilibrium much more readily otherwise.

The advent of Thatcherism in Great Britain and Reaganomics in the United States at the outset of the 1980s created the right political climate for the implementation of neoliberal ideas. Their chief proponent was Milton Friedman, who took advantage of a certain inconsistency of Keynes, suggesting that also in his theory real wages must eventually adjust themselves to the

---

[1] See pp. 52–3.

(physical) marginal product of labor when employment rises. While the sequence of Keynesian adjustments is different, the final outcome is identical. In time, this analysis was further "improved" to imply that aggregate demand is a decreasing function of prices, indicating that there exists such a level of prices which balances aggregate demand with aggregate supply.[2] One can hardly conceive of a more blatant example of the victory of the old way of thinking over the remnants of Keynesian economics.

It seems that the departure from Keynesian economics, the welfare state, and the social market economy, and the shift towards market fundamentalism, were also facilitated by the experiences of real socialism. The Polish October 1956, the concurrent Hungarian uprising, and the 1968 Prague Spring sent signals from Central and Eastern Europe suggesting the political disintegration of the socialist experiment, compounded by glaring evidence of the failure of the centrally planned economy. All of this encouraged criticism not only of the socialist system, but also of the role of government in the economy. However, every victory may contain the seed of a future demise. In this case, that seed was sown by the arrogance of neoliberal ideology, whose exponents came to the conclusion that there was no viable alternative to an unfettered market economy.

The new ideology called for small government and an unconditionally free market. Unemployment and output downturns were no longer blamed on deficiencies of the market mechanism but on the state's interventionist attempts to counteract them. It was claimed that the market, if left to its own devices, operates optimally and finds solutions that are in the best interest of both business and society. Thus, true friends of the people should not oppose the market, but let it act in an unrestrained manner, as that would benefit even the poorest strata thanks to the trickle-down effect. As Thomas Palley noted, orthodox macroeconomists interpret the current crisis as an unfortunate event resulting from a rare confluence of adverse factors, while the advocates of the effective demand theory consider it an inescapable consequence of the neoliberal triumph of the early 1980s.[3] The new neoliberal paradigm promised faster growth with prosperity for everybody. However, as was mentioned at the very beginning of this chapter, actual growth was slower rather than faster, while the lopsided allocation of the benefits derived from it led to unprecedented inequality of income and wealth. It is little wonder that, with such a distribution of national income between wages and profits, household debt spiralled out of control, precipitating the current crisis.

Every economy is deeply affected by currency exchange rates and the prices of basic raw materials, which largely depend on those exchange rates. After the

---

[2] For criticism of this interpretation of Keynes's theory, see Łaski (2000).
[3] See Palley (2009).

fall of the Bretton Woods system, the exchange rate of the US dollar to the major European currencies has been extremely volatile. While crude oil is sold at cartel prices, they are expressed in dollars, and so they are also sensitive to its exchange rate and have become an object of speculation, similarly to basic food commodities. However, it is the stock market that is the main arena of speculation, and in this respect the current crisis is neither the first nor the last one of the kind. It was preceded by the 1998 collapse of Long-Term Capital Management (LTCM) and the bursting of the dot-com bubble in the years 1995–2001. Some blame Alan Greenspan, former chairman of the Federal Reserve, for fuelling mortgage speculation in the United States with his cheap money policy. In fact, through his actions he postponed the outbreak of the crisis. However, being a market fundamentalist, Greenspan is co-responsible for doing away with the restraints (e.g., on mortgage lending) that were previously in place and he opposed any attempts to introduce new restrictions. Thus, in his congressional testimony he was forced to admit that his ideology failed in some critical ways.[4]

The most urgent task at hand remains to contain the consequences of the crisis and return the economy more or less to business as usual. The place of financial capital in a normal economy remains an open question. There exist gambling casinos and one cannot ban those dealing in financial capital. However, casinos should be closely controlled and regulated. In particular, the real economy must not be allowed to remain merely an adjunct to the financial market casino, and a potential victim of that casino. It is necessary to overcome the ideas that have brought the world's economy to where it is now and to extend access to theories that have turned out to be more useful in explaining the causes of the crisis and in identifying measures for preventing future global downturns.

Today's economic teaching largely determines what the social elites think tomorrow. This also applies to the mass media, which shape people's attitudes and reactions. In the absence of discerning, precise responses to real-life challenges in the form of alternatives, societies eventually turn to populists and witch doctors. That is why it is so vital to familiarize students of economics with alternative schools of economic thought and equip them with the ability to think critically.

---

[4] See Greenspan (2009).

References

AMECO, European Commission, Annual Macro Economic Database.

Bhaduri, Amit, 1972 [1993], "Unwanted Amortization Funds: A Mathematical Treatment," *Economic Journal*, June; reprinted in Amit Bhaduri, *Unconventional Economic Papers: Selected Papers of Amit Bhaduri*. Oxford Economic Press, Delhi.

Bhaduri, Amit, 1986, *Macroeconomics: The Dynamics of Commodity Production*. Macmillan, London.

Bhaduri, Amit, 2014, "What Remains of the Theory of Demand Management in a Globalised World," Public Policy Brief No. 130, Levy Economics Institute of Bard College, New York.

Chojna, Janusz, 2008, "Udział podmiotów z kapitałem zagranicznym w polskim handlu zagranicznym," in *Inwestycje zagraniczne w Polsce, Raport roczny* ["Share of Foreign Firms in Polish Foreign Trade," in *Foreign investment in Poland, Annual Report*], Instytut Badań Rynku, Konsumpcji i Koniunktur, Warsaw (in Polish).

Chojna, Janusz, 2013, "Firmy z kapitałem zagranicznym w polskim handlu zagranicznym," in J. Chojna (ed.), *Inwestycje zagraniczne w Polsce, 2011–2013*, ["Foreign Firms in Polish Foreign Trade," in J. Chojna (ed.), *Foreign Investment in Poland, 2011–2013*], Instytut Badania Rynku, Konsumpcji i Koniunktur, Warsaw (in Polish).

Dalziel Paul C. and Geoffrey C. Harcourt, 1997, "A Note on 'Mr. Meade's Relation' and International Capital Movements," *Cambridge Journal of Economics* 21(5): 621–31.

Eatwell, John, 2003, *The Anatomy of the "Pension Crisis" and Three Fallacies on Pensions*, Cambridge Endowment for Research in Finance and Judge Institute of Management Studies, Cambridge.

European Commission, 2013, "Statistical Annex of European Economy," Spring, European Commission, Brussels.

European Commission, 2013, "Statistical Annex of European Economy," Autumn, European Commission, Brussels.

European Commission, 2014, "Statistical Annex of European Economy," Spring, European Commission, Brussels.

Falkinger, Josef, 1995, "Zastosowanie zasad ekonomii publicznej dla krajów przechodzących transformację: aspekty redystrybucyjne i efektywnościowe. Analiza teoretyczna ilustrowana doświadczeniami Niemiec i Austrii," ["Redistribution and Efficiency Consequences of Applying Principles of Public Economics to Countries in Transformation"] in: Josef Falkinger, Kazimierz Łaski, and Leon Podkaminer (eds), *Polityka fiskalna w warunkach transformacji* [*Fiscal Policy in the Course of Economic Transformation*], "Studia i Prace Zakładu Badań Statystyczno-Ekonomicznych", No. 23, Warsaw (in Polish).

References

Flassbeck, Heiner and Freiderike Spiecker, 2013, "Investitionen in Sachanlagen—die ungenannte Achillesferse der deutschen Wirtschaft," July 26, http://www. Flassbeck-economics.de.

Flassbeck, Heiner and Heiner Lapavitsas, 2013 (May), "The Systemic Crisis of the Euro—True Causes and Effective Therapies," May, Rosa-Luxemburg Stiftung, Berlin.

Galbraith, James K., 2012, *Inequality and Instability: A Study of the World Economy just before the Crisis*. Oxford University Press, Oxford.

Greenspan, Alan, 2009, Hearing at the US Congressional Committee on Oversight and Government Reform, http://www.youtube.com/watch?v=55-A1-D3MR0.

Johnston, David Cay, 2005, "Class Matters: Richest Are Leaving Even the Rich far behind," *The New York Times*, June 5.

Hicks, John, 1974, *The Crisis in Keynesian Economics*. Basil Blackwell, Oxford.

Kaldor, Nicolas, 1960 [1971], *Alternative Theories of Distribution*, in *Essays on Value and Distribution*. Duckworth and Co., London.

Kalecki, Michał, 1935 [1990], "The Essence of the Business Upswing," in *Collected Works of Michał Kalecki, Vol. I: Capitalism: Business Cycles and Full Employment*. Oxford University Press, Oxford.

Kalecki, Michał, 1937 [1990], "A Theory of the Business Cycle," in *Collected Works of Michał Kalecki, Vol. I: Capitalism: Business Cycles and Full Employment*. Oxford University Press, Oxford.

Kalecki, Michał, 1943 [1990], *"Political Aspects of Full Employment,"* in *Collected Works of Michał Kalecki, Vol. I: Capitalism: Business Cycles and Full Employment*. Oxford University Press, Oxford.

Kalecki, Michał, 1945 [1990], "Full Employment by Stimulating Private Investment," in *Collected Works of Michał Kalecki, Vol. I: Capitalism: Business Cycles and Full Employment*. Oxford University Press, Oxford.

Kalecki, Michał, 1970 [1993], "Theories of Growth in Different Social Systems," *in Collected Works of Michał Kalecki, Vol. IV: Socialism: Economic Growth and Efficiency of Investment*. Oxford University Press, Oxford.

Keynes, John Maynard, 1936 [1967], *General Theory of Employment, Interest and Money*. MacMillan, London.

Kornai, Janos, 1980, *Economics of Shortage*. North-Holland, Amsterdam.

Łaski, Kazimierz, 2000, "Aggregate Demand and Aggregate Supply in Modern Macro-economics—a Critical Appraisal," in Tadeusz Kowalik and Jerzy Hauser (eds), *Polish Economists in the World*. Wydawnictwo Naukowe PWN, Warsaw (in Polish).

Łaski, Kazimierz, 2009, "The Government Expenditure Multiplier and its Estimation for Poland," Monthly Report No. 7/2009, WIIW, Vienna.

Łaski, Kazimierz, Jerzy Osiatyński, and Jolanta Zięba, 2010, "Government Expenditure Multiplier and its Estimate for Poland," National Bank of Poland Working Paper No. 246 (in Polish).

Łaski, Kazimierz, Jerzy Osiatyński, and Jolanta Zięba, 2012, "Fiscal Multipliers and Factors of Growth in Poland and in the Czech Republic in 2009," National Bank of Poland, Working Paper No. 117.

Lavoie, Marc, 1992, *Foundations of Post-Keynesian Economics Analysis*. Edward Elgar, Cheltenham.

Lopez, Julio G. and Michael Assous, 2010, *Michal Kalecki*, Palgrave Macmillan, Basingstoke.

Maddison, Angus, 2001, *The World Economy: A Millennial Perspective*. OECD Development Centre Studies, Paris.

Meade, James, 1975, "The Keynesian Revolution," in Milo Keynes (ed.), *Essays on John Maynard Keynes*. Cambridge University Press, Cambridge.

Moore, Basil, J., 1988, *Horizontalists and Verticalists: The Macroeconomics of Credit Money*. Cambridge University Press, Cambridge.

Most Important Economic Chart, The, 2014, *Economist's View*, March 18, https://economistsview.typepad.com.

Nikiforos, Michalis, 2014, "Distribution-led Growth in the Long Run," Working Paper No. 814, Levy Economics Institute of Bard College, New York.

Osiatyński, Jerzy, 1978, *Capital, Income Distribution and Value—the Crisis of Neomarginalist Economics*. Państwowe Wydawnictwo Naukowe, Warsaw (in Polish).

Palley, Thomas I., 2009, "After the Bust: The Outlook for Macroeconomics and Macroeconomic Policy," Public Policy Brief No. 97, The Levy Economics Institute of Bard College, New York.

Palley, Thomas I., 2012, *From Financial Crisis to Stagnation: The Destruction of Shared Prosperity and the Role of Economics*. Cambridge University Press, Cambridge.

Palley, Thomas I., 2013, "Horizontalists, Verticalists, and Structuralists: The Theory of Endogenous Money Reassessed," *Review of Keynesian Economics* 1(4): 406–24.

Pasinetti, Luigi L., 2000, "Critique of the Neoclassical Theory of Growth and Distribution," *Banca Nazionale del Lavoro Quarterly Review* 53(215): 383–431.

Piketty, Thomas, 2014, *Capital in the Twenty-first Century*. Harvard University Press, Cambridge, MA.

Piketty, Thomas and Emmanuel Saez, 2014, "Inequality in the Long Run," *Science* 344(6186): 838–43.

Robinson, Joan, 1962, *Economic Philosophy*. Penguin, Harmondsworth.

Robinson, Joan, 1971, *Economic Heresies: Some Old-fashioned Questions in Economic Theory*. Basic Books, New York.

Robinson, Joan, 1972, "The Second Crisis of Economic Theory" (Richard T. Ely Lecture), *American Economic Review* 62(1/2): 1–10.

Statistical Annex of European Economy, Spring 2014, European Commission.

Steindl, Joseph, 1979 [1990], "Stagnation Theory and Stagnation Policy," *Cambridge Journal of Economics* 3(1); reprinted in Joseph Steindl, *Economic Papers: 1941–1988*. Macmillan, London.

Tscherneva, Pavlina, 2014, "The Most Important Chart about the American Economy You'll See This Year," https://www.vox.com/xpress/2014/9/25/6843509/income-distribution-recoveries-pavlina-tcherneva.

UNCTAD, 2013, "Trade and Development Report," UNCTAD, Geneva.

WIIW Database, http://data.wiiw.ac.at/annual-database.html.

Wolff, Edward, N. and Ajit Zachariasz, 2006, "Wealth and Economic Inequality: Who's at the Top of the Economic Ladder?" Levy Institute Measure of Economic Well-Being, The Levy Economics Institute, Bard College, New York, http://www.levyinstitute.org/pubs/limew1206.pdf.

Index